Fareham

in old picture postcards

by
John Emery

European Library - Zaltbommel/Netherlands MCMLXXXV

GB ISBN 90 288 3285 8 / CIP

European Library in Zaltbommel/Netherlands publishes among other things the following series:

IN OLD PICTURE POSTCARDS *is a series of books which sets out to show what a particular place looked like and what life was like in Victorian and Edwardian times. A book about virtually every town in the United Kingdom is to be published in this series. By the end of this year about 175 different volumes will have appeared. 1,250 books have already been published devoted to the Netherlands with the title* **In oude ansichten.** *In Germany, Austria and Switzerland 500, 60 and 15 books have been published as* **In alten Ansichten;** *in France by the name* **En cartes postales anciennes** *and in Belgium as* **En cartes postales anciennes** *and/or* **In oude prentkaarten** *150 respectively 400 volumes have been published.*

For further particulars about published or forthcoming books, apply to your bookseller or direct to the publisher.

This edition has been printed and bound by Grafisch Bedrijf De Steigerpoort in Zaltbommel/Netherlands.

INTRODUCTION

The Borough of Fareham is situated in the south of England in the County of Hampshire. It lies to the north of Gosport and extends from Portsmouth Harbour in the east, to the River Hamble in the west, covering an area of some 18,000 acres.

Finds of flint arrowheads and knives in the area indicate that man has lived here since the earliest days. In the Iron Age, the Celts are believed to have used the River Meon as a harbour for their boats. More imposing proof of early occupation of the area stands in the form of a large Roman fortress at Porchester, dating from the end of the 3rd century.

The Domesday Book of 1086 showed the present Fareham Borough to be comprised of the Hundred of Fareham (FERNEHAM), The Hundred of Titchfield (TICEFELLE) and the Manor of Porchester (PORCESTRE). The reign of King Edward I saw the formation of the first English Parliament. Fareham was one of only a handful of Hampshire towns invited to send representatives. The entitled two members from the area duly attended the assembly in 1306. Unfortunately the cost of such representation eventually became too heavy for Fareham to bear. In 1345 a petition to King Edward III begging to be excused this honour received the royal assent.

By the 14th century Fareham had become an important port for shipping, in the days when much of the trade of the Kingdom was conducted by small coastal vessels. Ships were loaded in Fareham Creek and in the Haven at Titchfield, where in those days there was a passage for vessels right into the township. At that time also the area was heavily wooded, and timber from the vast Fareham and Titchfield Parks was transported by sea via Fareham and Warsash to ship-building centres around the coast. Other industries carried out in the Borough over the years have included brick-making, leather-tanning, strawberry growing and the production of woollen goods, sacking, pottery, clay-pipes and parchment dressing.

From the time of King Henry II in 1163 Fareham has had links with royalty. Several reigning monarchs have visited and stayed in the area, which may explain why Fareham supported the royal cause in the Civil War of 1642-1646. As a result of its allegiance to King Charles I the district suffered badly at the hands of the victorious Cromwellians on several occasions.

Moving on through the 18th century, the population of the area was gradually increasing. A drastic rebuilding programme became necessary and during the course of this many of the older, more squalid dwellings were pulled down. These being replaced by some of the fine, stately buildings for which the Georgians were renowned, and happily many of these have survived to the present time. Indeed Fareham High Street today presents one of the finest examples of

Georgian architecture in the south of England. The population of 6,996 in 1801 had doubled by 1891, and grown to 21,817 by 1931. In 1932 the old town of Fareham joined with the ancient villages surrounding it to form the Urban District of Fareham. The Urban District eventually became a separate Parliamentary Constituency in 1970. Four years later it achieved the status of a Borough and today boasts a population of over 90,000.

Fareham Borough with its heavy residential building programme, industrial estates, shopping precincts, superstores, motorways and flyovers now stands as a prime example of modern development. This serves to accentuate the dramatic changes that have taken place in our villages and towns and to our way of life over the last few decades. Hopefully readers will enjoy the opportunity to return for a time, through the pages of our book, to those more tranquil days that now seem to belong to another world.

The pictures in this book are from the period 1880-1930; this broadly coincides with the years when picture postcard production and collecting was at its height. Although it was 1902 before postcard publication in this country really got underway, many of the early cards showed scenes that the respective photographers had taken years before. Edwardian times saw the 'golden age' of the postcard, when just about every family in the land had albums of cards which would be proudly exhibited before all visitors to the house. Even through the long years of the Great War the flood of postcards continued. It was not until 1919 and the doubling of the postage rate to 1d that the demand for postcards really began to wane, and by the late 1920's the flood had become a trickle. By that time, however, a marvellous photographic record of the life and times of the years surrounding the Edwardian era had been safely tucked away in the albums of those early collectors.

Many of the pictures in this book were the work of local photographers, for this part of Hampshire was rich in such men. There was F.G.O. Stuart of Southampton, responsible for over one thousand different Hampshire cards. A.H. Sweasey of Southsea also produced some superb photographic cards of the area as did William Smith of Gosport. Fareham could also boast two of its own postcard publishers in Hector Duffet and Sutton and Sons. Local photographers like Sidney Smith and Frank Pannel also did much to record the Fareham area on film in the early days of our period. With today's growing interest in local history, the old postcard has become much sought after. With prices rising alarmingly, these rectangular pieces of card are truly becoming treasures of the past.

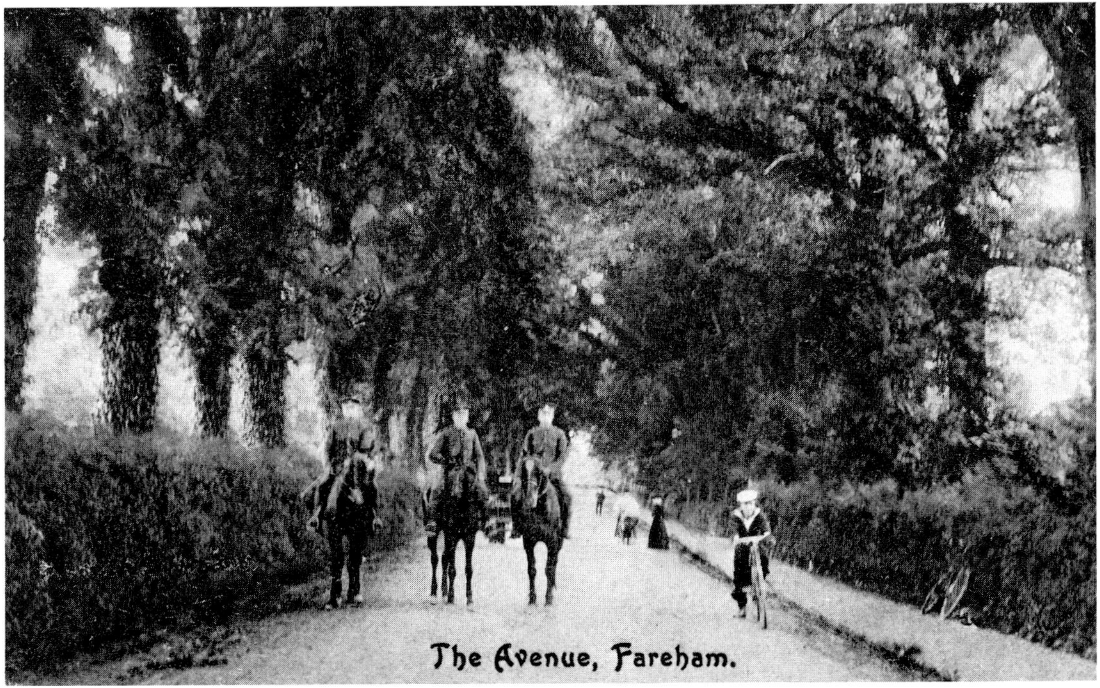

1. This rural scene of the Avenue, Fareham was photographed by William Smith of Gosport. The postcard on which it appeared was postally used on 5th July 1907. The Avenue is the final stretch of the road from Southampton before it passes under Fareham Railway bridge and enters the town itself. As pictured here, the branches from the tree-lined hedgerows each side of the road interlaced overhead and provided welcome shade for the Edwardian traveller on a hot summer's day. Today the Avenue is part of the busy A27. Most of the greenery has long since been sacrificed in repeated roadwidening operations to accommodate the ever increasing volume of traffic.

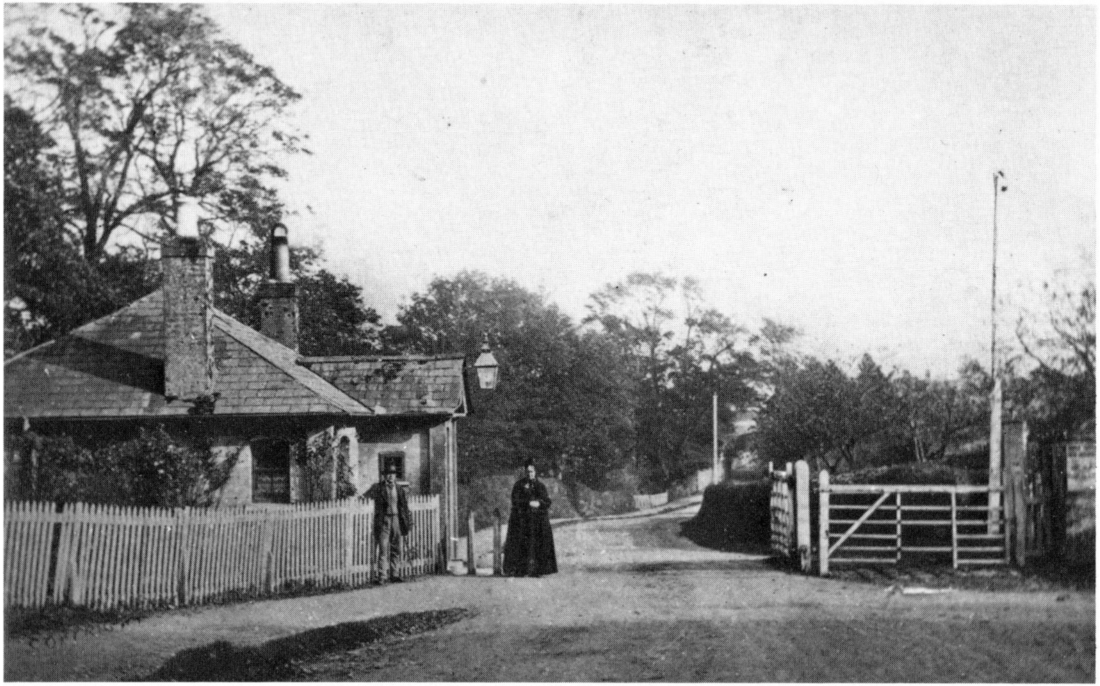

2. This toll house on the Titchfield road was situated at the corner of Gudge Heath Lane and what is now the A27. It was called Blackbrook toll house and was owned by the Titchfield and Cosham Trust. It had a weighing machine which stood on the opposite side of the main road. As well as a gate across this road, there were also bars across both Gudge Heath Lane and Redlands Lane. Just peeping through the trees in the background can be seen the railway bridge which stands adjacent to Fareham Station and which dates from 1840. Toll gates were a common sight in this country in the 19th century. Today they are a rarity, although road toll barriers are still encountered frequently on the continent. This picture was taken by Fareham photographer Sidney Smith about 1885.

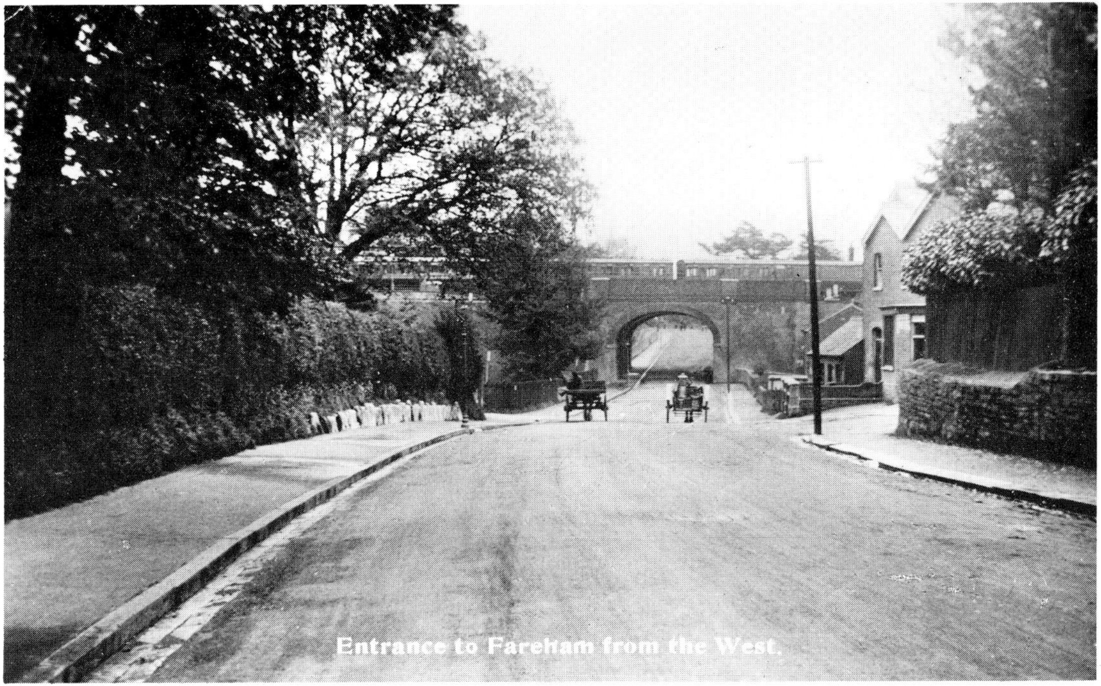

3. Moving on along the Southampton to Fareham road past Gudge Heath Lane, this was how the approach to Fareham Railway Station arch appeared in 1914. The road leading off to the right is Paxton Road. The building standing on the corner of the road served for many years as Paxton Road Post Office. This business continued to operate well into the post-war era before finally becoming another statistic in the Post Office Authority's economy drive. The rear carriages of a train from Portsmouth can be seen crossing the railway bridge as it pulls into Fareham Station. The station itself is screened from view by the large trees on the left of the picture.

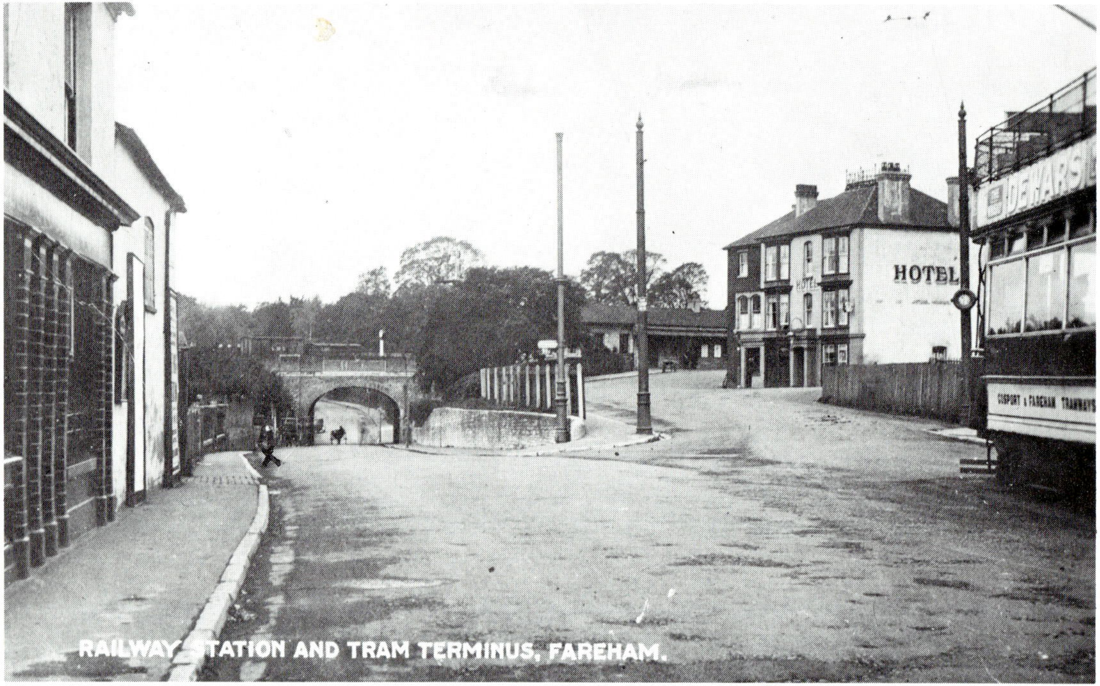

4. This picture by A.H. Sweasey shows the approach to Fareham Railway Station in 1928. The station entrance is tucked just behind the large hotel on the right. In later years this hotel was converted to a factory producing lady's underwear and today it is a bingo club. In the 1930's and 1940's many double-decker buses came to grief trying to negotiate the old railway bridge shown here. It was so low that the buses had to halt oncoming traffic by moving into the middle of the road in order to pass under safely. The new bridge built after the last war comfortably spans four lanes of traffic. The actual approach road and station exterior have changed very little since 1928. The tram just shown here was to run only one more year before being replaced by the motor bus.

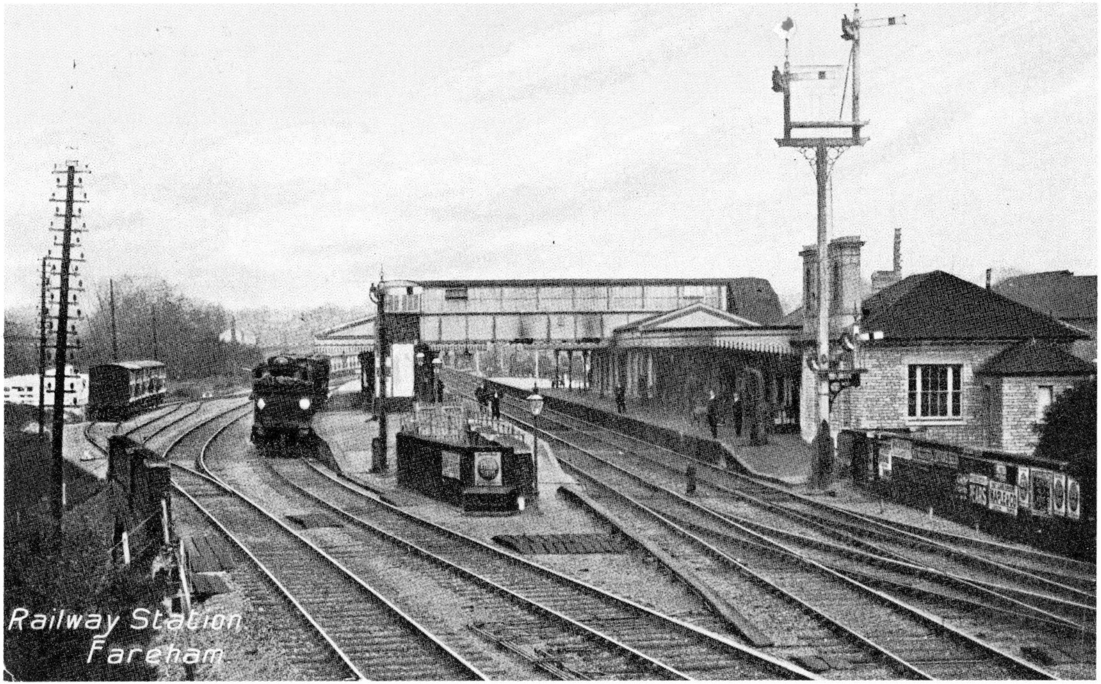

5. This interior view of Fareham Railway Station is from another card by A.H. Sweasey. This card was postally used in 1913 and the message reads 'bike arrived safely, the roads here are shocking'. Fareham Station was opened in 1841 when the first extension line of the London to Southampton railway allowed trains to run from Eastleigh through Botley and Fareham to Gosport. In 1848 the railway was extended from Fareham to link with Cosham and Portsmouth. It was later extended westward to Netley in 1889 to link up with the existing Netley to Southampton line. Finally in 1903 the opening of the Meon Valley Line to Alton gave Fareham a picturesque and direct route to London. Sadly after little more than fifty years, the Meon Valley Railway was closed as uneconomic on 5th February 1955. The same fate was also suffered by the Fareham to Gosport line. Happily Fareham Station as an important link on the South Coast route, remains as busy as ever. All it lacks today is the glamour that disappeared from the railway scene with the passing of steam.

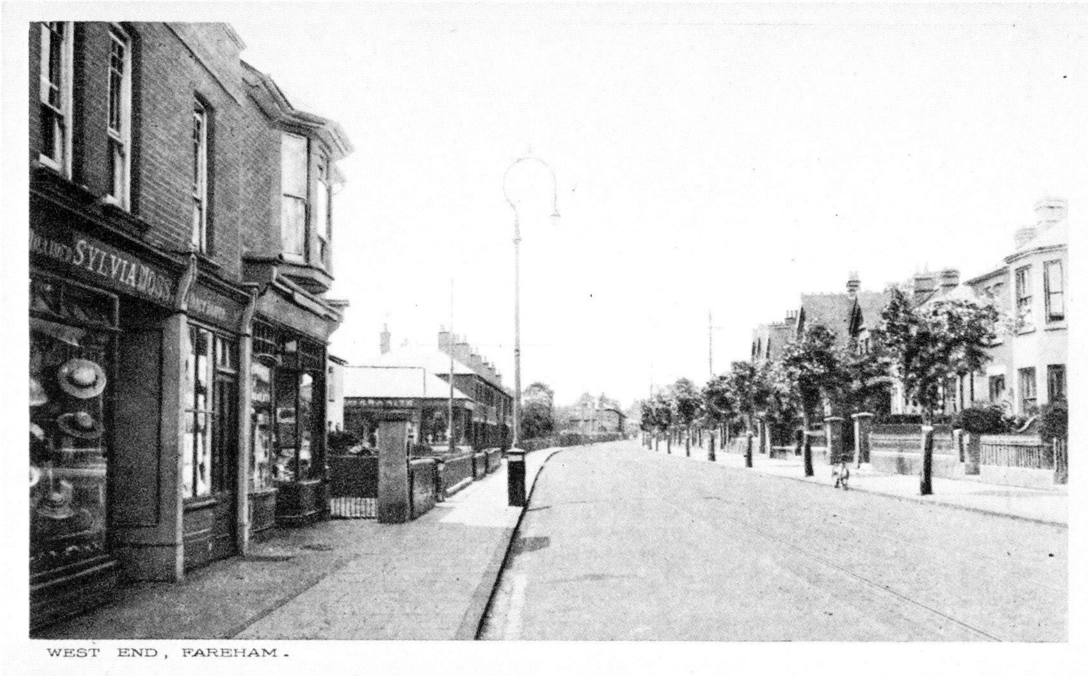

6. The buildings in the left foreground of this 1910 view of the western end of West Street are still there today. The shop nearest the camera was then a milliners owned by Sylvia Moss, whose window display of assorted hats really caught the eye. Like its neighbours, it is now trading in other goods under a different name. Just past this row of shops was the entrance to the Gillies. In those days the Gillies was entirely surrounded by open fields and a large number of allotments. The latter are still there today, but the open fields have seen the gradual encroachment of residential development. The row of houses on past the entrance to the Gillies is now replaced by large garage and motor cycle concerns. Across on the north side of the street many of the houses still survive, but have for the most part been converted into office premises.

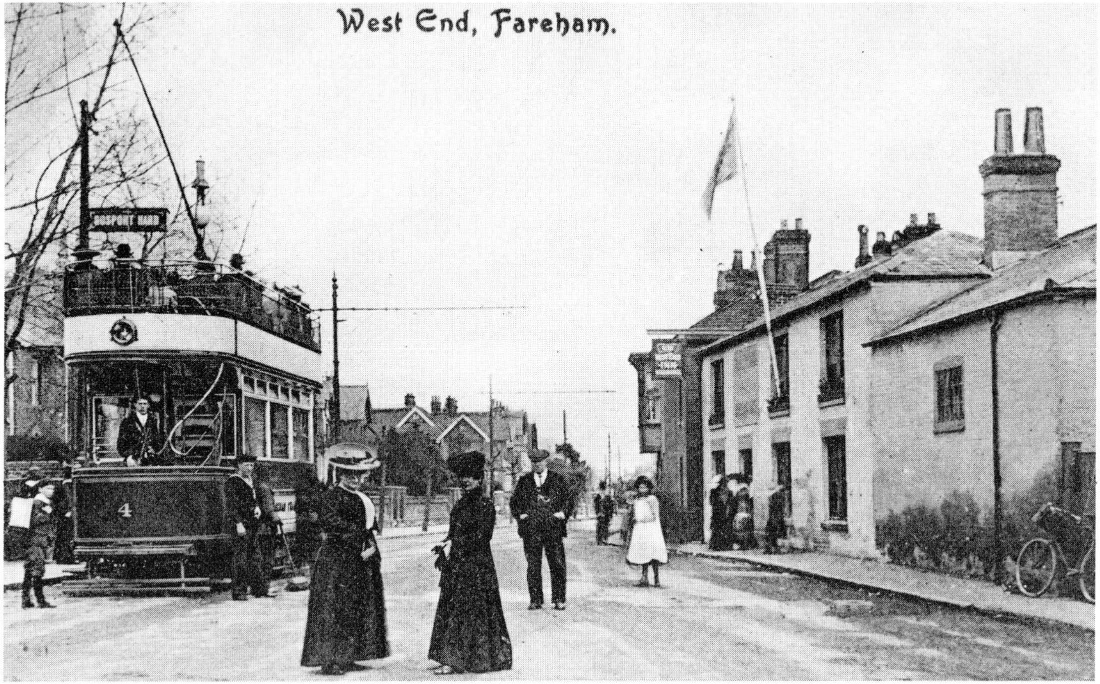

7. The Gosport and Fareham Tramways operated a service from the Hard at Gosport to Fareham Railway Station. The fare for the five mile journey was 4d and the tram ran every fifteen minutes. The service opened in 1906 and continued until the end of 1929. The trams then being replaced by motor buses owned by several small private companies. This picture by William Smith of Gosport, circa 1908, shows a tram at the Fareham end of the route, as well as some nice examples of Edwardian fashions. The public house on the right of the picture is the old West End Inn. This and the adjoining buildings were knocked down in the 1940's. The public house being rebuilt some thirty yards back on the new main road. Since then it has again been demolished this time to be replaced by a giant traffic roundabout at the start of the southern Fareham by-pass road.

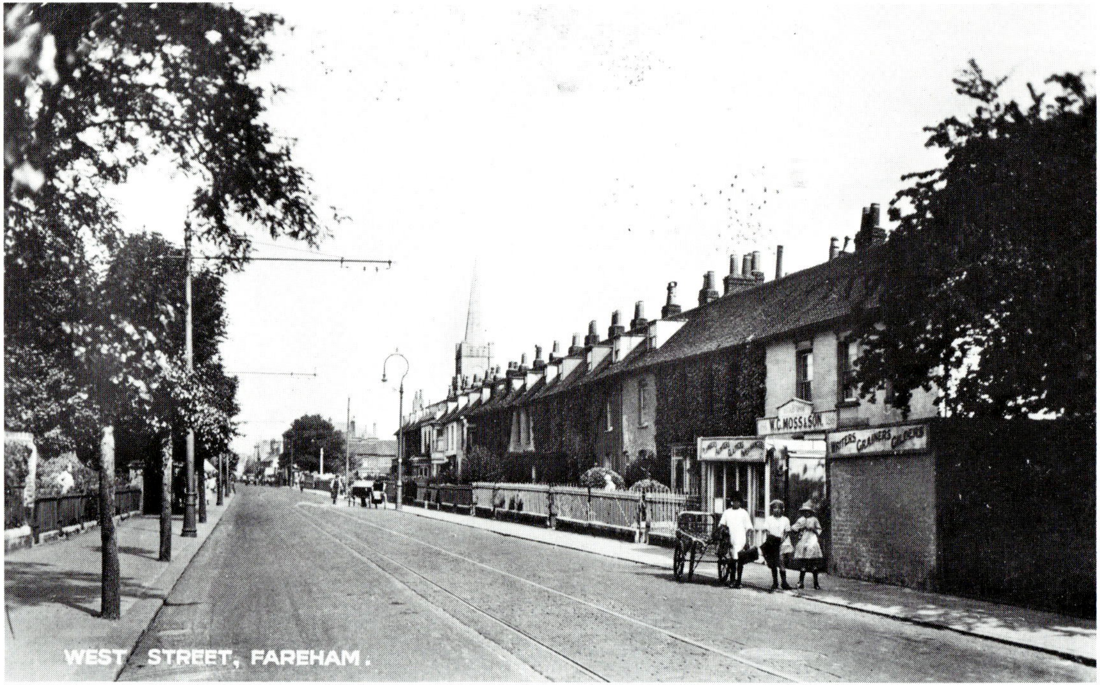

8. Approaching Trinity Church from the west this was how Fareham West Street looked in 1928. With the exception of the Stonemason W.G. Moss and Son, this part of the town was entirely residential. The fenced front gardens lined the pavements and people can be seen standing in their gardens conversing across the road. The overhead tram lines are still much in evidence. Today both sides of the road are full of shops and office premises. The front gardens having been replaced by pavement forecourts for car parking. Only some of the old upper storeys remain, where just the lower living rooms have been converted into business premises. This photograph was some more of the work of A.H. Sweasey of Southsea.

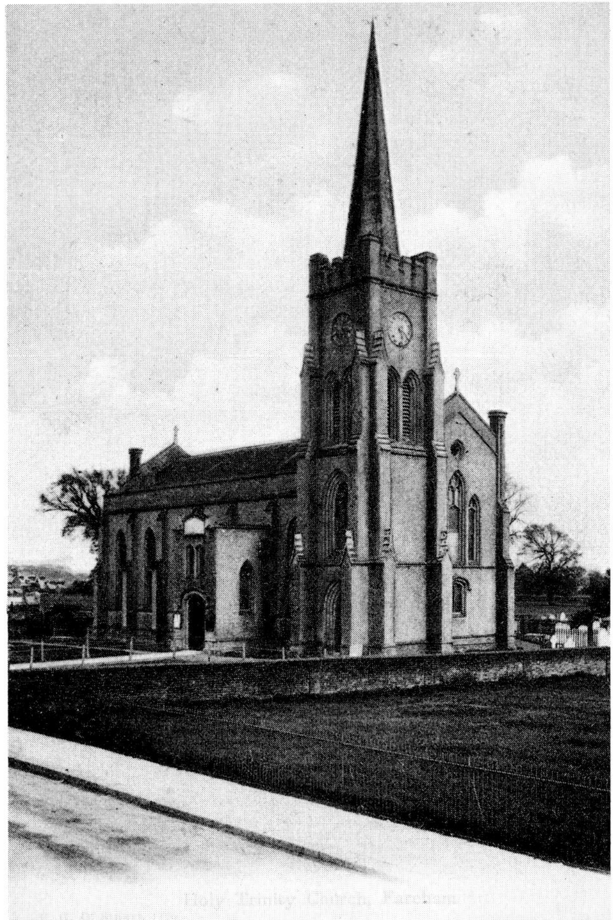

9. Holy Trinity Church still stands today as a considerable landmark in Western Fareham. It was built in 1835 by Jacob Owen in that loosely Gothic style of architecture so popular in early Victorian times. The church was dedicated in 1836. The imposing tower and spire were added a year later. The site had been purchased by public subscription and the building of the church was funded by monies bequeathed for this purpose in the will of Lady Thompson. This picture was taken by F.G.O. Stuart of Southampton in 1911. The church in those days stood in splendid isolation. The greenery that surrounded it has long since given way to the seemingly inevitable bricks and mortar.

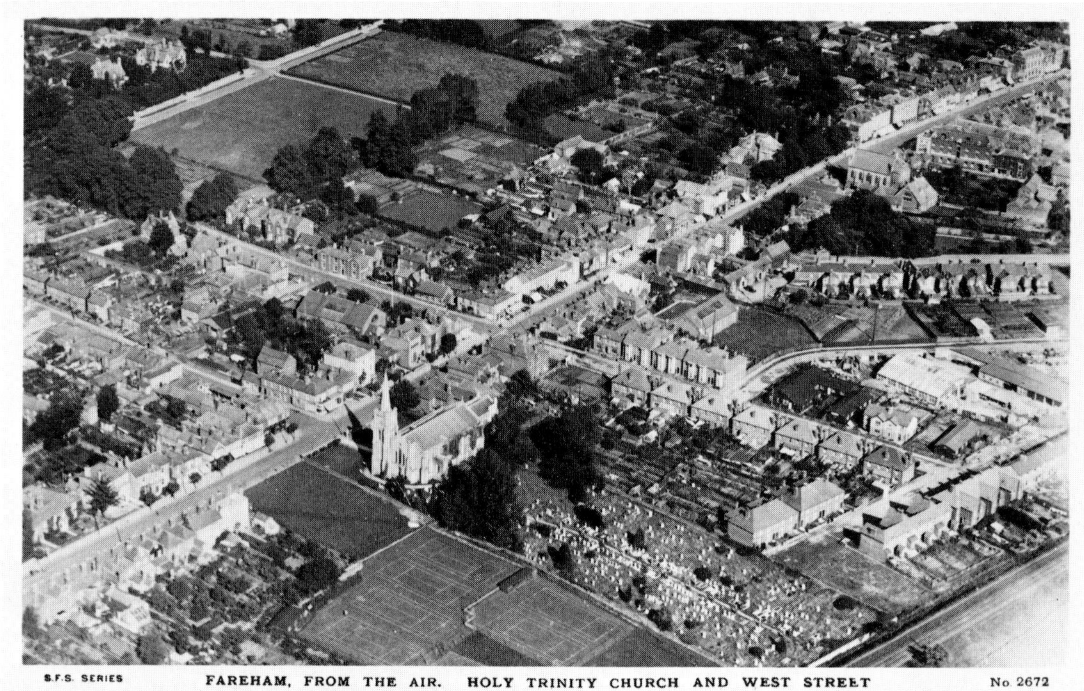

10. This aerial view of central Fareham was taken by the Surrey Flying Services of Croydon in 1925. It presents an interesting picture of the layout of the area at that time. Prominent in the foreground is Trinity Church and its graveyard. On the open space next to the church was soon to be built the old church halls which themselves were pulled down in the post-war days and replaced by a parade of shops. Behind this space, on land owned by the church, can clearly be seen a series of grass tennis courts once the home of Fareham Tennis Club. Among other interesting features are the cottages on the east side of Trinity Street and the large open space to the south of upper Osborne Road. Kings Road has altered little, but Queen's Road can be seen before the houses were built on its northern side.

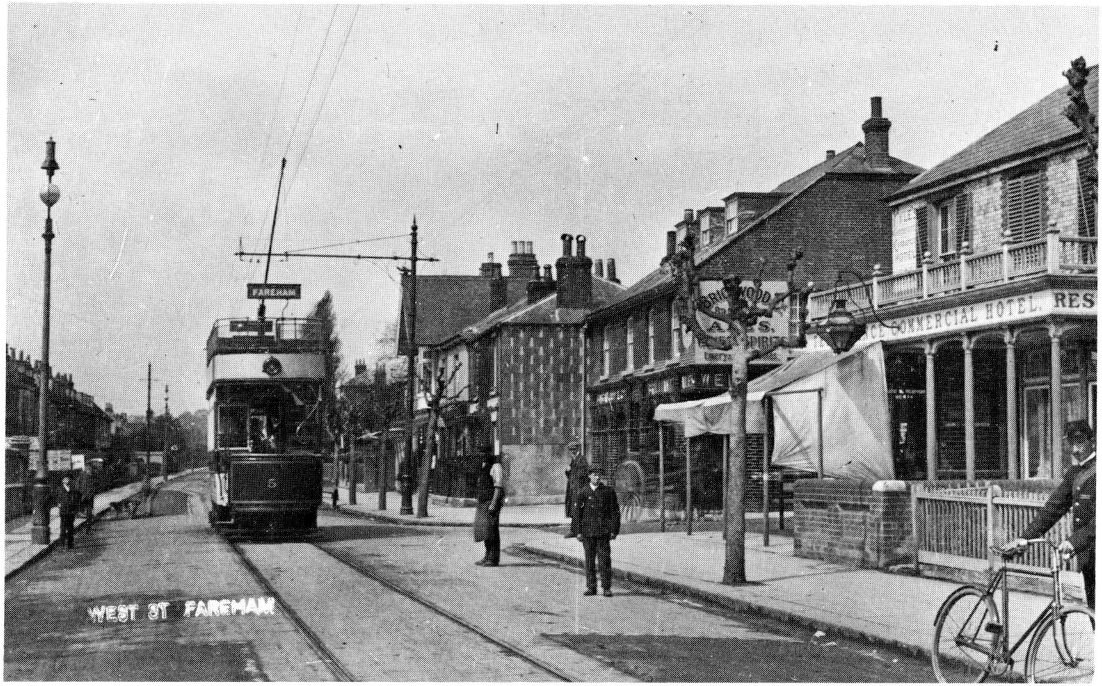

11. This was the scene at the bottom of Trinity Street as photographed by William Smith in August 1909. Trinity Street faced the church and on its nearside corner can be seen Pyle's Temperance Commercial Hotel. This building after many alterations and changes of use over the years, now houses the Southern Gas Company's showrooms. The Royal Oak public house building on the other corner still stands today. Next to this were two small shops, then another public house, the old King's Head. The oncoming tram is on its way from Fareham Station through the town, and on to Gosport. The local inhabitants, however, appear to find the camera more interesting.

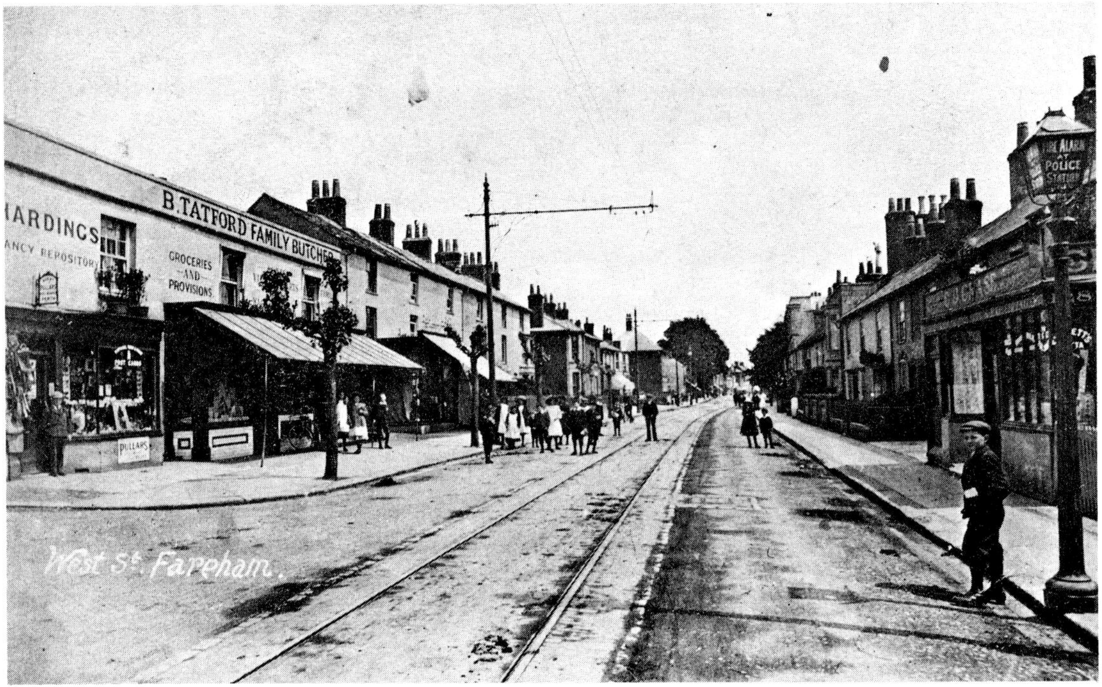

12. Pictured here is that part of the West Street at the junction with Osborne Road. Harding's toy shop is on the corner, then comes Tatfords the butchers. Opposite where the group of people stand awaiting the next tram, is the entrance to Malt House Lane, in which was half a dozen small cottages. On the far corner of the lane was a music shop which today sells goods in aid of the Spastics Society. On the right of the picture, facing Osborne Road, is the shop of shoemaker and repairer Mr. C.J. Chase. The message on the nearby lamp-post concerning the fire alarm, refers to the police station a few yards up Osborne Road. Incidentally the police vacated this for a bigger and better station at the bottom of quay street in 1980. The old building now being the Registry office. This picture was from another William Smith card and it was postmarked Fareham 10th December 1907 at 10.00 p.m.

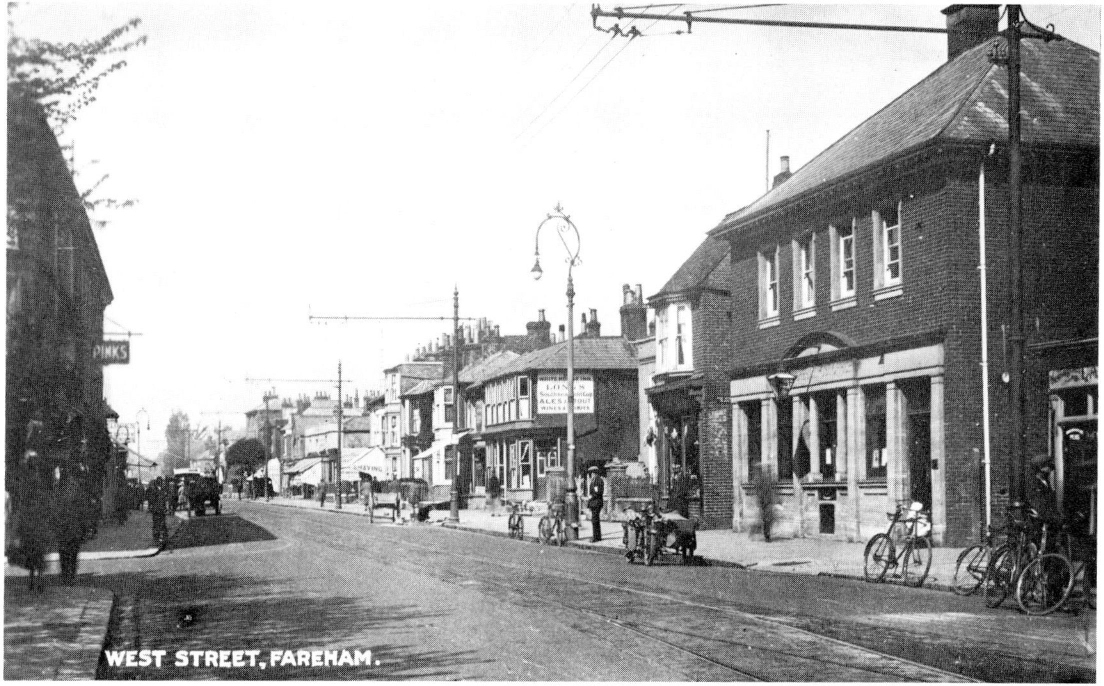

13. Fareham General Post Office stands in the foreground of this West Street scene. The Post Office moved from its old site opposite Portland Street to this new building about 1909. It remained there for almost sixty years, when the increased volume of business caused it to be moved just a few yards along the road to its present larger premises. Just on down the road from the Post Office stands the old White Horse Inn which had a fine bowling green to the rear. Across on the shady south side of the street can just be seen the sign of 'Pinks'. This dairy and provision shop was a branch of that well-known company and survived there until post-war days. This A.H. Sweasey card bears the message 'For your collection', indicating that as late as 1927 postcard collecting was still a popular pastime.

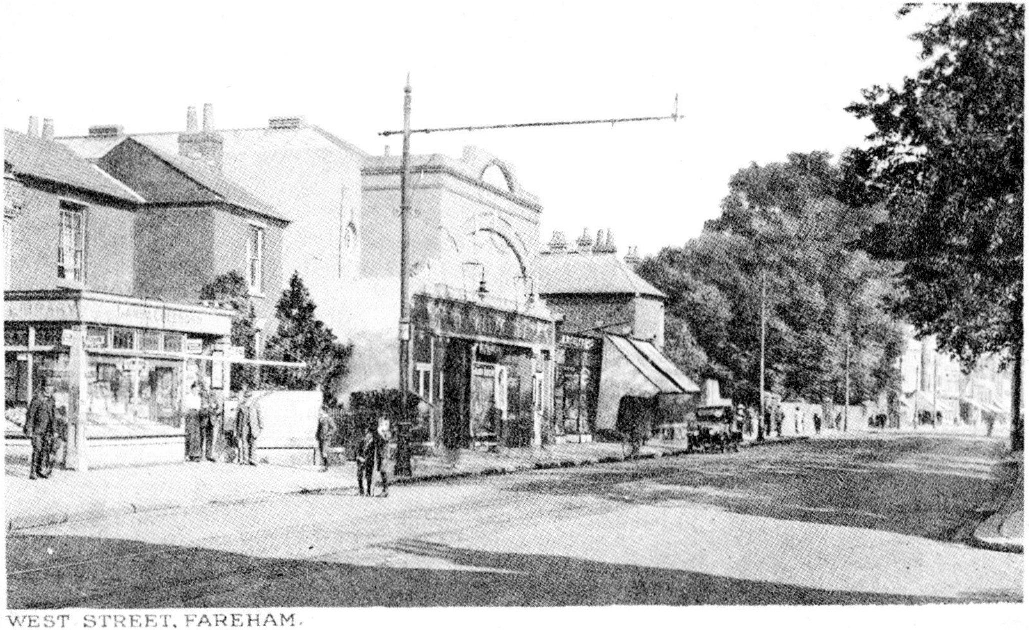

14. This was the view from the top of Hartlands Road looking east in 1921. The newsagent's shop on the left incorporated a library in those days. At the turn of the century it was owned by a french couple trading under the name of Madame Radigue. It was later taken over by a Mr. Spencer Lamb and by the time of this postcard had become Lamb and Coleborn. Today the shop trades as Bartlett and Sons. Interesting that this postcard was actually published by Lamb and Coleborn. Just along from the newsagents stands the old Alexandra Cinema. This was Fareham's only cinema from 1910 until it showed its last film in 1933, that same year the new Savoy Cinema opened just opposite the bus station. The Savoy served Fareham until 1959 and was joined in 1938 by the impressively luxurious Embassy Cinema, which survived until 1983.

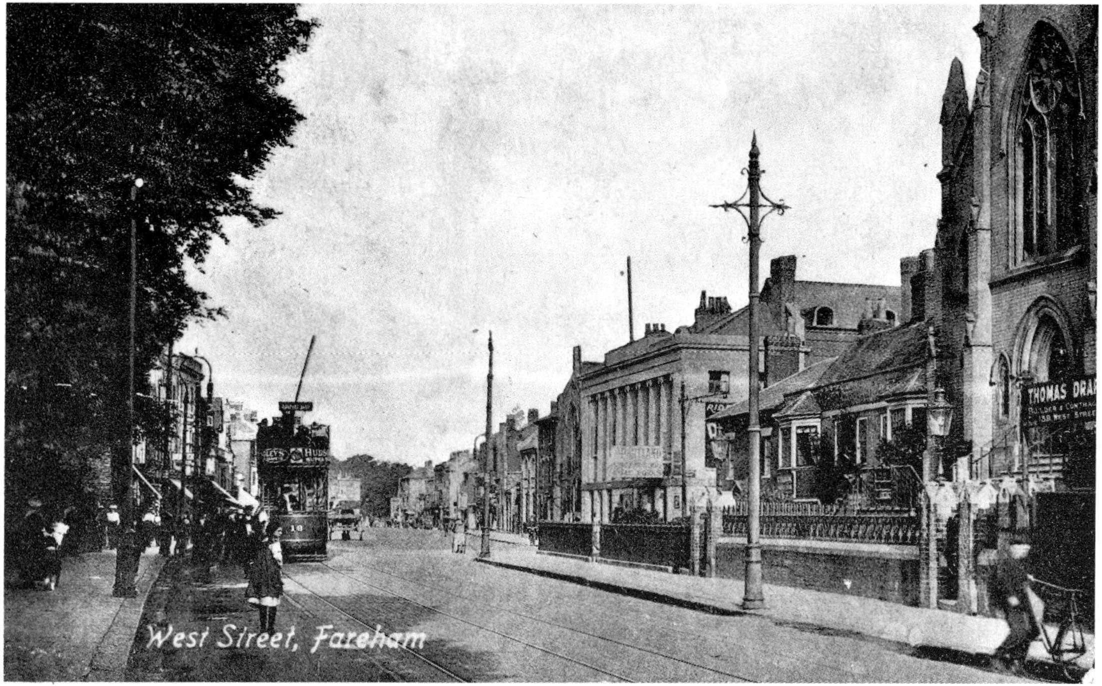

15. This is a rare card by A.H. Sweasey dating from 1919. It is interesting for the view it gives of the houses and the church standing on the site of the present bus station. The house next to the church was once the home of the famous author William Thackeray. It later served as a library and reading room. The Wesleyan Methodist Church was a most attractive building with numerous steps leading from the pavement up to its front doors. It was built in 1875 as a replacement for the old church that had stood there since the early part of the century. What a pity that it was to last for barely fifty years.

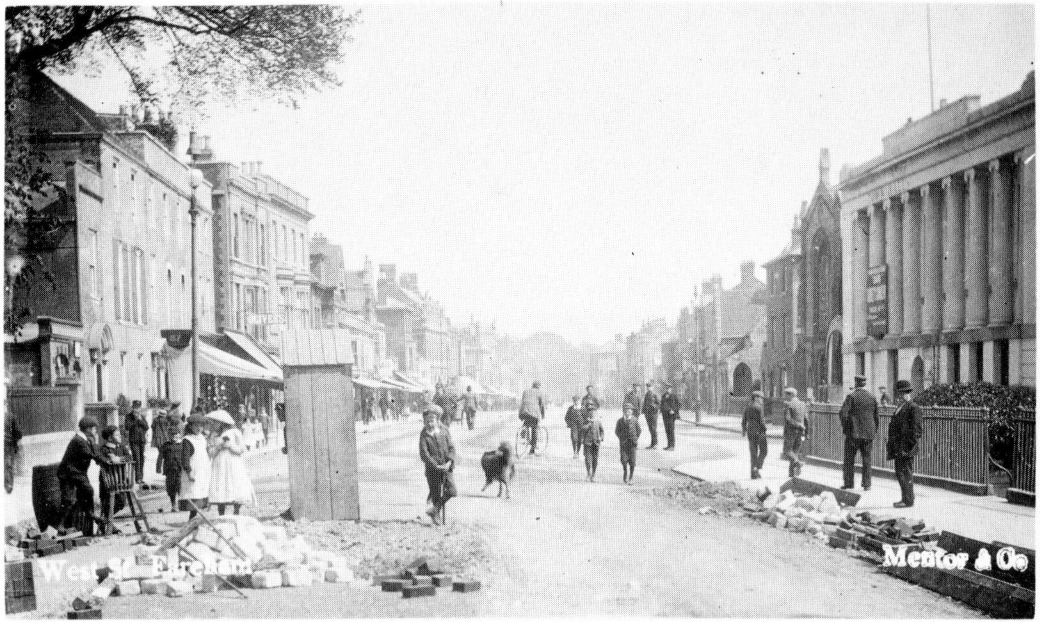

16. This card which captures such a lot of local activity is the type much sought after by today's collectors and local historians. It was the work of national photographers Mentor and Company and was sent through the post on 29th August 1905. It appears that even in those days road repairs were necessary. This despite the fact that being the pre-tram era in Fareham, the principal traffic consisted of the cycle and the horse and cart. This is obviously why the watchman feels he can risk siting his hut in the middle of the main road. From this picture he appears to have his hands full with the local youngsters. Possibly they want to know why he needs a brazier in August.

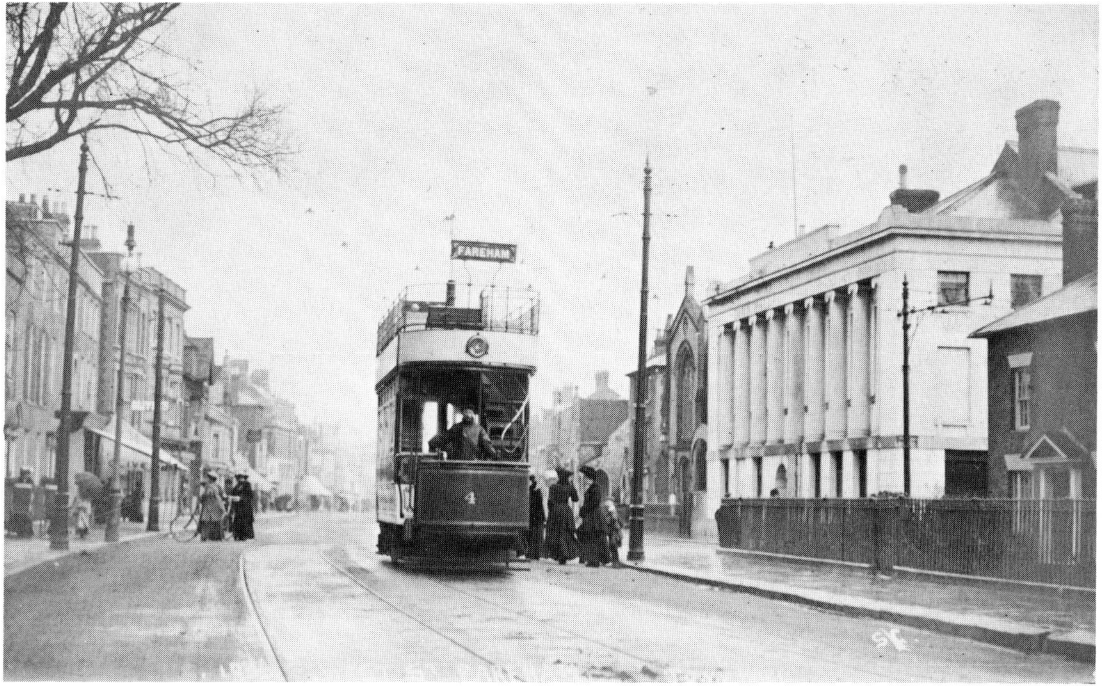

17. The number 4 tram en route from Gosport to Fareham Railway Station dominates this picture. It has just travelled up Portland Street and turned left into West Street. The tram drivers, like their passengers on the top deck, had no protection against the weather. This driver with cap pulled down and mackintosh buttoned up to the neck must have wondered why the photographer chose such a wet day to take this picture. The imposing, white building on the right is Portland Hall. This was the old Town Hall where downstairs was carried out all the work of local government. Except for the office in the left hand corner of the building which belonged to Mr. Warner the solicitor. The top floor of the hall was used for staging dances, plays and other entertainments.

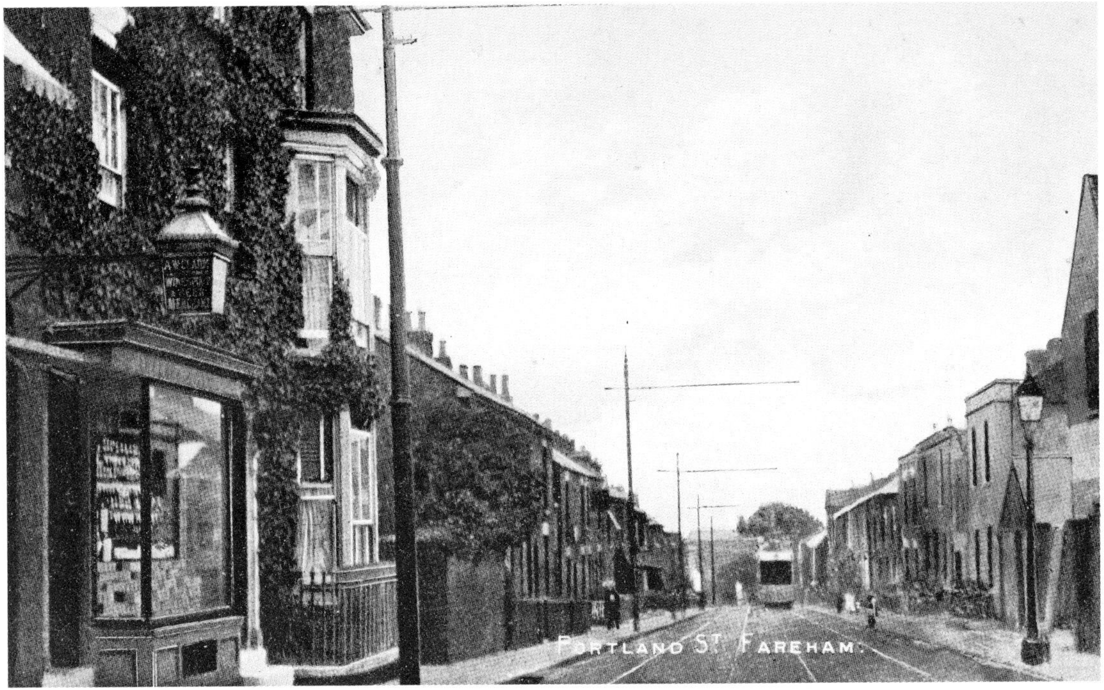

18. Portland Street, a turning off West Street, was the main route for traffic to and from Fareham from the south. The distant tram in this picture is returning from Gosport. It has just skirted Fareham Creek, passed under the railway viaduct and is on its way up Portland Street to the town centre. The wine, spirits and beer merchants shop of A.W. Clark is prominent on the left of the picture. This appears to be the only shop the street possessed when A.H. Sweasey took this picture in 1912. Today the lower left side of the street is little changed. The buildings on the right have been replaced by a series of small shops and lower down by a link road running into the bottom of Hartlands Road.

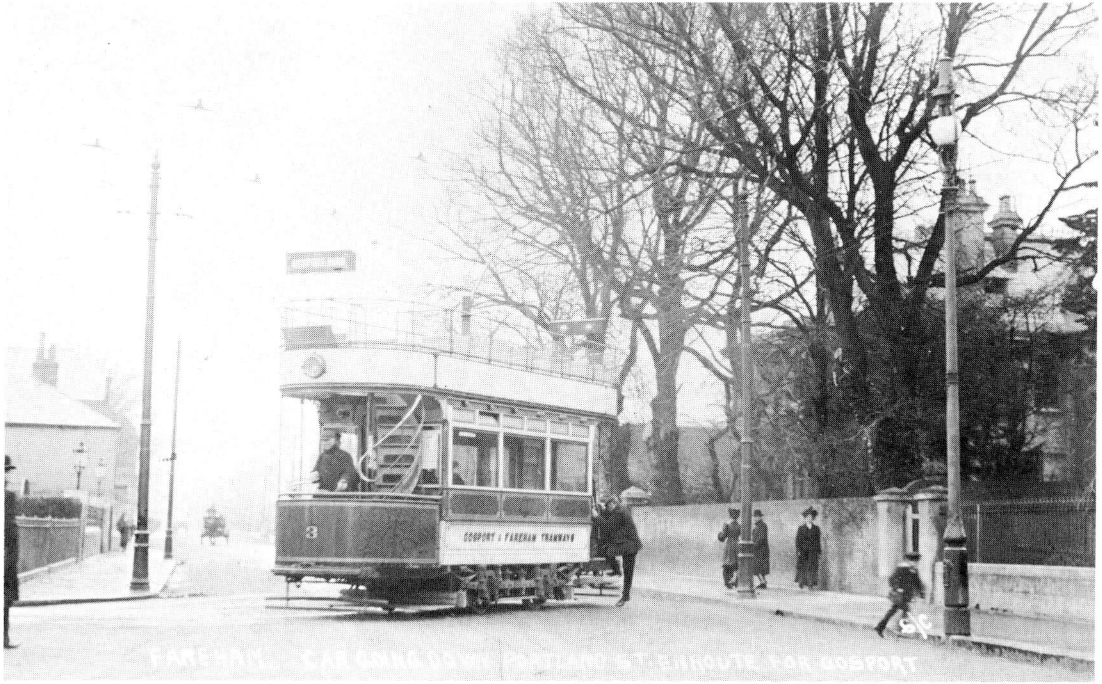

19. It was 1907 when this photograph was taken of a tram turning out of West Street into Portland Street en route to Gosport. The sender of the postcard writes: 'Do you recognise the boy just stepping on to the pavement?' The recipient would have needed good eyesight to answer this question correctly. The large building standing beyond the trees was Westbury House. Many servants were employed here, and there was a fine drive for carriages leading up to the front of the house. Leading off the West Street on the other side of Westbury House was Westbury Path which led to Westbury Farm. This footpath is still there today, unlike the farm, which was soon to give way to the housing needs of a growing population.

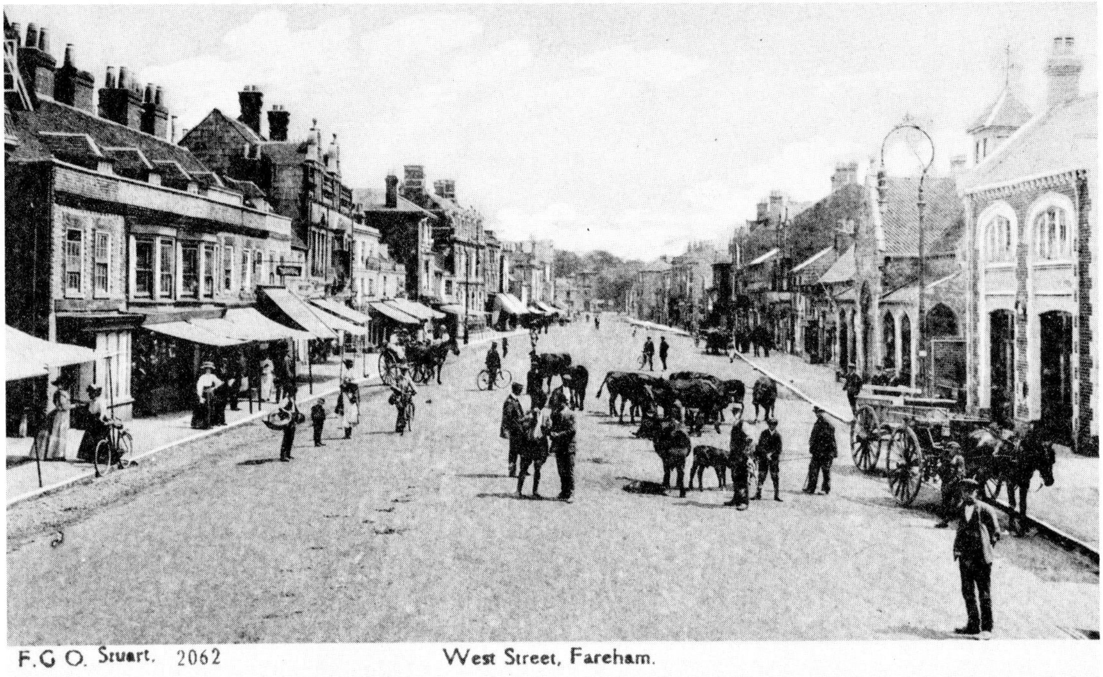

20. Animals standing patiently outside the Market gates in the West Street were a common Monday morning sight earlier this century. The cattle, sheep or pigs having been sold by auction in the market place were ushered out here to await their new owners. They were then herded through the streets either to the Railway Station, or directly to one of the many farms surrounding the town. This practice caused growing problems during the 1920's, when traffic in the town was on the increase. Confrontations between trams and herds of animals causing many tempers to be lost. This picture was taken by F.G.O. Stuart in 1918. The building on the right was the old Fire Station. Hopefully the brigade did not receive too many emergency calls on Monday mornings.

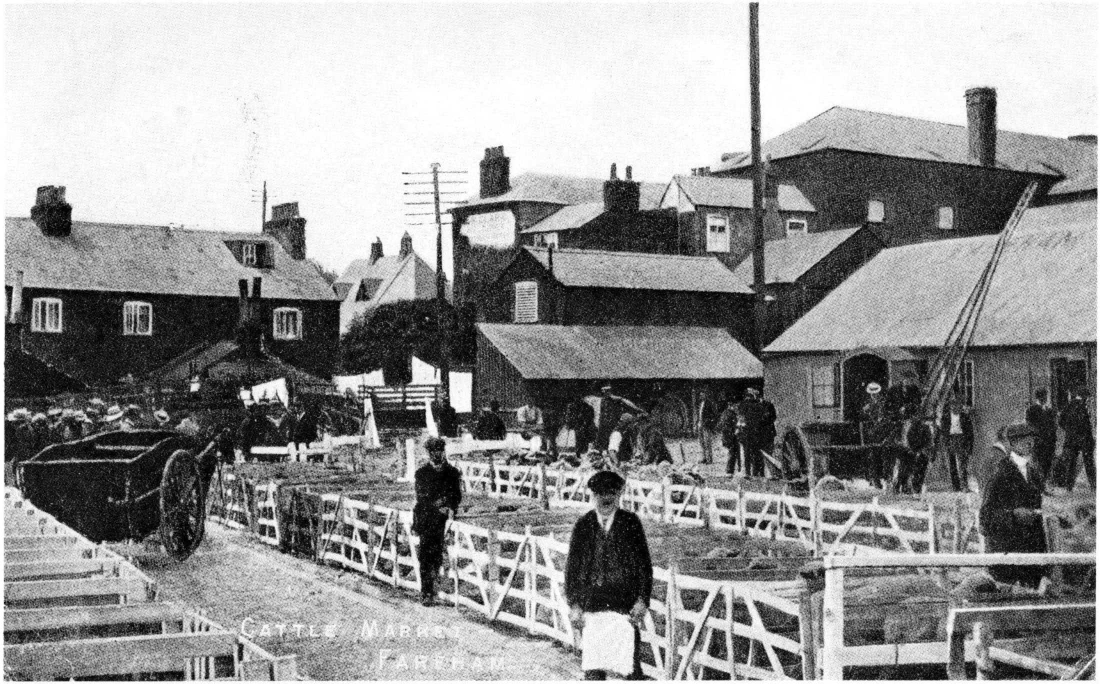

21. It was around the turn of the last century that several local farmers formed a Market Company, to be run by High Street auctioneers Austin and Wyatt. One of the Company's first actions was to move the market to its present site. Prior to this it had been held outside the old Town Hall in the West Street. In earlier days still, a Borough Market House had stood in the middle of the West Street. Then the market was a more flexible affair where private bartering went on anywhere along the streets adjacent to this building, often to be finalised in the local tavern. Today development threatens the market place but hopefully an alternative location can be found to allow this age-old Fareham tradition to survive. In this interior view of Fareham market taken in 1910 the camera of A.H. Sweasey is centreed on the sheep pens.

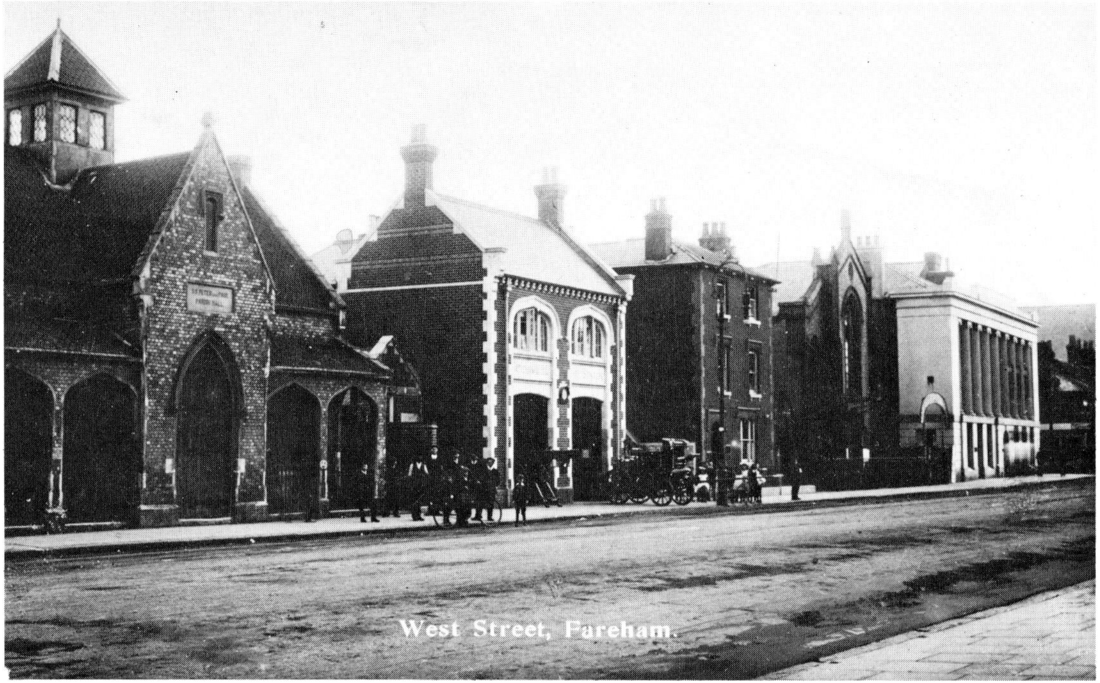

22. Fareham's first fire station came into being in the High Street in the 1860's. In 1888 it was moved to a site in Quay Street. Then in 1910 a more suitable location was found for it in West Street. Here it remained until recent years, when a new ultra-modern station was opened at the end of West Street near the Railway Station. This view of the West Street Station was photographed by A.H. Sweasey in 1914. One of the period's fire-fighting appliances can be seen on the pavement outside the building. Next door to the Fire Station stands the Parish Church Hall of St. Peter and Paul's Church.

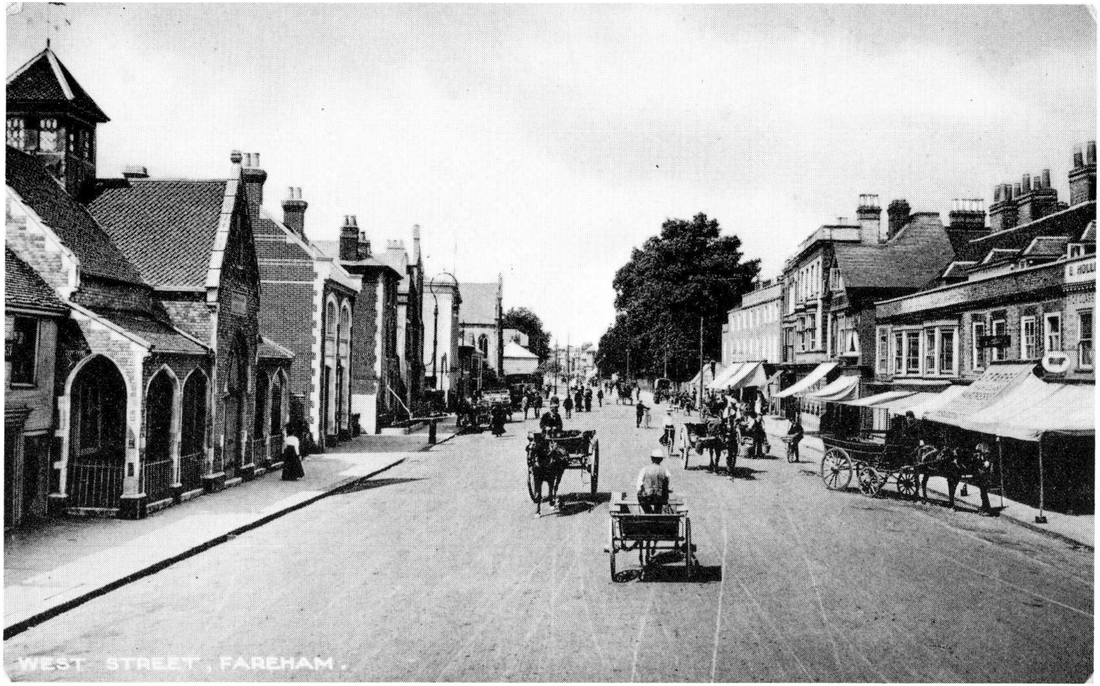

23. It would only take a few Red Indians to convince readers that this was a picture of one of the old American cowboy townships. As F.G.O. Stuart observed in 1916, with the exception of the odd cycle, there was not a trace of mechanisation in sight. Admittedly the trams did not operate at this end of the West Street, but it is pleasing to see the horse and cart and pony and trap having the run of the road. It is also apparent that nobody was too concerned about keeping to the left or right of the roads in those days. The lovely old flint building in the left forefront of the picture is the old Parish Hall. Today this stretch of West Street is the entrance to the town's ultra-modern shopping centre.

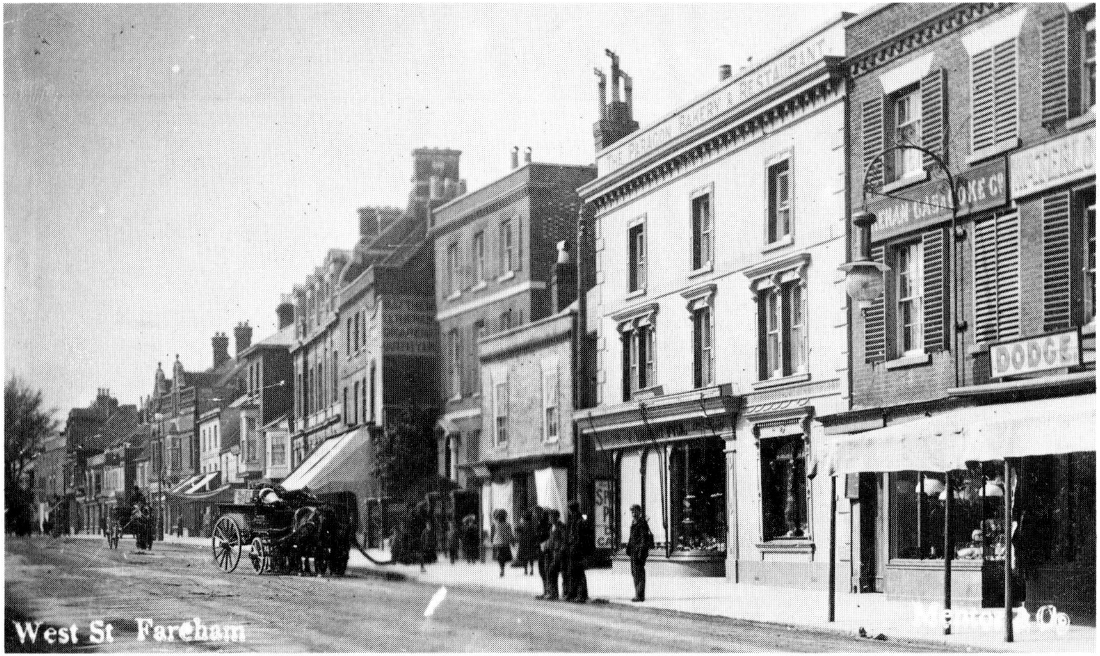

24. This 1905 view of the north side of eastern West Street was photographed by Mentor and Company. On display are some famous old Fareham trading names, alas now disappeared. At this time Dodge's the drapers and gents outfitters had already been established over fifty years. Next door is the Paragon Bakery and Restaurant. This owned by Mr. Pyle, a baker and confectioner whose cakes were a legend in the town. Running along the side of Pyle's bakery was Church Path often referred to as Pyle's Alley. This was believed to link the Parish Church of St. Peter and Paul with Fareham Harbour. It is one of a network of such ancient footpaths in the town and could well date back some two thousand years. On the other side of the path was Millard's, a corn merchants, then further along Vimpany's the jewellers and Letheren's the drapers followed by the Capital and Counties Bank. The latter an imposing building that has changed but little since the 1860's when it belonged to the Hant's Banking Company. It was taken over by Lloyds in 1918.

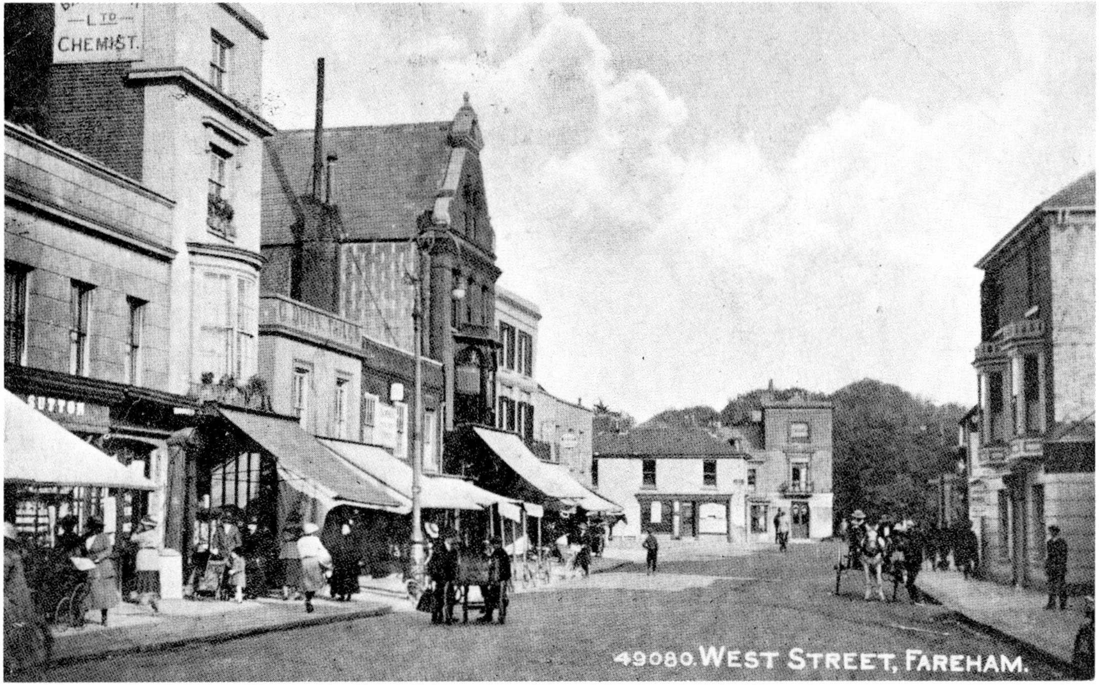

25. Three more well-known old Fareham trading names appear on this 1925 picture postcard. They are Dunn and Sons, the gentlemen's tailors and outfitters, Batchelors the chemist and Suttons the newsagents, printers and stationers. All three of them survived well into the post-war period. The business of Suttons was run by two brothers and this postcard is an example of the work done by them as printers. It is interesting how often photographers were tempted to include a glimpse of their own business premises in their work. Standing at the bottom of the High Street facing the camera is the office of Austin and Wyatt. These estate agents and auctioneers are still in business there today. Just behind them, on the corner of Union Street, can be seen the large square-fronted building that for many years now has been Soothill's Corner House Bakery.

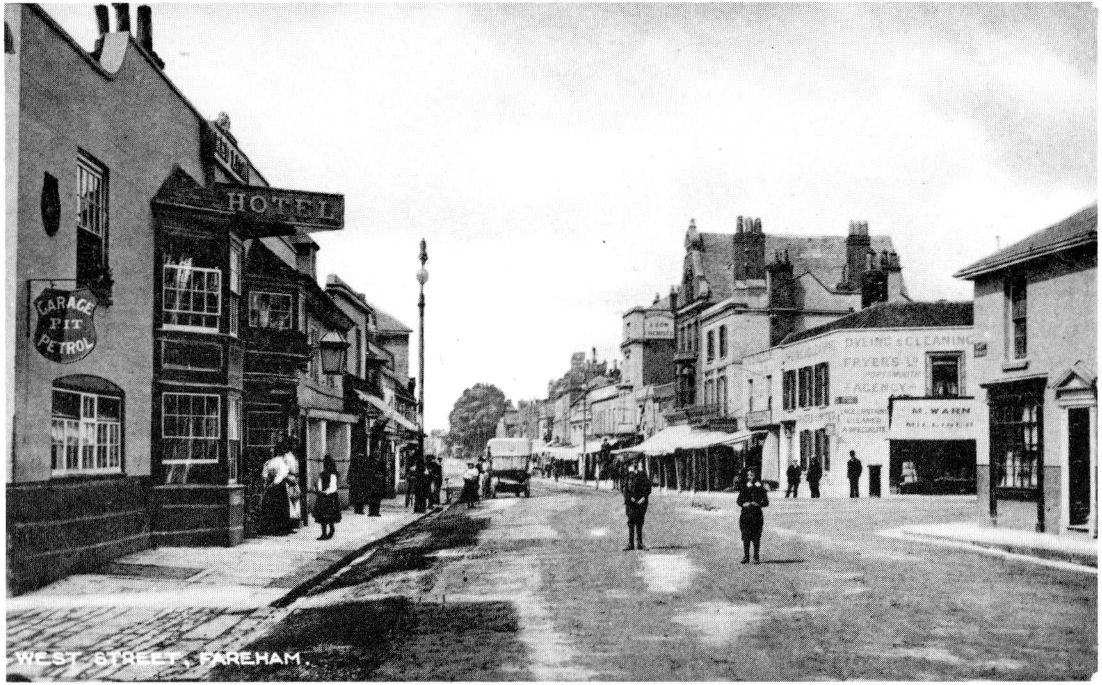

26. F.G.O. Stuart was standing in East Street at the bottom of Union Street when he pointed his camera westwards to capture this view on 26th July 1917. West Street running from here through to the Railway Station in practically a straight line had by the Second World War become filled with an almost unbroken sequence of small shops. It was at this time that it became known as Fareham's 'golden mile'. The Red Lion on the left of the picture happily still appears much the same today. It is now one of Fareham's prime hotels having been a coaching inn in days gone by. On the right are the offices of Austin and Wyatts. Prominent on the facing corner of High Street stands the premises of draper Mr. M. Warn.

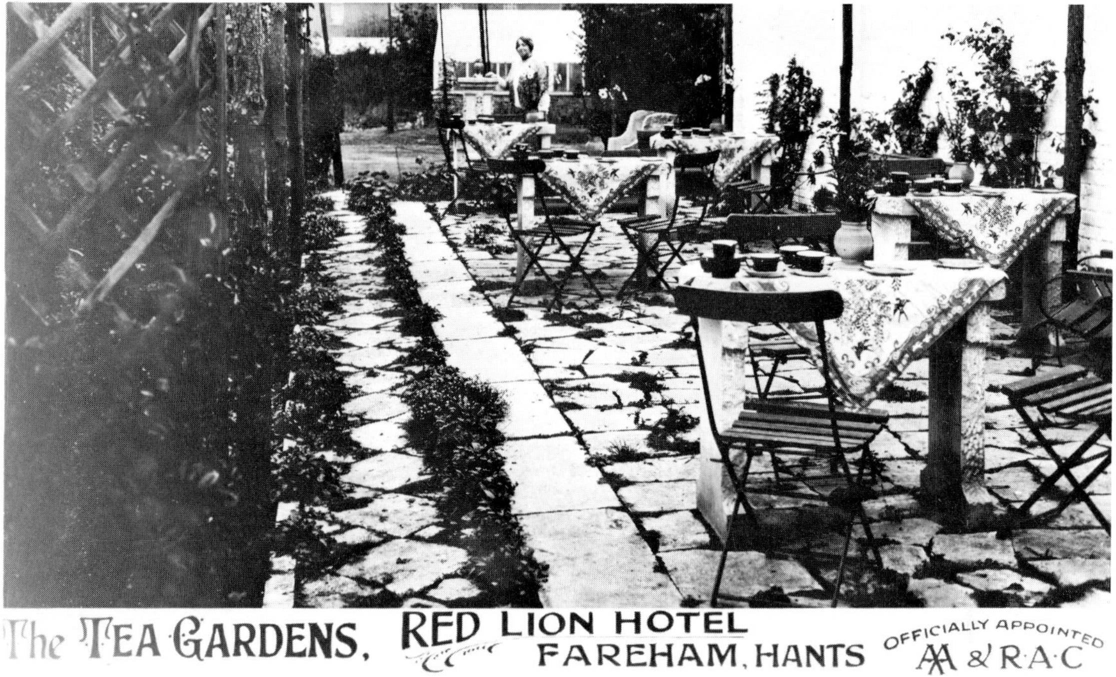

27. This is a rare advertising card for the Red Lion Hotel. The photograph was taken by Thomas Humphries of Portsmouth and the card passed through the post on 16th July 1929. Interesting to see that even in those days the hotel had the approval of the two motoring associations. The Red Lion for centuries had offered a haven for weary travellers to rest and refresh themselves. Standing in the perfect position at the top of a sharp incline on the road into town, it was much appreciated as a place to rest panting horses, and years later, over-heating engines. With the coming of the railway to the western end of Fareham, the enterprising landlord ran a twice daily horse-drawn carriage service to the station for the benefit of travellers. As well as serving as a residential hotel it has also been the venue for many of the district's grander social occasions over the years.

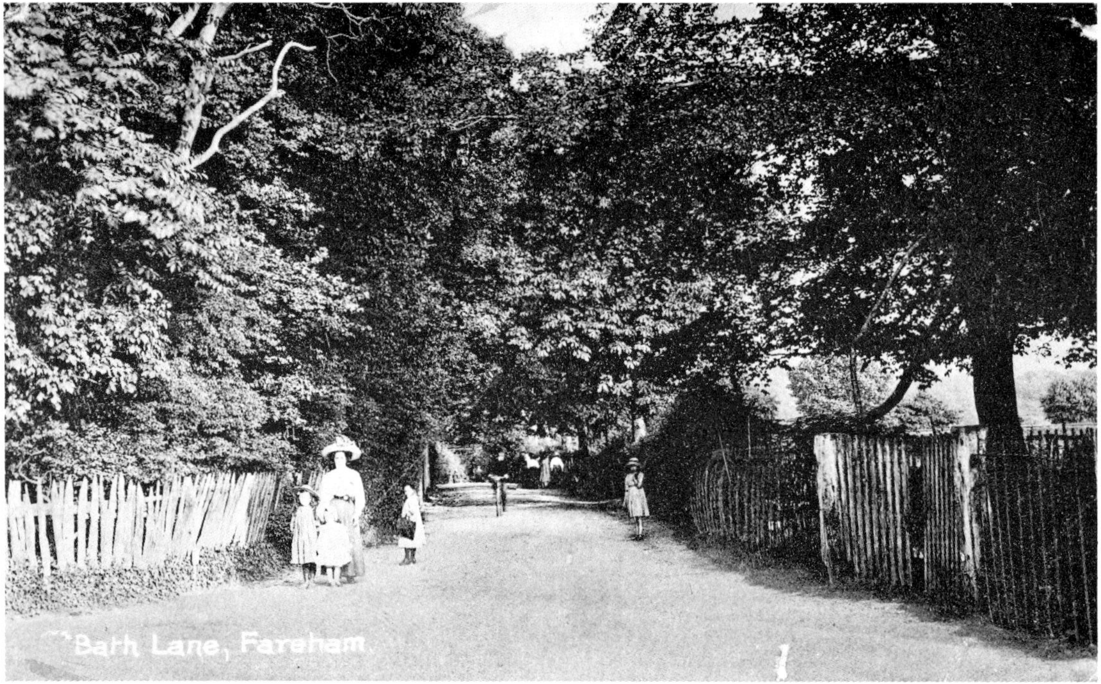

28. Bath Lane ran from East Street down to the upper reaches of Fareham Creek, and in earlier days was known as Park Lane. A sea-water bathing house was erected at the bottom of the lane in 1838. Because mixed bathing was not even thought about by any right-minded Victorian, two large baths were installed, one for men and one for women. The two baths being supplied with water from the creek at high tide. In the following years Park Lane became known locally as Bathing House Lane and eventually the name was officially changed to Bath Lane. Fareham's Park Lane today is the extension of Trinity Street. This picture shows Bath Lane as it appeared to A.H. Sweasey in April 1926.

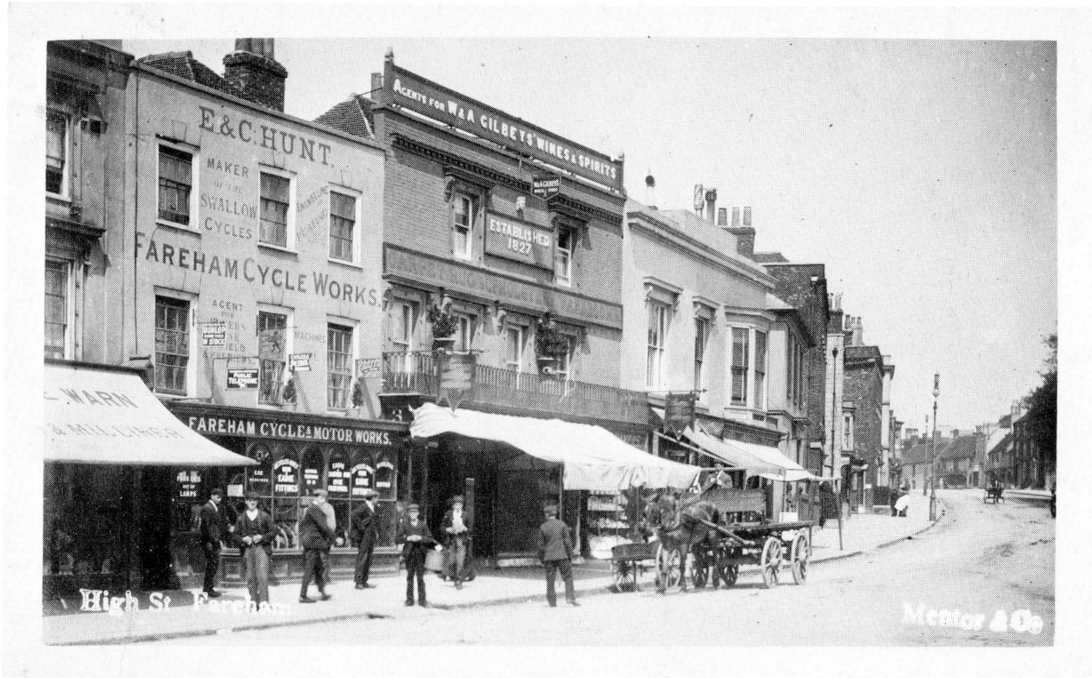

29. There was always something going on outside the premises of 'Hunts' and 'Abrahams' at the bottom of Fareham High Street. Here Mentor and Company have captured a typical scene in July 1905. The Fareham Cycle and Motor Works owned by the Hunt family was a thriving business in those days. Apart from general retailing and repairs they also made and marketed their own 'Swallow' cycles. Some of the products they sold such as 'Carless Petrol' and 'Pratts Motor Spirit' being promoted by a fascinating array of signs projecting from the front of the building. This business was later taken over by a Mr. May who traded on through the 1920's but found competition in the town becoming very keen. Next door to E. and C. Hunts, under the huge awning, stood the long established business owned by the Abraham family. They were primarily furnishers and cabinet makers, but also had the agency for Gilbey's Wines and acted as estate agents and auctioneers in their spare time. Outside the shop, patiently waiting for the next load, can be seen the horse and cart of Powell's, the local delivery agents.

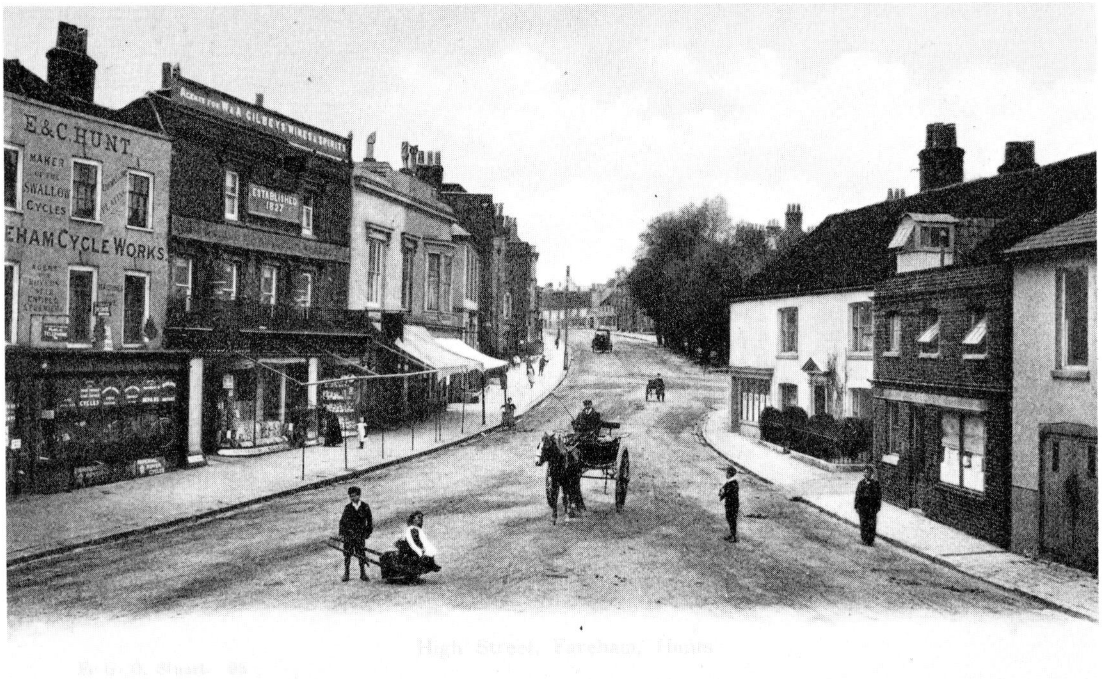

30. This is a common card by F.G.O. Stuart but it gives a nice overall view looking north up the High Street in 1913. The bottom part of the street had a few shops on each side, and featured prominently on the right of the picture are the premises of Edney's the corn chandlers. Further up, the street was mainly residential and contained many stately buildings. Leading off the High Street on either side were several courts and alleys which often passed under picturesque archways to arrive at secluded mews cottages. The fine parade of trees just visible in the centre of the picture adds even more character to a street which today is acknowledged to contain some of the finest examples of Georgian architecture in the country.

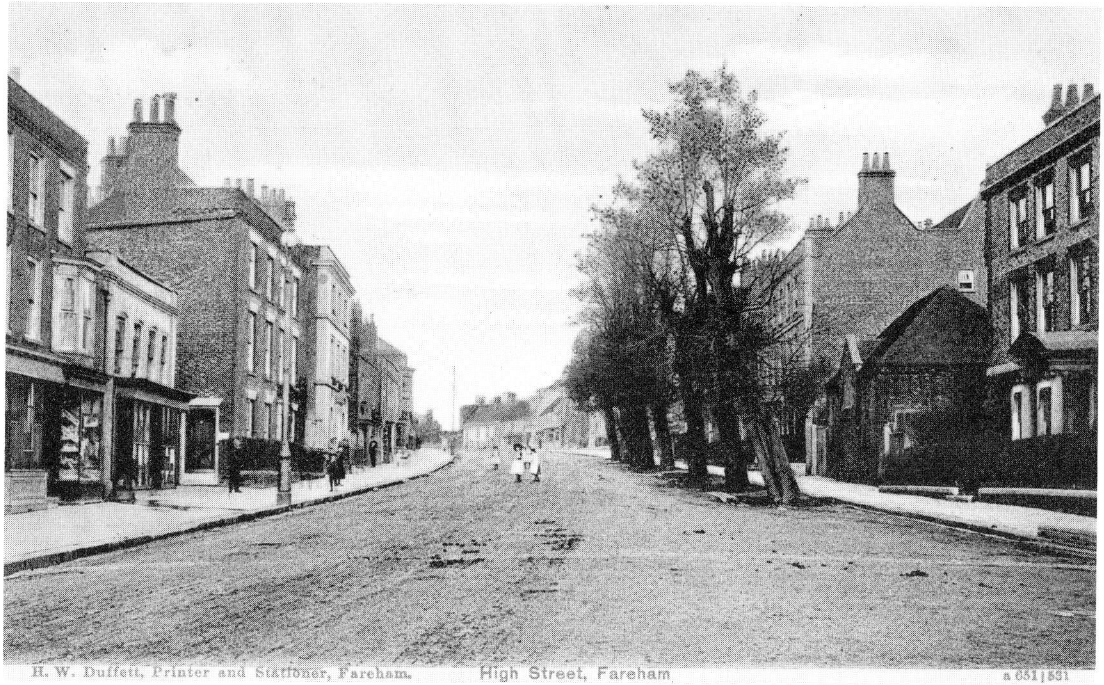

31. Fareham photographer Hector Duffett was responsible for this picture of a tranquil upper Fareham High Street in 1905. In earlier days, for a short time each year the whole street was transformed. It was back in the 13th century that the town was granted the right to hold a cheese, horse, sheep and cattle fair on 29th and 30th June each year. On those days stalls the length of the High Street were piled high with all sorts of cheeses as well as hundreds of other commodities. Supporting the stalls and sales of livestock was always a traditional pleasure fair with its swings, roundabouts, coconut shies etc, whilst a regatta was held on nearby Fareham Creek. Sadly by the middle of the last century interest was waning, the last fair was held in 1871, after which unbroken peace returned to the High Street.

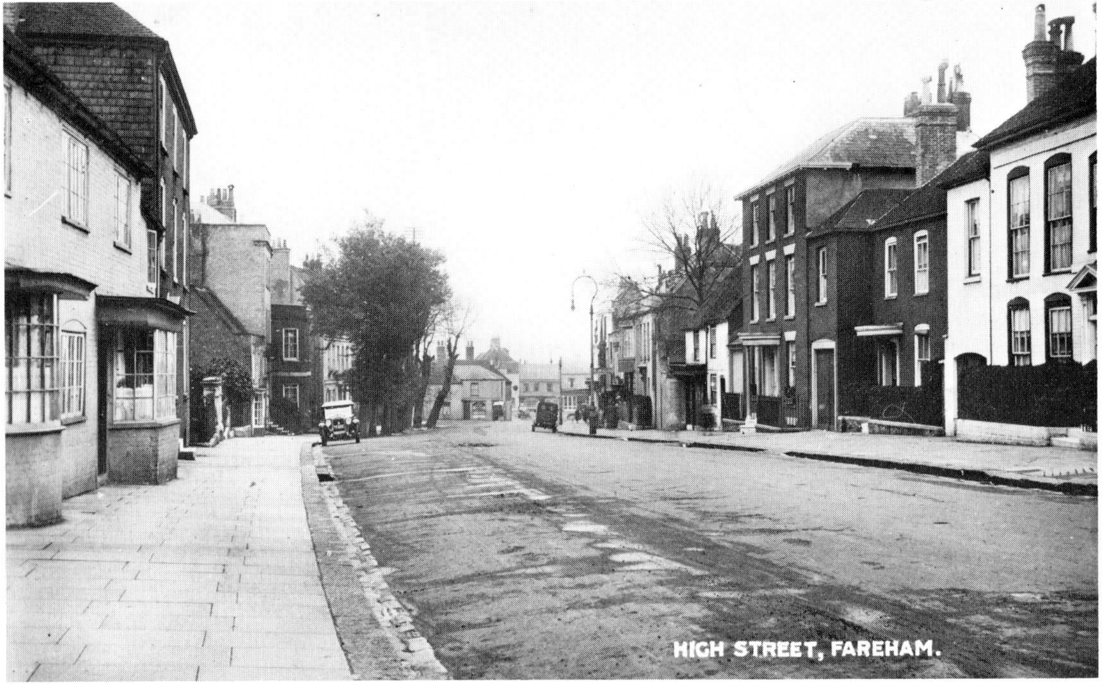

32. This 1920's view of the High Street is another example of the work of that prolific local photographer A.H. Sweasey. It was taken from a position near the top of the hill looking south towards West Street. This part of the High Street was largely residential and standing aloof from the hustle and bustle of West Street, presented a quiet air of elegance and charm. Little has changed here since the 1920's, apart from a dramatic increase in the amount of activity in the street. As the population has grown and the volume of motorised traffic in the town has increased, so has the High Street lost much of its tranquility. Although in recent years various new roads and traffic re-routing schemes have helped to ease the situation.

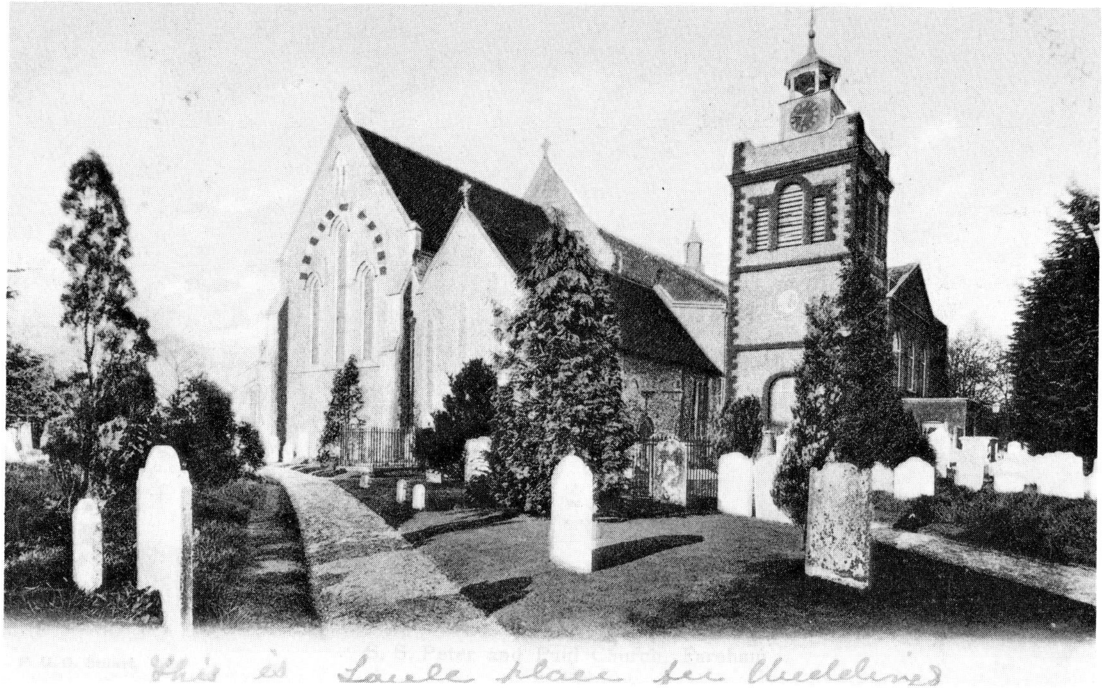

33. Predictably the most photographed building in Fareham is the Old Parish Church, here pictured by F.G.O. Stuart in 1906. The church was dedicated to St. Peter and Paul and existed in much smaller form at the time of the Domesday Book. Since then it has been rebuilt several times and today only one chancel reveals traces of mediaeval construction. The Georgian style tower was added in 1742 and there is a peal of ten bells, the tenor being cast in 1745. The bells have since been recast and two bells added as a memorial to the late George Privett, for many years Verger and Parish Clerk. Mr. Privett was also a local historian of great repute and responsible for that fine volume 'The Story of Fareham', published in 1949.

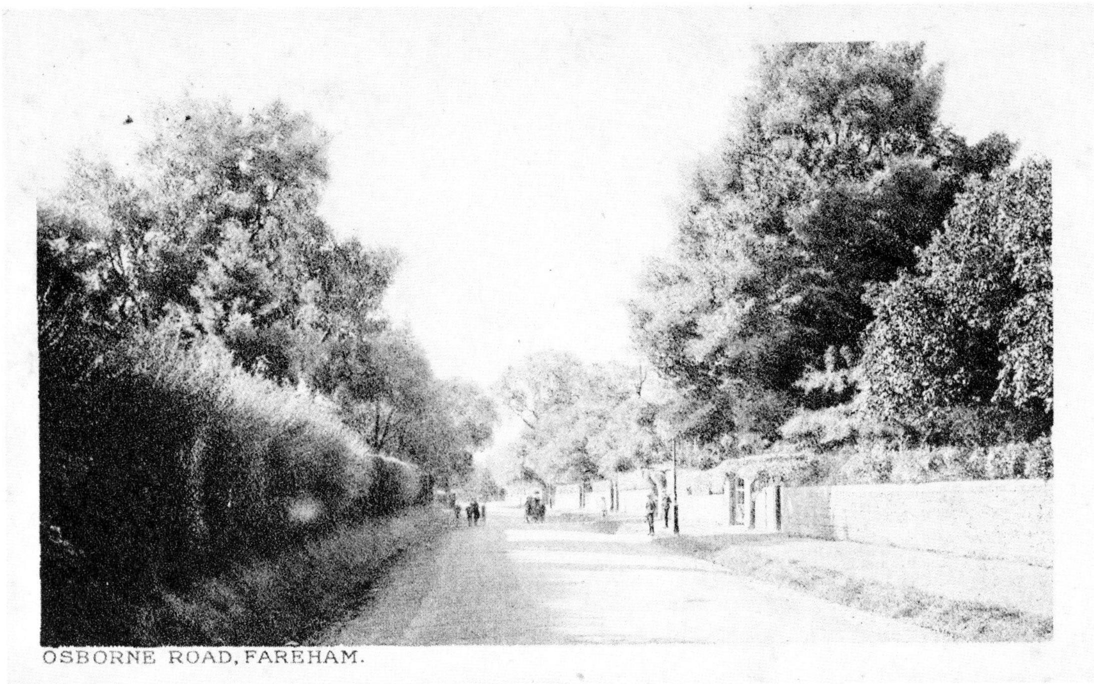

34. Leading away from the parish church in a westerly direction is Osborne Road. After a quarter of a mile it takes a ninety degree turn to the south to join up with West Street. The stretch of road pictured here was always called Osborne Road. The southern part used to be Charles Street, thus naming in full Charles Osborne, the man responsible for developing the area. Osborne Road runs along a gravel platform that marked a temporary halt in the ancient seas gradual retreat from the land in pre-historic times. This picture was published by Lamb and Coleburn of Fareham in 1919. Today the right-hand side of the road remains much the same but the hedgerows on the left have given way to the approach to Ferneham Hall and a multi-storey car park.

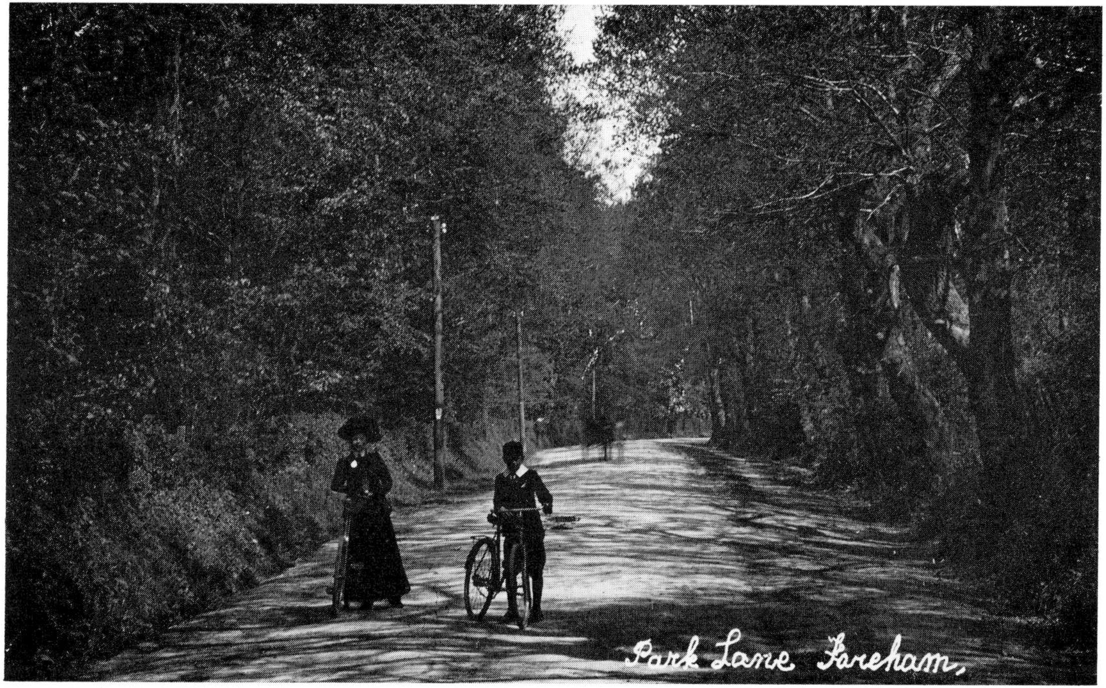

35. This is how Park Lane appeared to the photographer in 1905. It was so peaceful in those days he was lucky to find anyone to pose for the camera. The two people who obliged present a lovely example of Edwardian dress. The boy with his large, stiff white collar and the lady with her grand hat and flowing ankle-length dress which must have presented considerable problems when cycling on a windy day. Very little had changed in this part of Fareham over the years except the name of the lane. This was originally Puxhold Lane then Puxel Lane before eventually becoming Park Lane. Today the lane is lined with pre-war houses and a college on one side and a recreation ground, swimming pool and post-war housing development on the other, but happily many of the old trees remain.

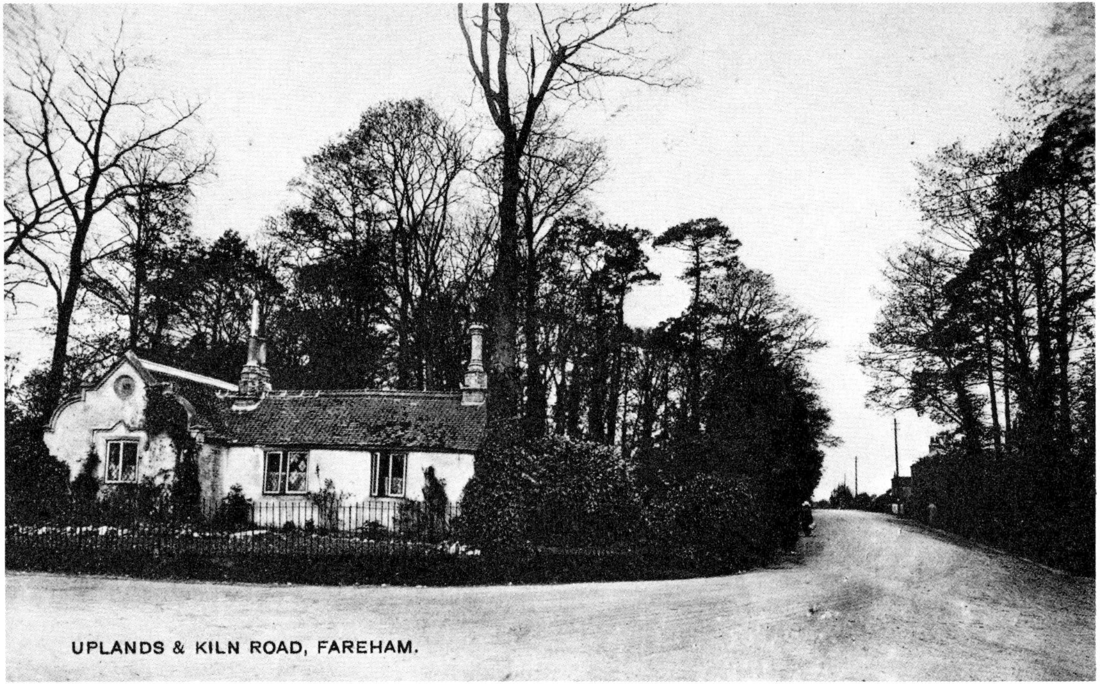

36. Close by the crossroads at the top of Park Lane, with its entrance just next to the cottage in the picture, stands Uplands House. This impressive old house dates back over two hundred years and was built for Samuel Jellicoe, a member of the famous naval family. Standing in extensive grounds at the top of the hill the house must have commanded superb views before the area was developed. Uplands is still there today and is now a home for the elderly. Kiln Road, which was the route to Fontley village and Knowle Hospital, can be seen here as it leads off Park Lane. This postcard was printed in France and published by R.H. Croker, a confectioner and tobacconist of West Street, Fareham in 1922.

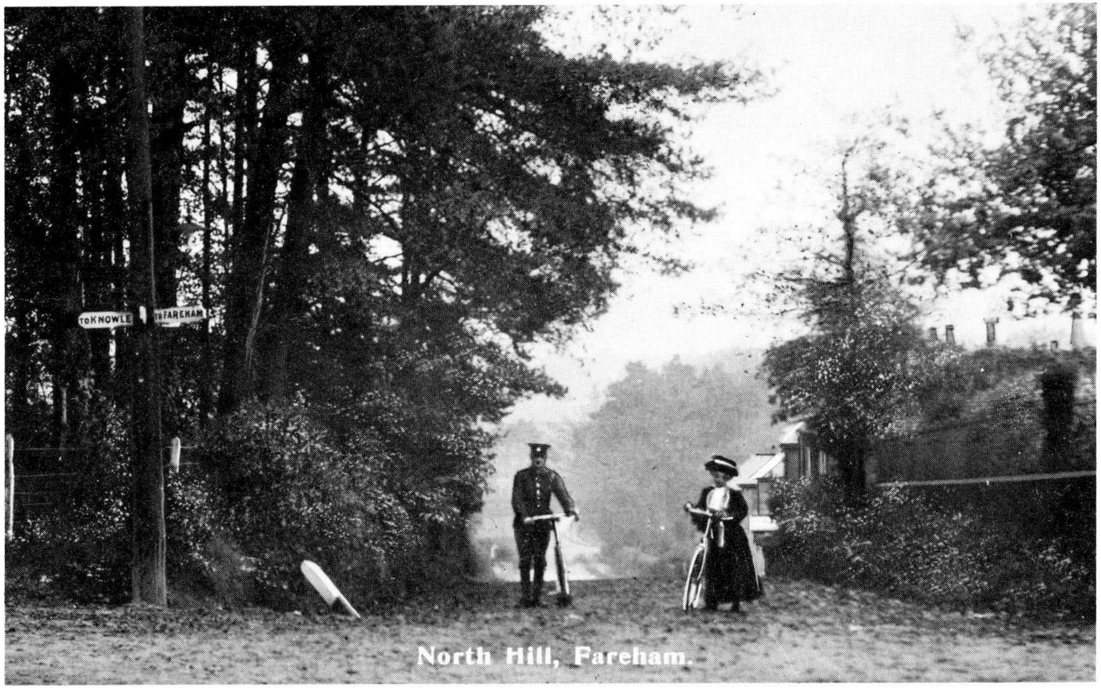

37. This is another of the roads forming the crossroads at the top of Park Lane. North Hill in the old days was the main road out of Fareham for travellers to Wickham and all points north. A toll gate used to be in operation at the crossroads, and no doubt the tollkeepers led a trouble-free existence, with travellers being far too exhausted from struggling up the hill to feel like arguing about the toll charges. Lined with just a few cottages, the hill really was a steep one, presenting a formidable obstacle to the coach horses of old and indeed to the engines and brakes of the earlier motorised transport. This view was on an A.H. Sweasey postcard dating from 1913.

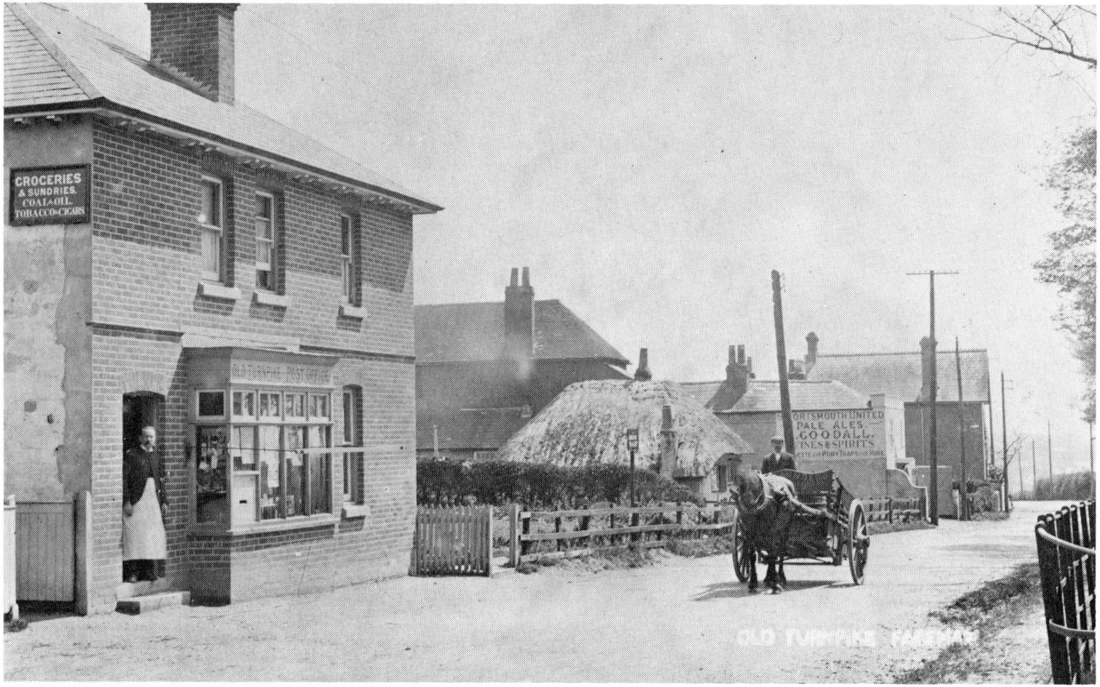

38. The fourth road forming the crossroads in north Fareham with Park Lane, Kiln Road and North Hill is Old Turnpike, formerly known as North Road. This was the view looking down the road from near the top in 1906. On the left is the Old Turnpike Post Office and General Stores that survived until just a few years ago, and still stands as a private residence. Further down the road, just past the establishment offering pony traps for hire, is the New Inn public house. This was no doubt the last calling place of the brewer's horse and cart seen climbing the hill. The tollgate at the top of the hill had been transferred to the bottom of Old Turnpike in time for the opening of the new low level route to Wickham.

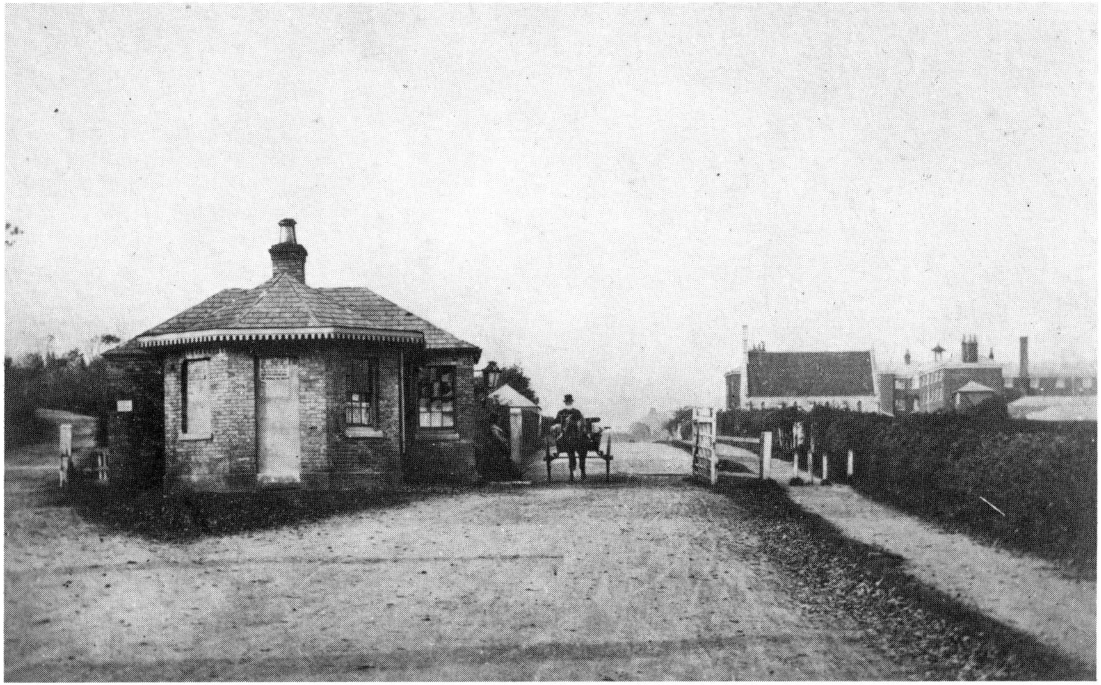

39. This picture of the Turnpike Tollgate was taken by Sidney Smith around 1880. The tollhouse stood on the site now occupied by the Turnpike Garage. The hill climbing off to the left of the picture is Old Turnpike. Having just journeyed along the Wickham Road to Fareham, the old gentleman on the pony and trap is seen paying his dues. The story goes that some devious travellers preferred to suffer a roundabout route through Wallington Village and a series of narrow, muddy lanes rather than pay the toll. In an era when time was of less importance, the financial savings of such a detour no doubt had attractions for those with a sound knowledge of the local geography. The buildings on the right of Wickham road are the old Fareham Workhouse which became St. Christopher's Hospital in 1948.

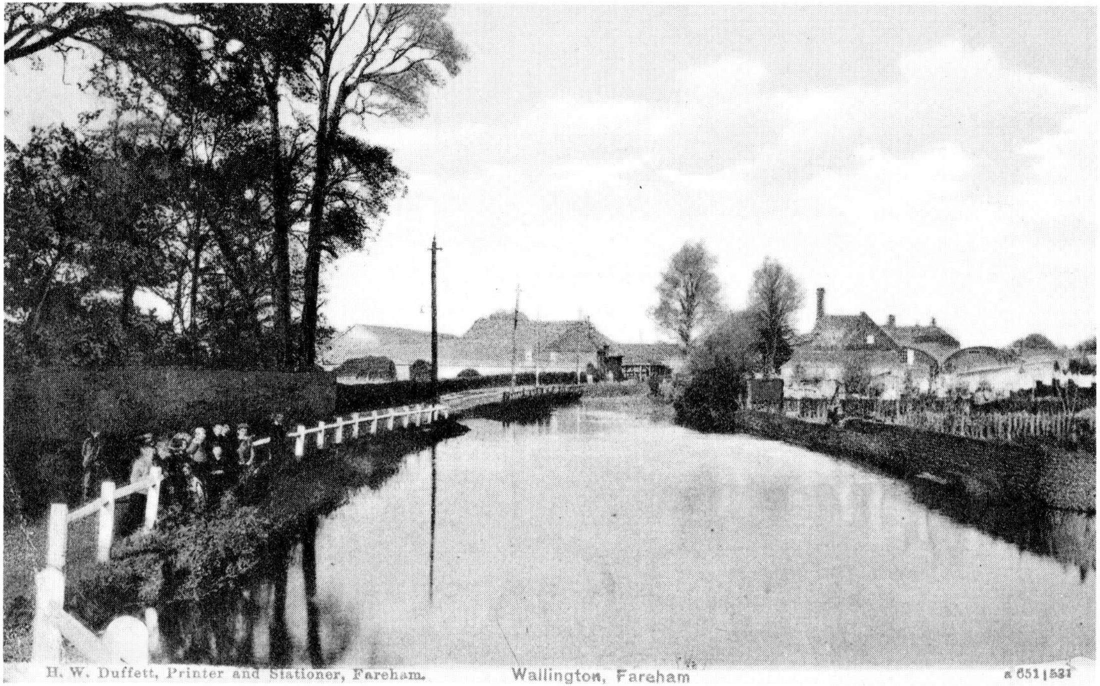

40. Standing on Wallington bridge and facing north, Hector Duffett photographed this view of the river and village of Wallington, before an attentive audience in 1908. Wallington was the first fording place on the river that rises in the South Downs and meanders down to empty into the upper reaches of Fareham Creek. The finding of flint implements in the area substantiates the belief that a settlement existed on the river banks around this lowest crossing point as far back as pre-historic times. Up until recent times the entire population lived in picturesque cottages in Wallington Shore Road and North Wallington. It is hard to believe that such a dreamy little hamlet could have supported two thriving industries over the years.

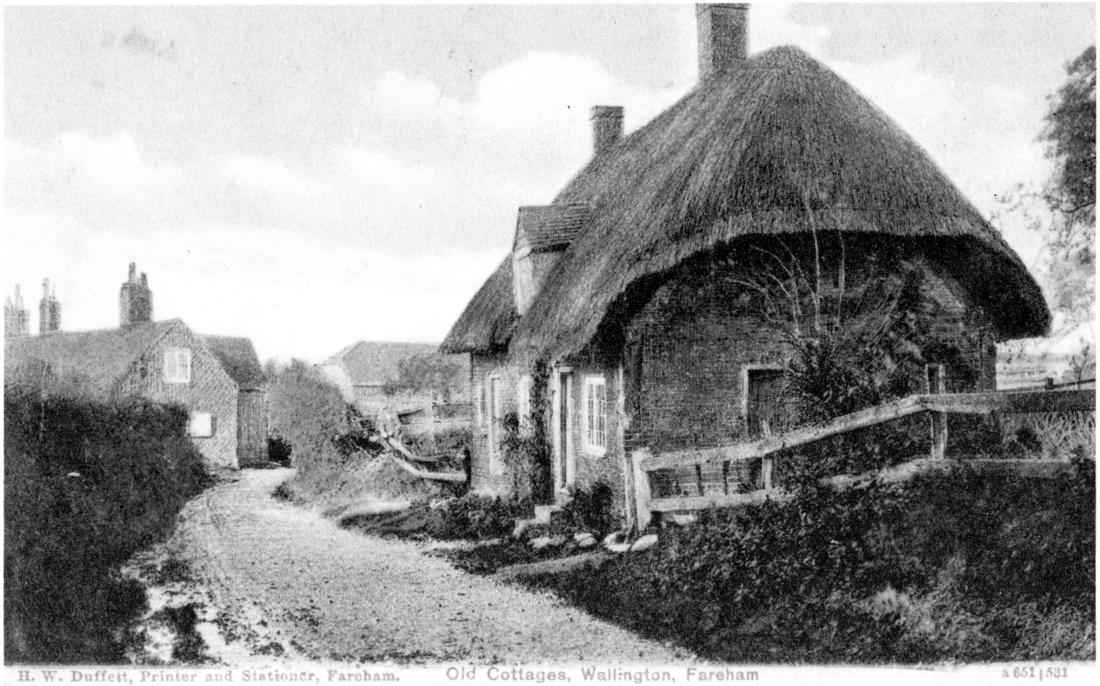

41. Wallington village, pictured here in close-up by Hector Duffett in 1908, was for many years the site of a high quality tannery. When it was first established in the 17th century, the hides and bark used in the tannery, and the finished products were all carried by sea via the Fareham Quays. With the coming of the railway, cartloads of hides and bark travelling between railway station and tannery became a common sight in the town. The tannery employed some three dozen men and was in operation right up to the First World War. The other local industry was in the form of Wallington Brewery. This was located in the north of the village and commenced operations in the early 19th century. It was to continue to produce an ale of considerable local repute for more than a hundred years.

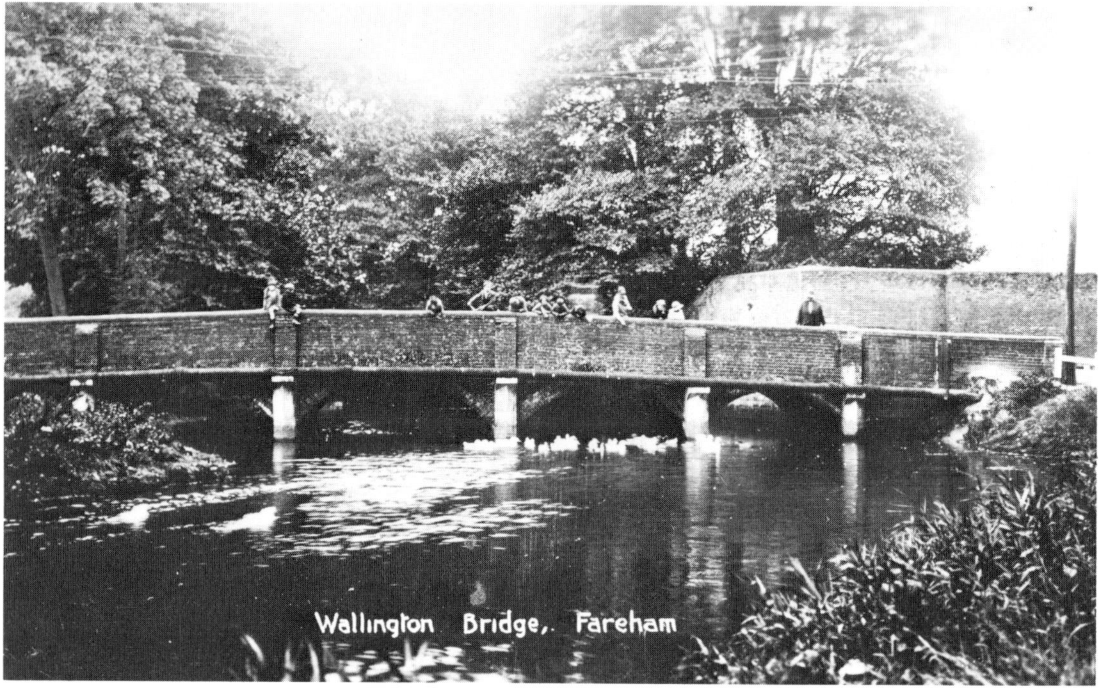

42. The old Wallington Bridge is pictured here in 1929 in a postcard published by Suttons of Fareham. It was obviously a peaceful spot where the local inhabitants liked to linger and fatten up the large duck population. The lovely old brick built bridge dates from the late 18th century and was a picturesque link between Wallington village and the rest of Fareham. Today the major road works in the area have tended to isolate the village. Whilst in 1978 the old bridge itself was under threat from the Southern Water Authority. The resolution of a group of local residents finally dispelled any plans for its demolition and the locality has now been declared a conservation area.

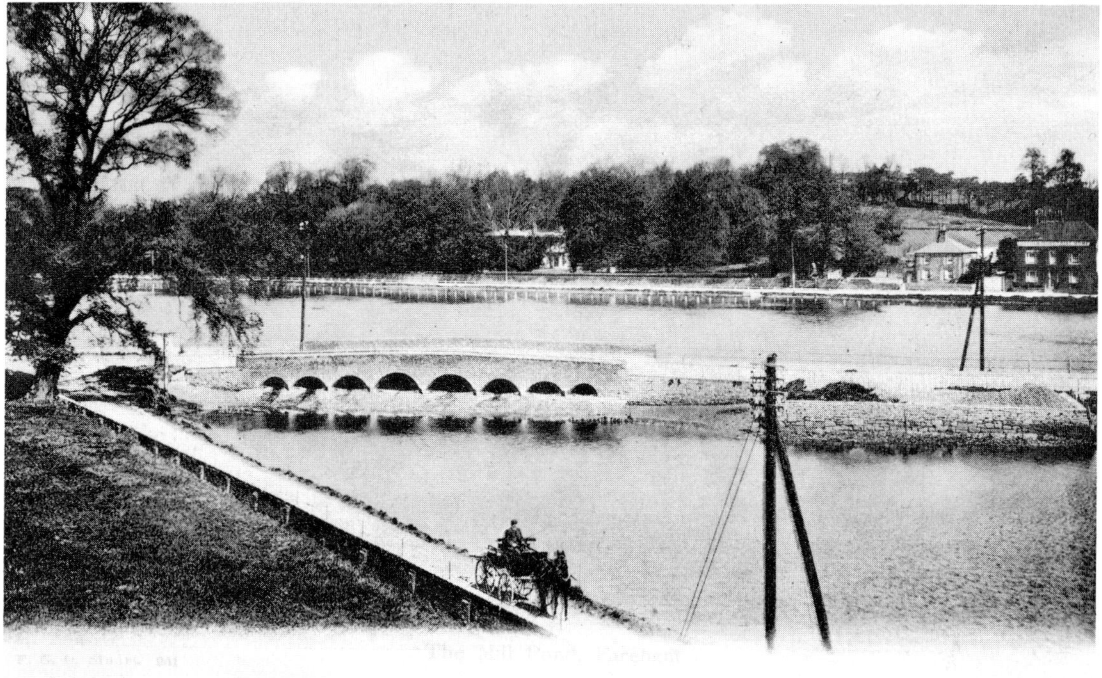

43. Just down the river from Wallington Bridge was the Millpond as pictured here by F.G.O. Stuart in 1905. Running along the background is Wallington Shore Road and on the gentle slopes beyond were large residences like Wallington House and East Hill Lodge where lived the local aristocracy. On the right of the picture stands St. Edith's Church of England Home. This was founded in 1869 as an industrial home where girls received training in domestic duties. Two years after this picture was taken the Church of England Society for Waifs and Strays had the building completely modernised. Today it survives as the Roundabout Hotel but most of the old millpond has disappeared beneath the Delme roundabout.

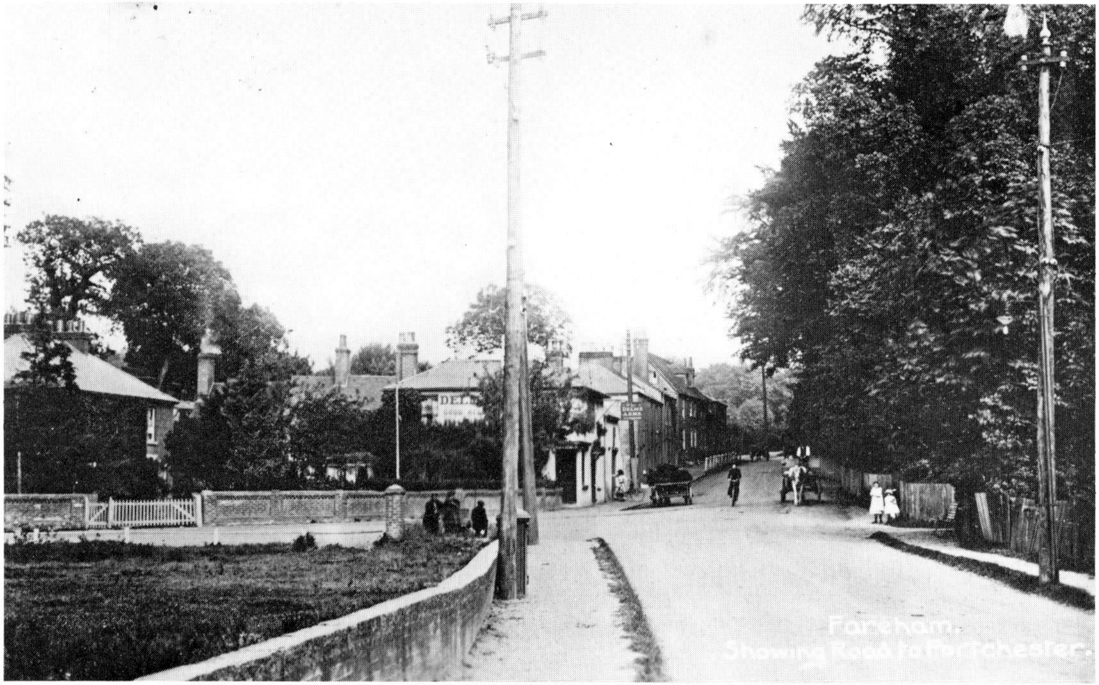

44. Pictured here is the point where Wallington Shore road meets the main Fareham to Porchester road at what used to be known as the Delme Arm's corner. Photographer Mr. Sweasey appears to have been standing on the bridge almost under the railway viaduct when taking this scene in 1912. The old Delme Arms public house, despite a disastrous fire, still graces the same spot today. The routing of the new main road to Porchester to the other side of those splendid trees in the picture meant that the public house, adjoining cottages and that part of the main road were all preserved in a pleasant backwater just off the new Delme roundabout.

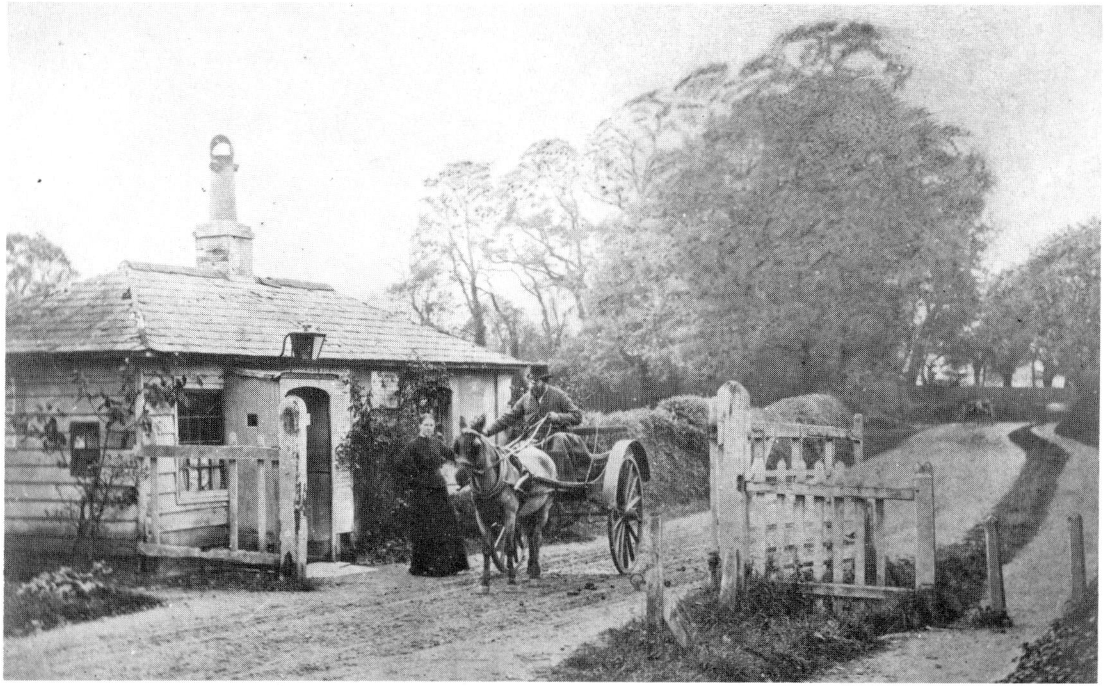

45. Just on past the Delme Arms public house, nearing the top of the incline leading out of Fareham towards Porchester, and guarding the eastern approach to the town stood East Cams tollhouse. It can still be seen today on the north side of the A27 just a few yards to the Fareham side of Downend Road. In this close-up picture by Sidney Smith circa 1885, the lady in charge can clearly be seen collecting the toll. The large five-bar gate stands open to allow the pony and trap to pass through and to await the next client who can be seen in the distance, approaching from Porchester. This was one of six tollgates, the one at Blackbrook having already been pictured, that lay along the Titchfield to Cosham road and belonged to the Titchfield and Cosham Trust.

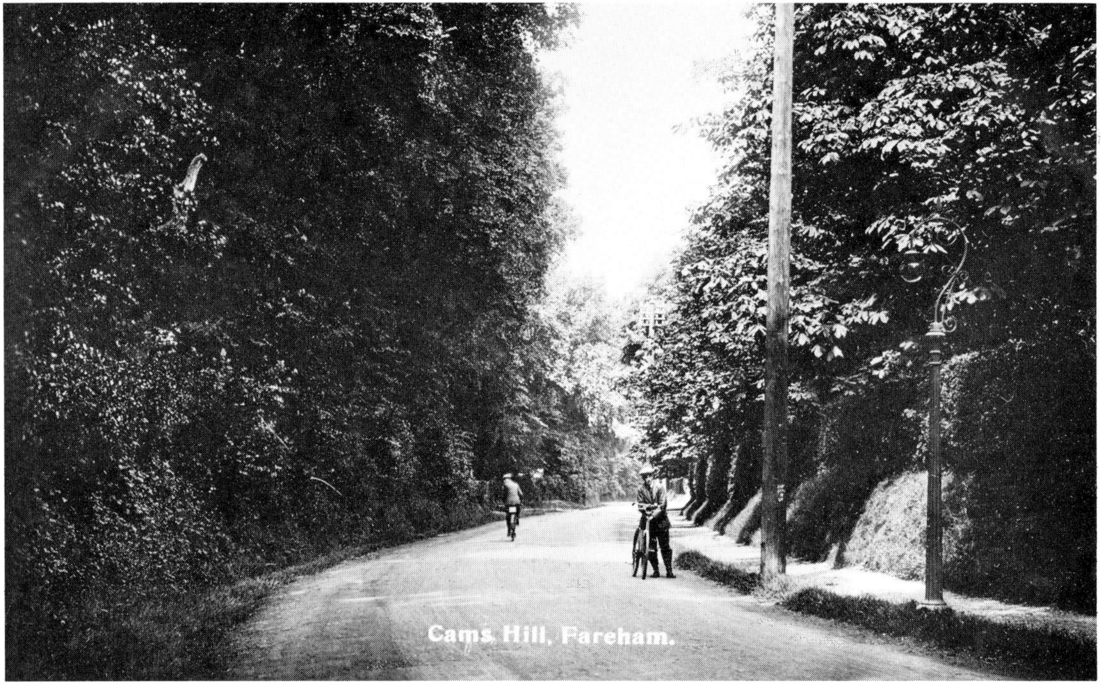

46. In 1927 this road leading into the town from the east was lined with rows of magnificent trees. Cams Hill itself though was still a steady climb, and the cyclist facing the camera was no doubt only to pleased to pause and pose. The free-wheeling cyclist on his way down the hill can only spare a backward glance. What a pleasant walk it must have been down the single, sheltered footpath to the millpond, or on into the town. It is very different today with most of the trees and hedgerows having disappeared. Four lanes of traffic career by in clouds of exhaust fumes, whilst the wind sweeps in unchecked from the open waters to the south.

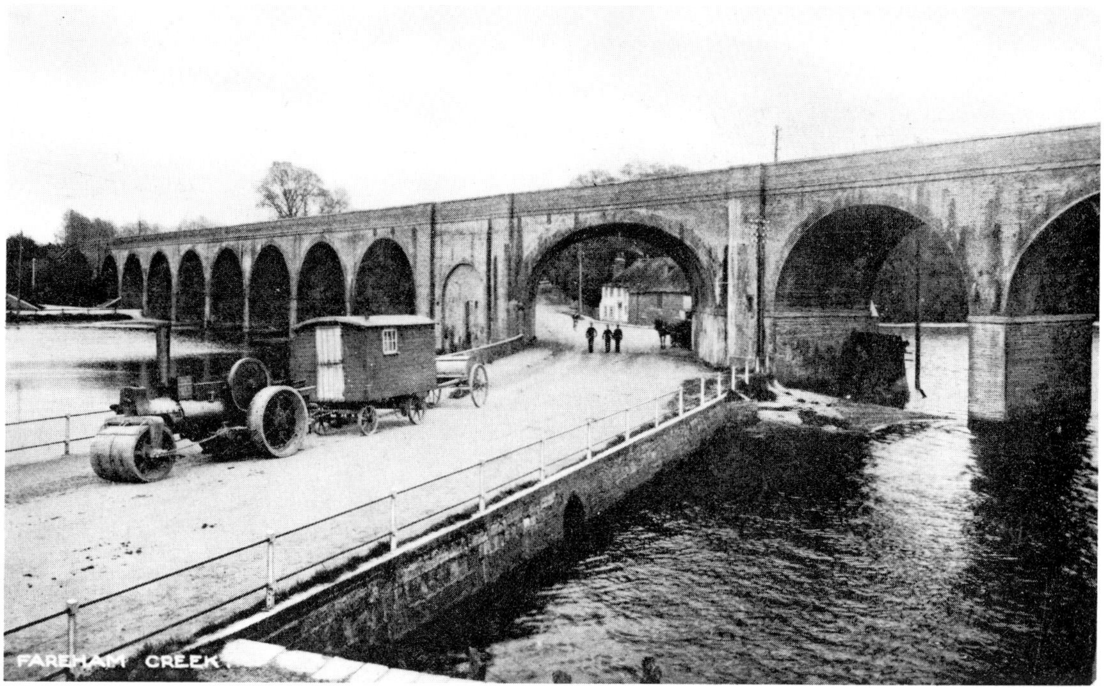

47. In pride of place in this 1916 photograph by F.G.O. Stuart are what appears to be an abandoned steam roller, workmen's caravan and trailer. Possibly the three figures walking under the railway viaduct are on their way to reclaim them. The road over the Creek passes under the viaduct and on up into the town. The building that can be seen through the archway is Cams Mill. The cameraman was clever enough to take his picture at high tide when Fareham Creek was looking at its best. Most of this scene is now replaced by new road systems and a large roundabout. The viaduct itself being almost dwarfed by an enormous concrete traffic flyover.

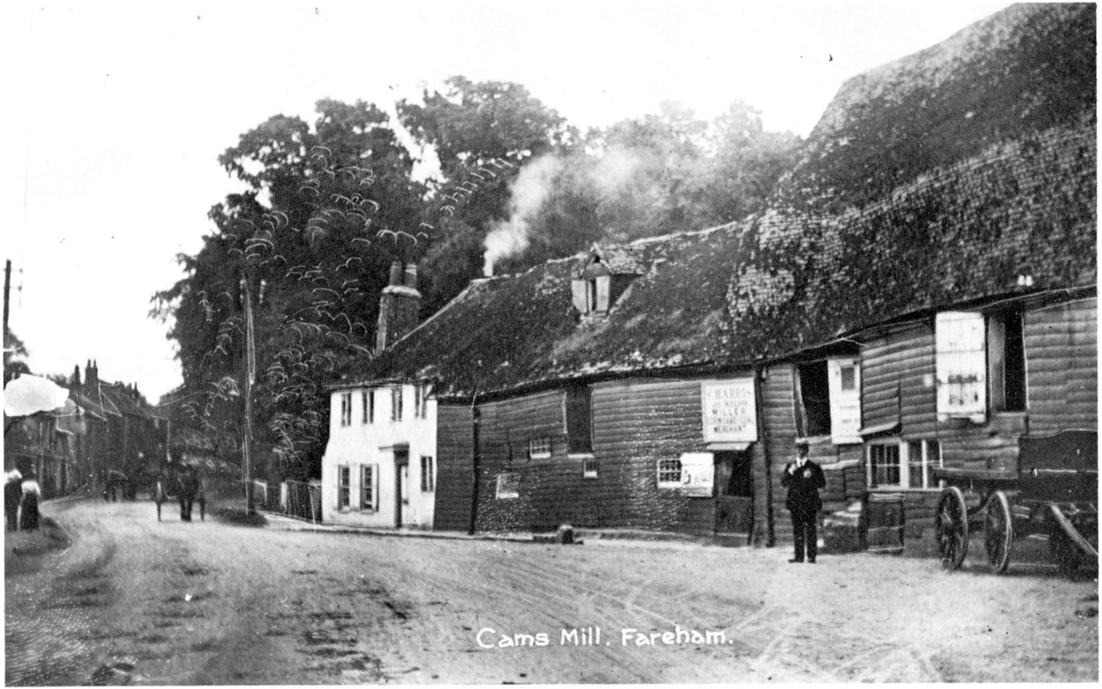

48. The Domesday Book referred to two mills at Fareham, one of which occupied the site of the old mill seen here. In this A.H. Sweasey photograph of 1915, the gentleman posing proudly outside the mill was presumably Mr. S. Harris, the owner at that time. The large sign board states the proprietor to be a miller, corncake and coal merchant. Before Mr. Harris the mill had been owned for many years by a Mr. Clark and was indeed known locally as Clark's mill. Cams Mill, to give it its proper name, fronted on to the main Fareham to Portsmouth road at the bottom of East Street. In the years previous to the taking of this picture the mill had been gradually lapsing into a poor state of repair. The situation continued on through the war years and in 1920 the decision was taken to demolish it, thus severing another of Fareham's links with the past.

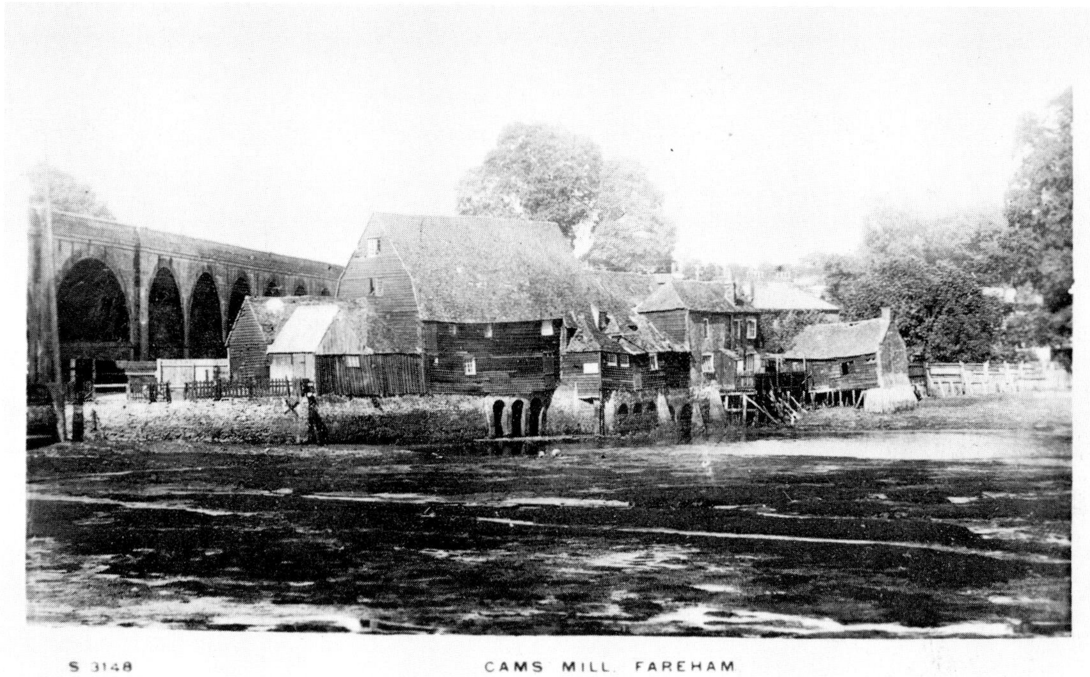

49. This is the rear view of the old mill standing on the water's edge at Cams. The railway viaduct seen to the left of the mill was constructed in the 1840's. This was to carry the trains across the upper reaches of Fareham Creek when the line was extended from Fareham to Portsmouth in 1848. The demolition of the mill in 1920 is said to have upset many of the local residents. The old tarred wooden building was certainly picturesque and is said to have attracted artists for many miles around. This seems to be borne out by the wide selection of sketches and paintings that exist of the old mill buildings and the Creek on which it stood.

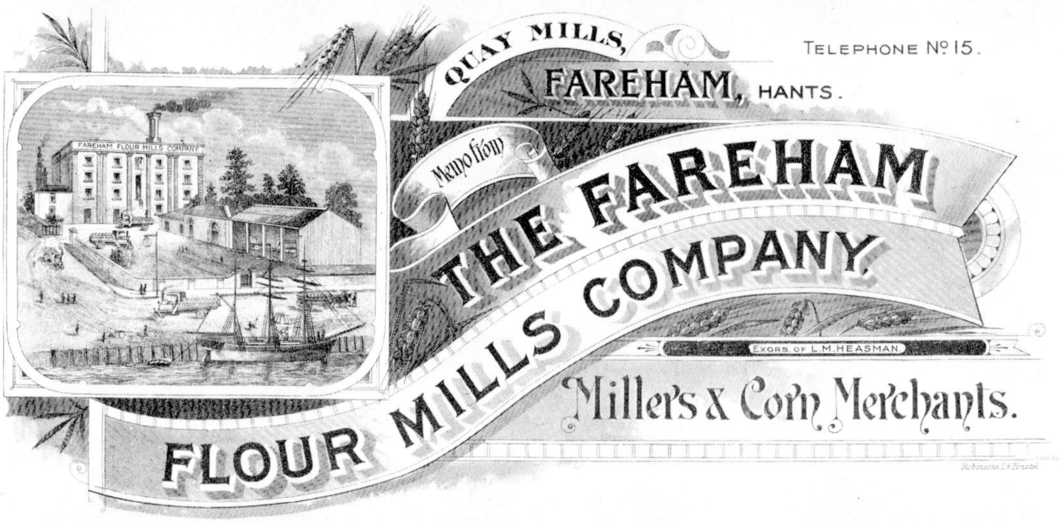

50. Further down Fareham Creek stood another large millhouse which had been built at the Lower Quay by Thomas Burrell in 1830. This mill was driven by steam and was taken over by the Heasman family towards the end of the 19th century. In their hands it was extensively modernised and became the first building in the town to have electricity. For over one hundred years the mill was at the centre of the hive of industry that surrounded Fareham's Lower Quay. It was not until 1960 that milling operations finally ended. The letterhead shown here was the type used by the Fareham Flour Mills Company around the turn of the century.

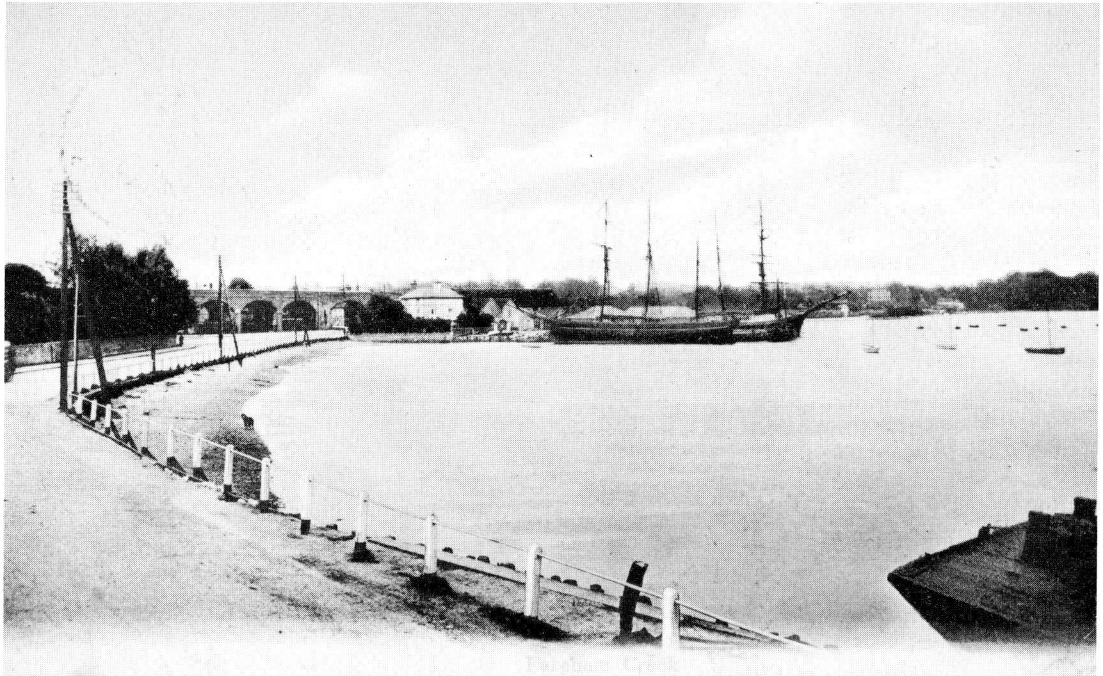

51. For many centuries Fareham was a flourishing seaport with vessels bringing such imports as coal, corn, salt, hides and bark to the town's quays. This cargo was then replaced with products of the Fareham area such as timber, leather bricks, pottery and grain. A ship-building industry had started up on the shores of Fareham Creek as far back as the 16th century. This was to give the town a big advantage when a boom in ship-building took place along the south coast in the late 18th century. This industry continued for one hundred years before starting to wane, although the early part of this century still saw a large number of smaller pleasure craft being built locally. The serene looking Creek here was photographed by F.G.O. Stuart in 1905. On the left can be seen the main road from Gosport leading under the distant railway viaduct and up to the town centre.

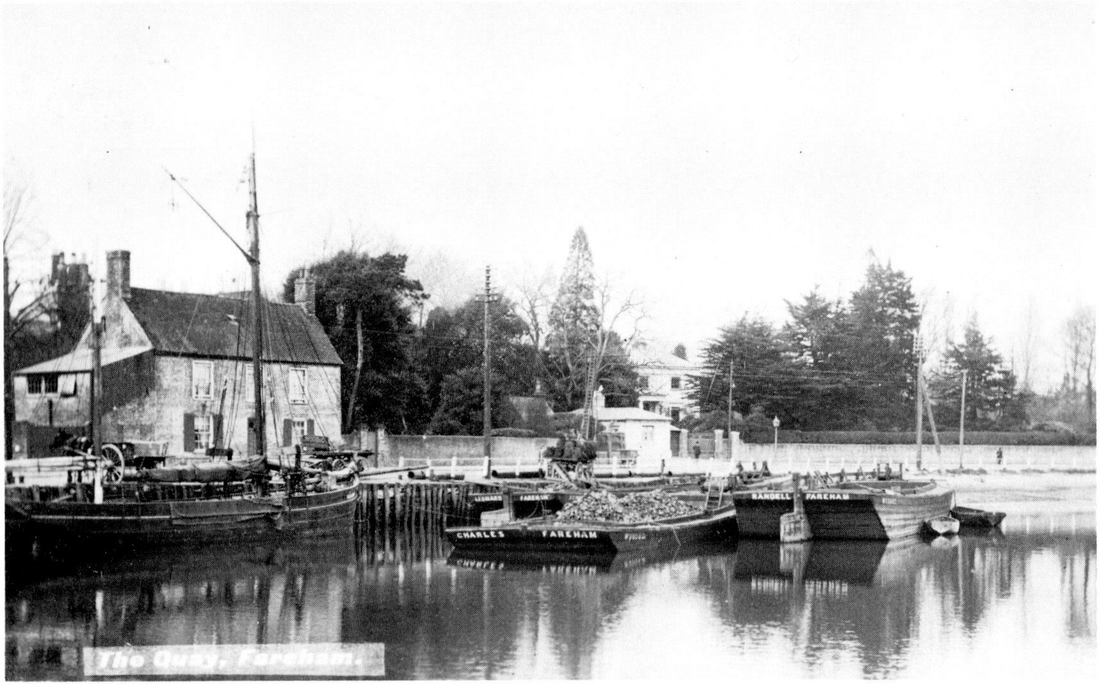

52. When this photograph of the quay was taken in 1906 there seems to have been a lull in the usual activity. Tied up alongside the quay are three coal barges in the process of being unloaded. These flat-bottomed craft belonged to local coal merchants Wood and Company and were towed up from Portsmouth by tugs. One of the old horse-drawn carts can be seen on the quay half loaded with sacks of coal. The house in the background stands on the far side of the main Gosport to Fareham road. It was one of several fine homes that were built overlooking the Creek. In the days before non-stop motor traffic roared along the main road these houses must have been the envy of all.

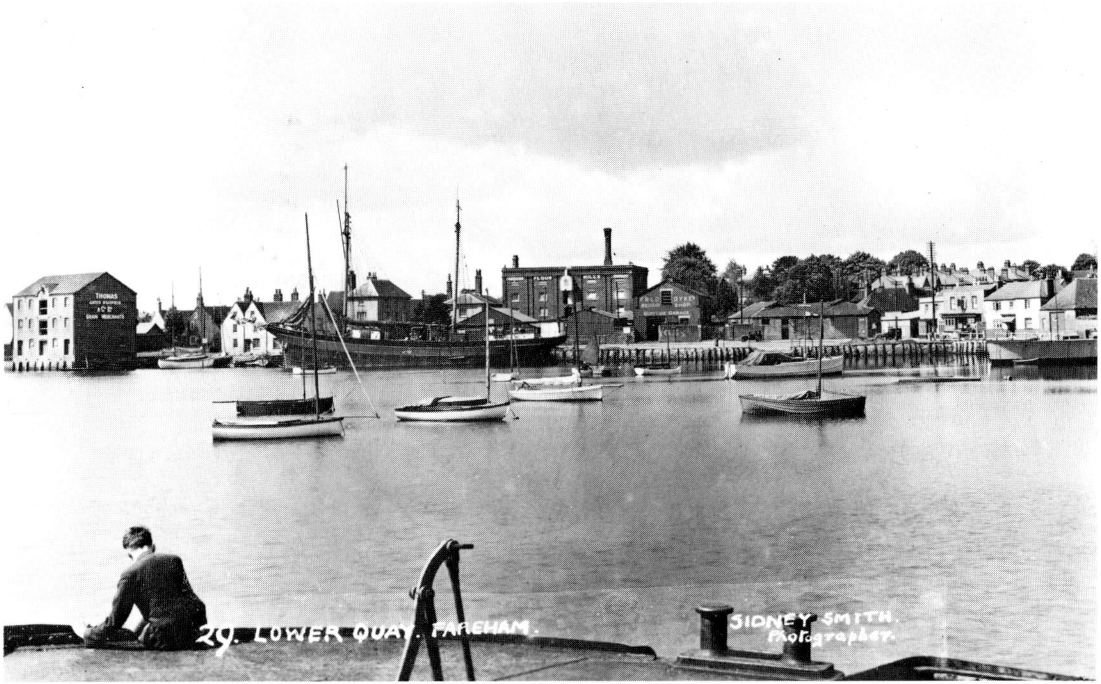

53. The Lower Quay area appears here as viewed by Sidney Smith from the upper quay in 1930. Prominent in the middle of the photograph is the Fareham Flour Mill. Next to this is the quayside garage and repair shop of Fred Dyke. Mr. Dyke went on to become one of the town's most prominent businessmen building up a large haulage and removals concern. His wife served on the local council for many years, and many charities owe her a debt of gratitude. By 1930 the gradual silting up of the deep-water channel, coupled with the vast advances made by road and rail transport, had drastically reduced the Creeks's commercial use. Only the occasional small coaster carrying corn or shingle continuing to call. As the picture shows, the pleasure boat was taking over the Creek and replacing work-stained old hulls with a colourful array of sails.

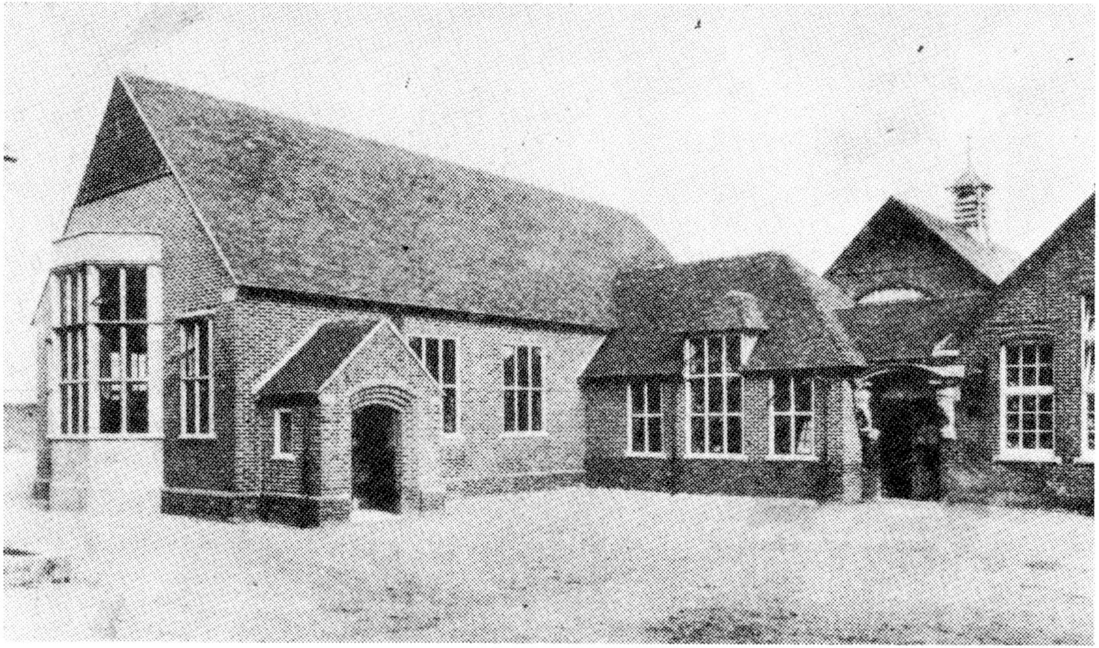

54. When wealthy Fareham Timber merchant William Price died in 1721 his will instructed that his West Street house be used as a school for thirty of the poorer boys and girls in the parish. The school, to be supported by the proceeds from his estate at Elson and Crocker Hill, was to have as trustees the vicar of the parish and his church wardens. Provision was also made for a resident schoolmaster and an annual clothing allowance for each pupil. The schoolhouse then stood on the site of the old Fareham Fire Station building. Having fallen into disrepair it was rebuilt on the same site in 1842 and remained there for another sixty-five years. In 1907 it was considered no longer suitable and a new school building was constructed in Park Lane. This picture of the new school building was taken in 1927.

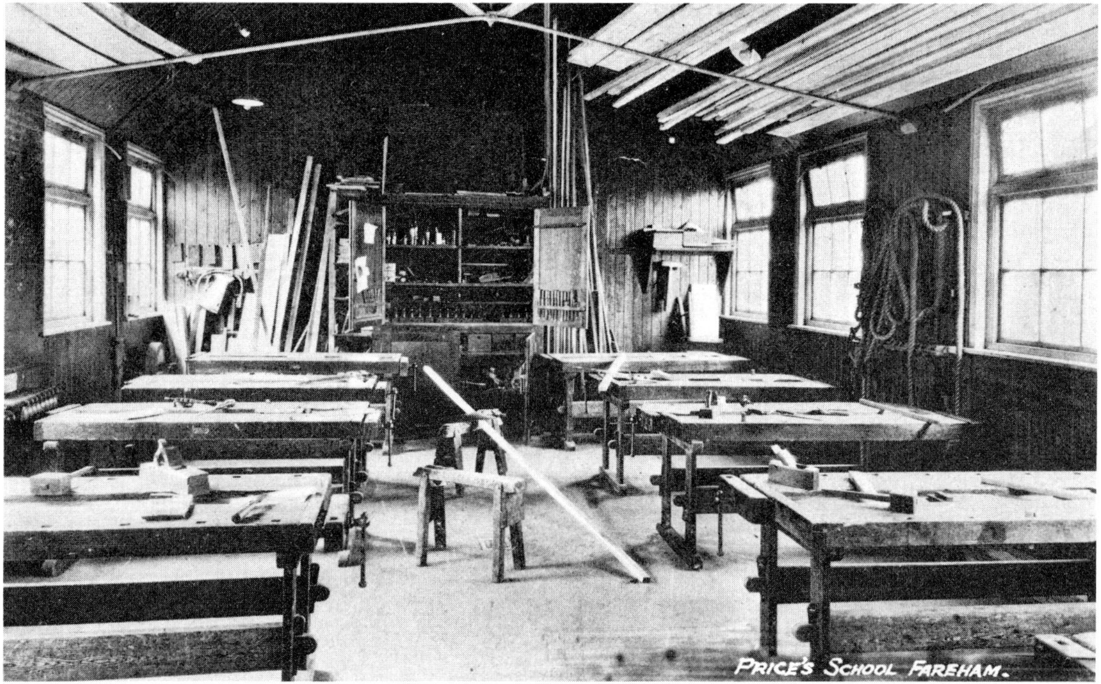

55. The new Price's school in Park Lane was equipped with many up to date innovations to widen the education of its pupils. One of these was the well-stocked and laid out woodwork room pictured here. When the old West Street school was rebuilt in 1842 it was turned into a school for boys only. The girls were transferred to the recently enlarged Fareham National School. This policy was continued in the new Park Lane School and allowed more time and space to be devoted to male orientated occupations like woodwork. In recent years Price's school became a sixth form college with the fair sex once more gaining a foothold. Soon now it will be moving to another site in Fareham to become part of a large educational complex. The one possible redeeming feature of the old school's loss of identity is that a badly needed hospital might one day rise in its place.

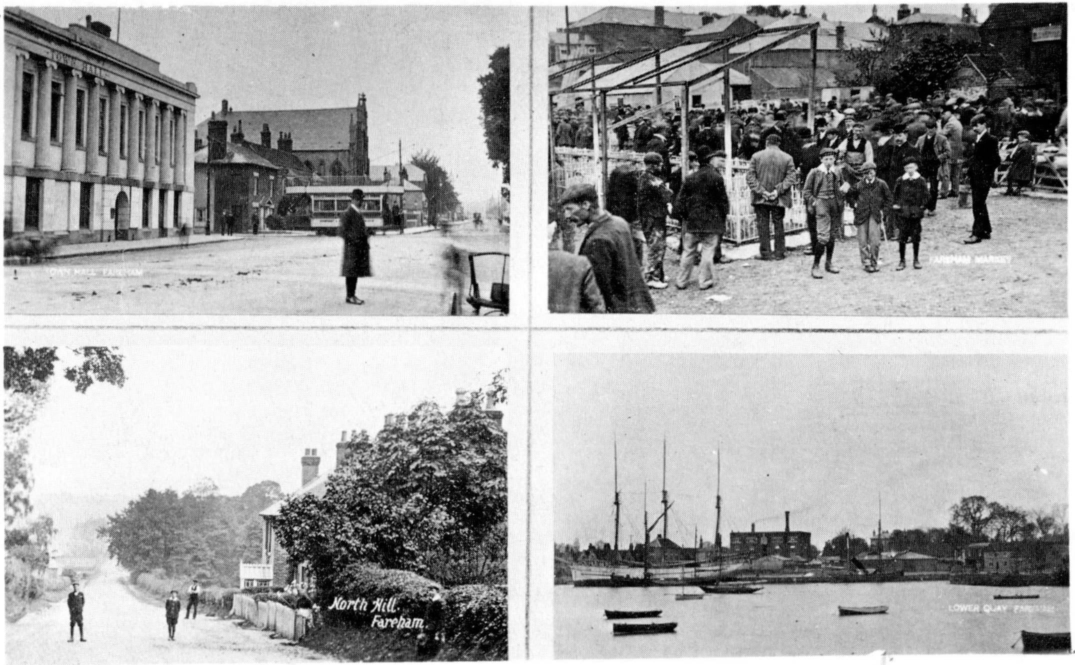

56. A few years after the start of the Edwardian postcard collecting boom, harassed postcard publishers were casting around for new ideas in postcard form, to help them to corner a larger share of the market. One such novel idea was born in the form of a multi-view card which showed several different views of a town on one card. Usually a quartered card pictured four scenes, and on occasion a rarely seen view was mixed with more common ones. In the William Smith card pictured here the view of North Hill and Fareham Creek are common whilst those of the tram at the top of Portland Street and the interior view of Fareham Market are very difficult to find today on single view cards.

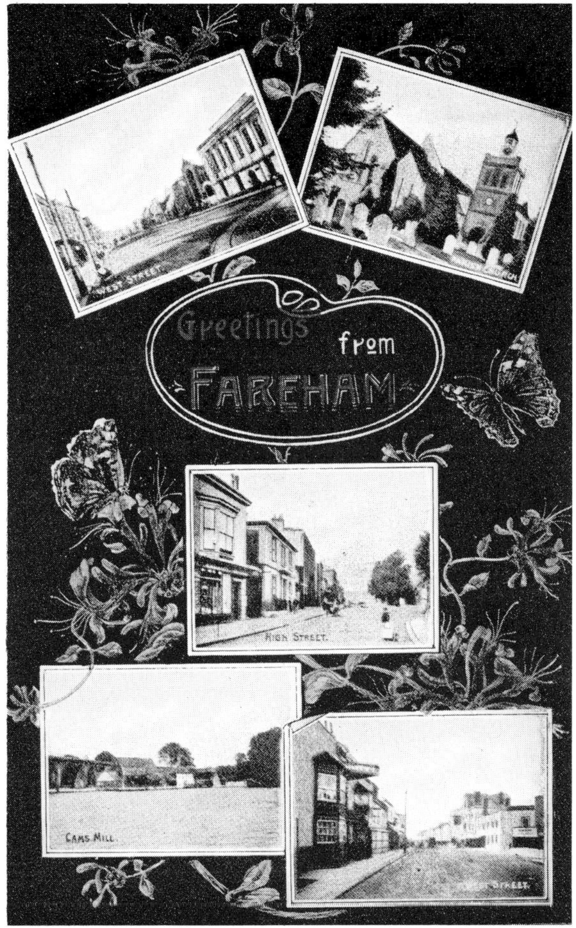

57. This is an example of a card by Hector Duffett of Fareham, who took the multi-view postcard idea even further. He has taken five different Fareham views, all fairly common, arranged them most artistically on a card and surrounded them with an attractive decor. Whilst the quality of the views leaves something to be desired, the card is different and on the whole quite pleasing. Eager collectors in 1917, the date on this card, were just as happy as they are today to snap up anything a little out of the ordinary. The multi-view card enjoyed considerable popularity, no doubt because at least four views for the price of one appears a bargain in any era.

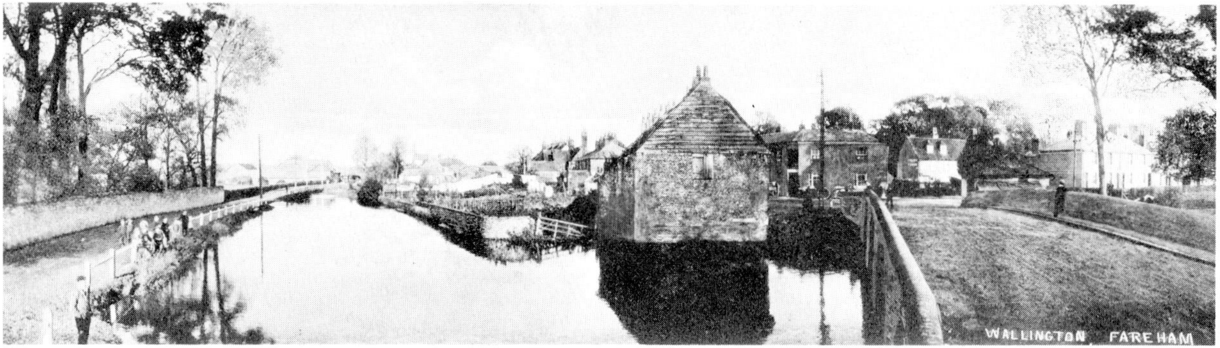

58. Taking the novelty topographic postcard idea another stage Hector Duffett produced sets of six 'Panoramicards' around 1905. The normal dimensions of a postcard are 5½ inches by 3½ inches but these monsters measured 11½ inches across. They were very effective and the example shown here gives a comprehensive impression of the village of Wallington, standing on the banks of the river. The main road is shown leading over the old bridge and into the heart of the village. The back gardens of the cottages in Wallington Shore Road lead right down to the river and it is clear to see why the inhabitants have experienced problems with flooding on occasions.

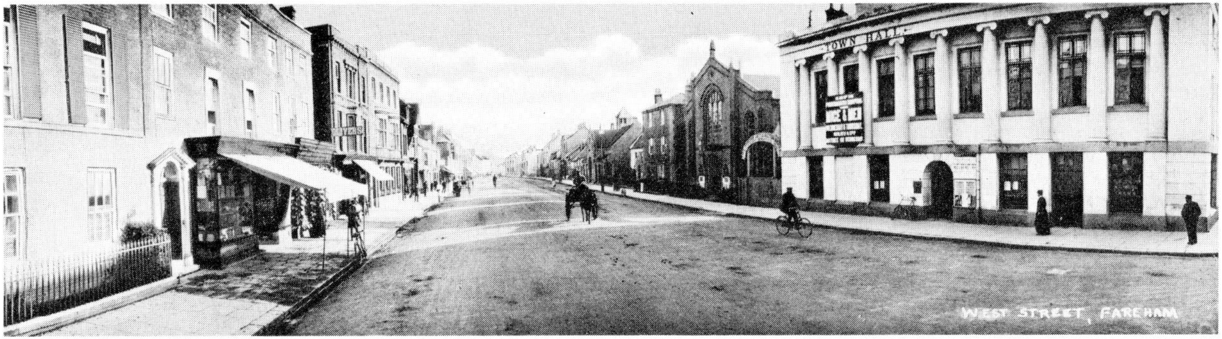

59. This second example of the panoramic view card shows a peaceful West Street pictured looking eastwards from the top of Portland Street. On the right, next to the Congregational Church, is the gateway to the market with the sign above reading 'The Fareham Cattle Auction Market Sales every Monday at 10.30 a.m.'. Next door, at the Town Hall, is showing a play called 'Mice and Men' in aid of the Portsmouth Hospital. This was a sample of the wide variety of entertainments held upstairs in this building, ranging from plays to concerts by military bands and Fareham's own Philharmonic Society, dances and even at one time a waxworks. Interesting to note on the lower right hand window of the building the words Working Men's Club. Presumably the club was held here before moving to Kings Road and more recently to Mill Road.

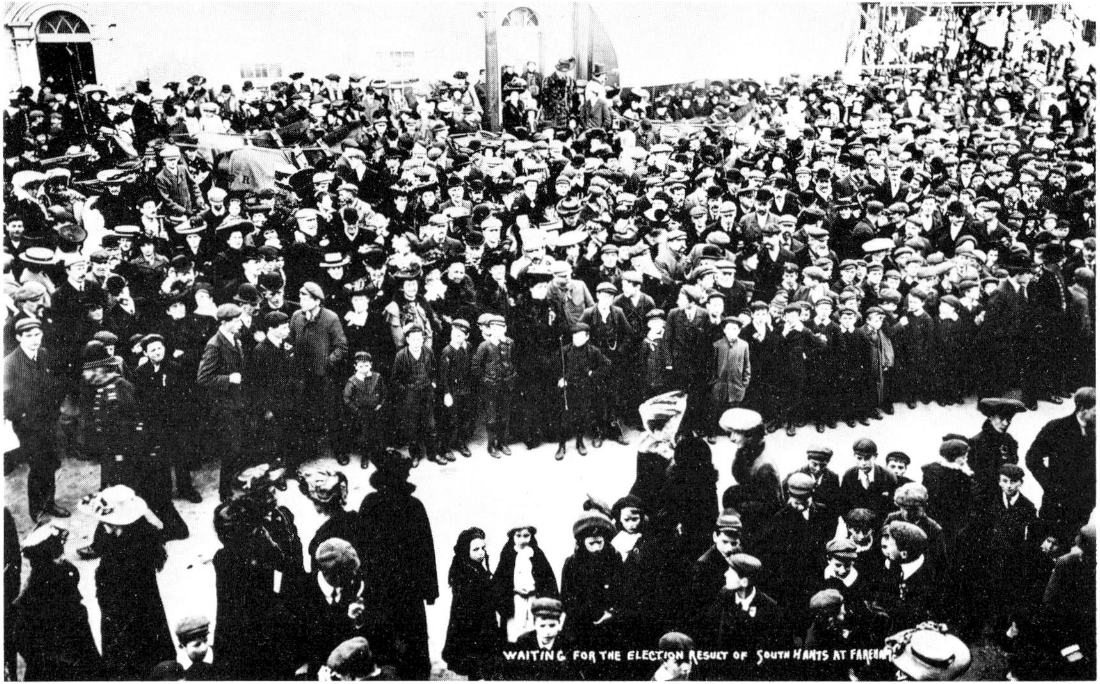

60. The top-hatted coachmen with their horses and carriages are lined up along the side of Fareham West Street opposite the town hall. They are entirely engulfed by the large crowd standing patiently awaiting the announcement of the result of the South Hants Division election result. This was in the general election held on 20th January 1906. A feature of this crowd scene is the wide variety of headgear on display. The top hats, bowlers and assorted caps of the men mixing with the Sunday best hats and bonnets of the ladies. Amazing that in all this crowd there is not a bare head in sight although there probably was when Mr. A.H. Lee was announced as the winner. In the right background of this picture can be seen the long established shoe shop of Mr. G. Oliver.

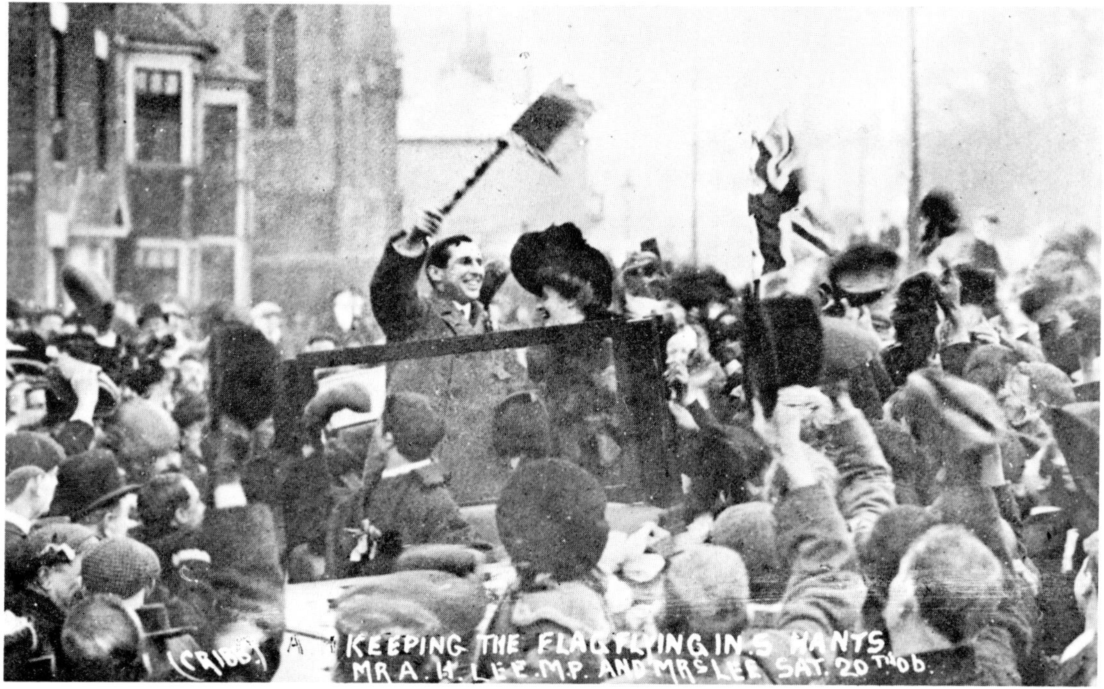

61. What scenes of jubilation on this postcard by Portsmouth photographer S. Cribb showing the events in Fareham on 20th January 1906. The successful Conservative candidate Mr. A.H. Lee and his wife are seen in their car outside Fareham Town Hall surrounded by enthusiastic supporters after the declaration of the election results. The message on the back of the card reads 'Ted went to Fareham to hear it declared, the crowd nearly went mad at the result. Arthur went with him and said he could hardly keep him in the cart'. Mr. Lee was defending the seat he had won for the Conservatives in 1900. In the Balfour Government of 1903 he had served as Civil Lord of the Admiralty. He was to go on to win another two elections in 1910 the second unopposed.

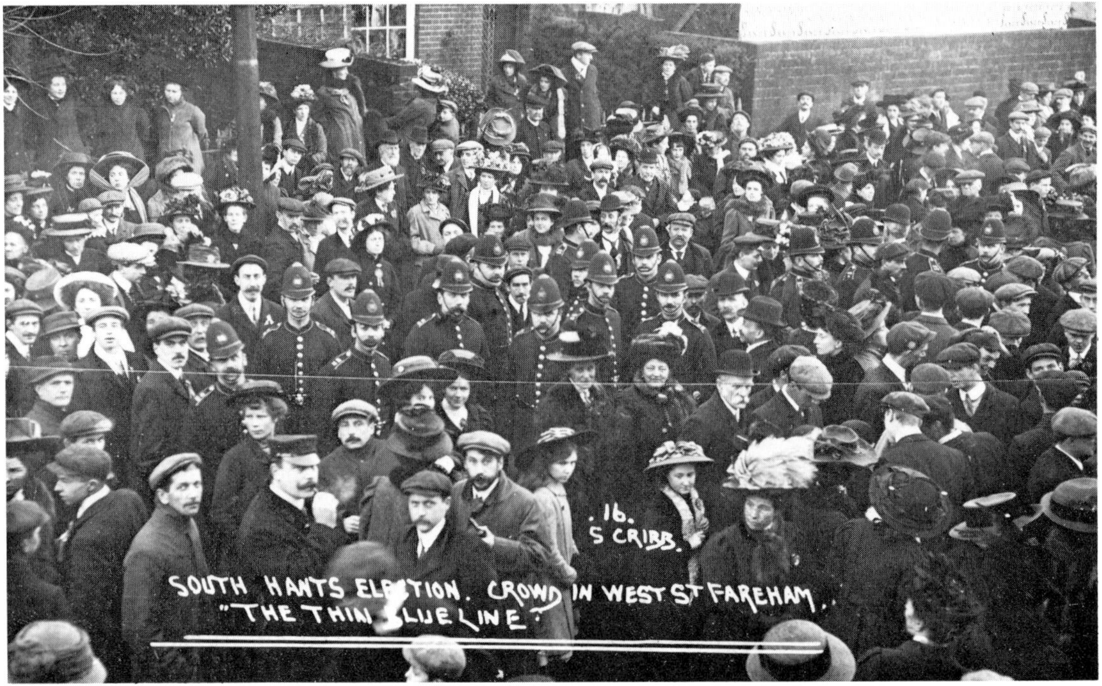

62. After four years in office the Conservative Government went to the country again in January 1910. This was the scene outside the Connaught Drill Hall in the West Street as the counting of the votes was nearing completion. As the photographer Mr. S. Cribb comments the crowd is being controlled by the 'Thin Blue Line' of policemen. From the look of the picture they do not appear to be experiencing any problems. No doubt things warmed up a trifle when the eventual announcement of the election result proclaimed that Conservative M.P. Mr. A.H. Lee had once again successfully defended his seat. The mass of opposition posters in the background encouraging everyone to 'Vote for Sandy' obviously had very little effect.

63. Mr. A.H. Lee is pictured here by S. Cribb at the scene of yet another election triumph. On this occasion he has just been returned as the successful candidate for the South Hants division in January 1910. He is seen standing at the second floor window of the Connaught Drill Hall building in Fareham's West Street. Fareham or Hampshire South constituency returned a Tory in all thirteen elections from 1900 to 1945. Arthur Hamilton Lee was born in Bridport, Dorset in 1868 and entered the Royal Artillery in 1888. He returned from the army in 1900 and successfully contested four elections in the next ten years. In 1917 as Lord Lee of Fareham he and his wife presented the mansion and estates of Chequers in Buckinghamshire on trust to the nation for the use of all future Prime Ministers.

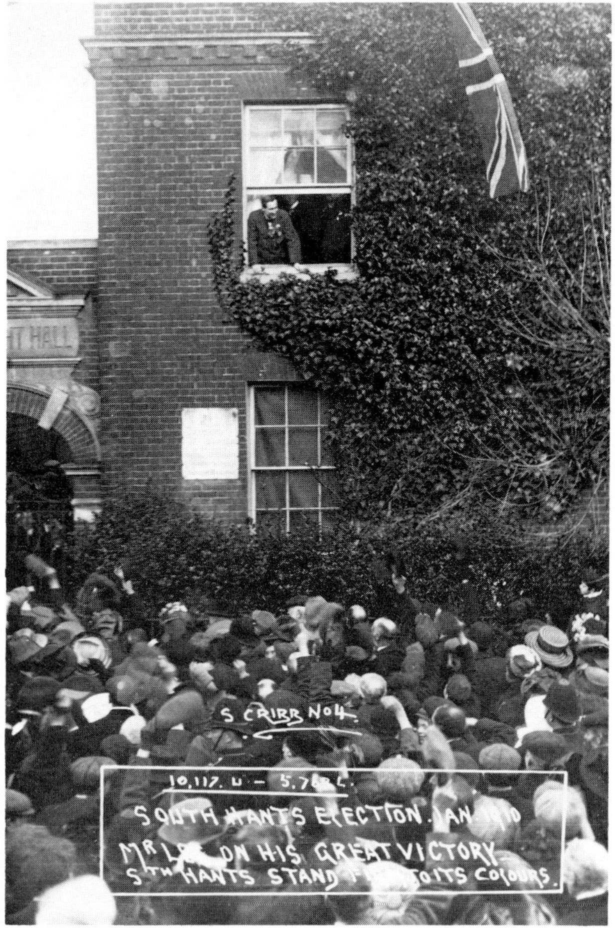

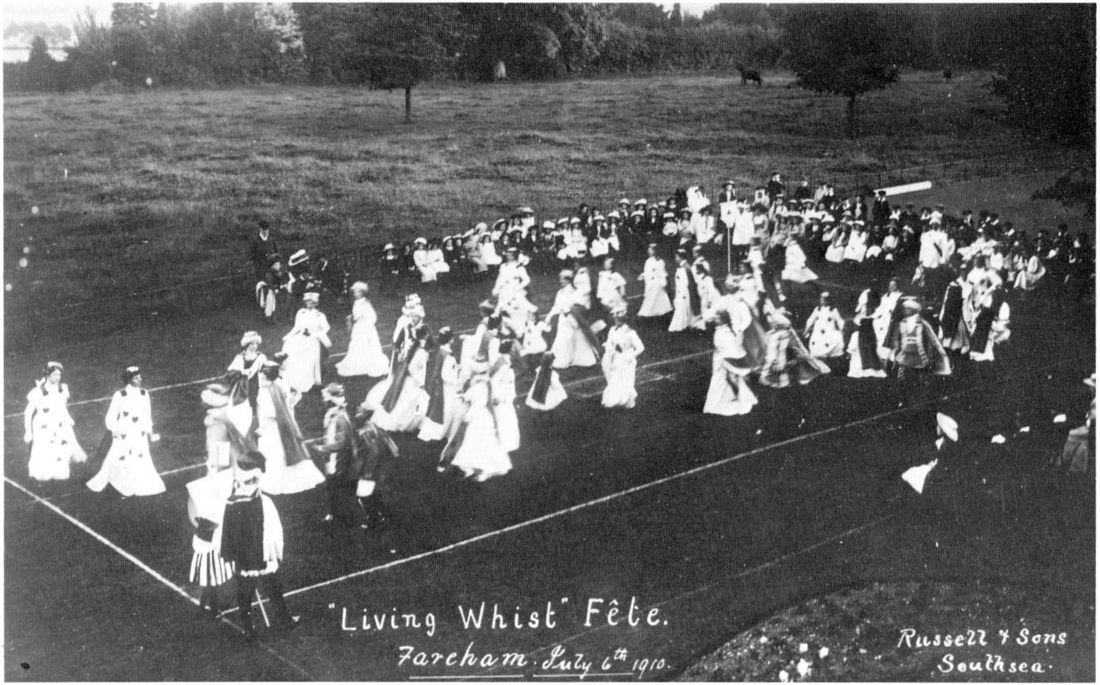

64. Before the days of radio, television and the cinema people had to make their own entertainment. In the summer all kinds of galas and fetes were held, whilst winter months saw friends gathering for musical evenings and whist or ping-pong parties. Always looking for new ideas, the Edwardians came up with the notion of combining an indoor and outdoor event in the form of a Living Whist Fete. On these occasions each participating person took the place of a playing card and were manipulated into tricks as the fete progressed. No efforts were spared in the making of the playing card costumes and these colourful events became very popular. This picture by photographer Russell of Southsea shows a Living Whist Fete being enacted before an attentive audience on 6th July 1910 in Fareham.

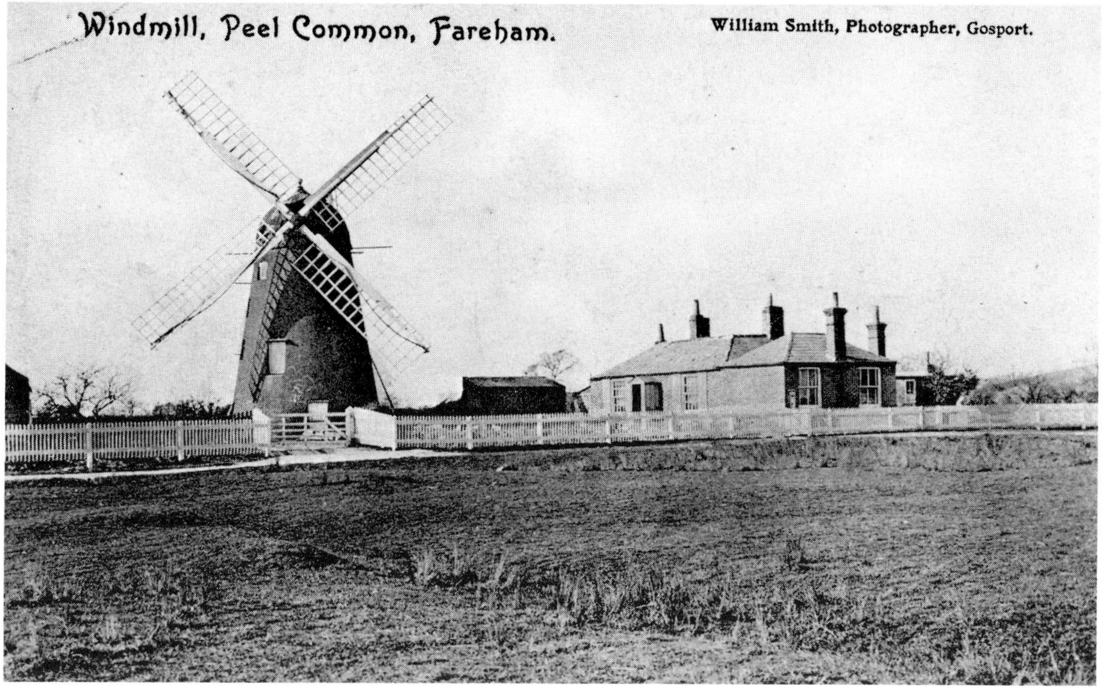

65. Windmills date back to at least the 12th century, although the man responsible for the original idea of harnessing the wind to provide power is not known. They were usually used to grind corn, with the wind driven sails transmitting power through linked gearing to drive the grinding stones. Records show that there were around two thousand windmills in operation in England at the turn of the century, most of them located in the south-eastern part of the country. Being dependant on catching the wind they needed to be sited on high or open ground. The mill at Peel Common pictured here by William Smith in 1908 was well placed to catch the prevailing south-westerly wind sweeping in from the Solent. This windmill stood in Newgate Lane and was a landmark for miles around before its demolition in 1926.

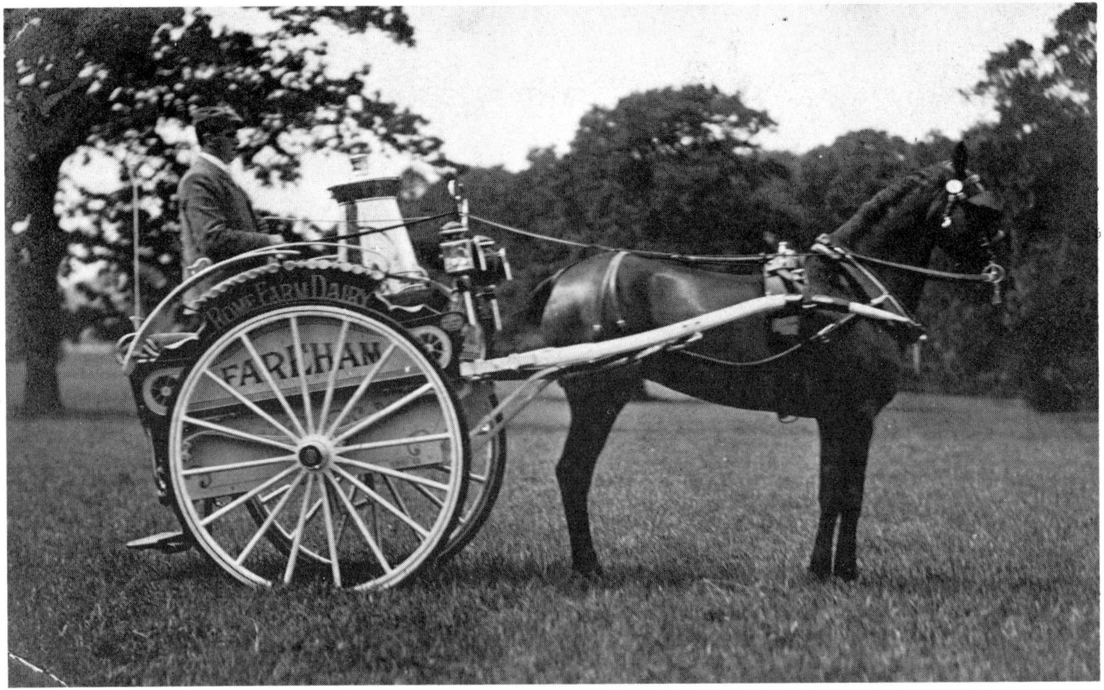

66. Most of the farmland surrounding the Peel Common Windmill was owned by the Holliday family of Rome Farm. The immaculate dairy cart and beautifully groomed horse posing for this 1904 photograph were no doubt heading for a local gymkhana. Horse-drawn dairy carts were a feature of Fareham roads long after they had disappeared from most other districts. This was mainly due to the town's most famous dairy farmer Tom Parker, who was distributing his milk this way as late as the 1960's. This hard working business man built up a large dairy farming concern in Fareham and played an active part in its running until his death in 1982, at the age of eighty-six.

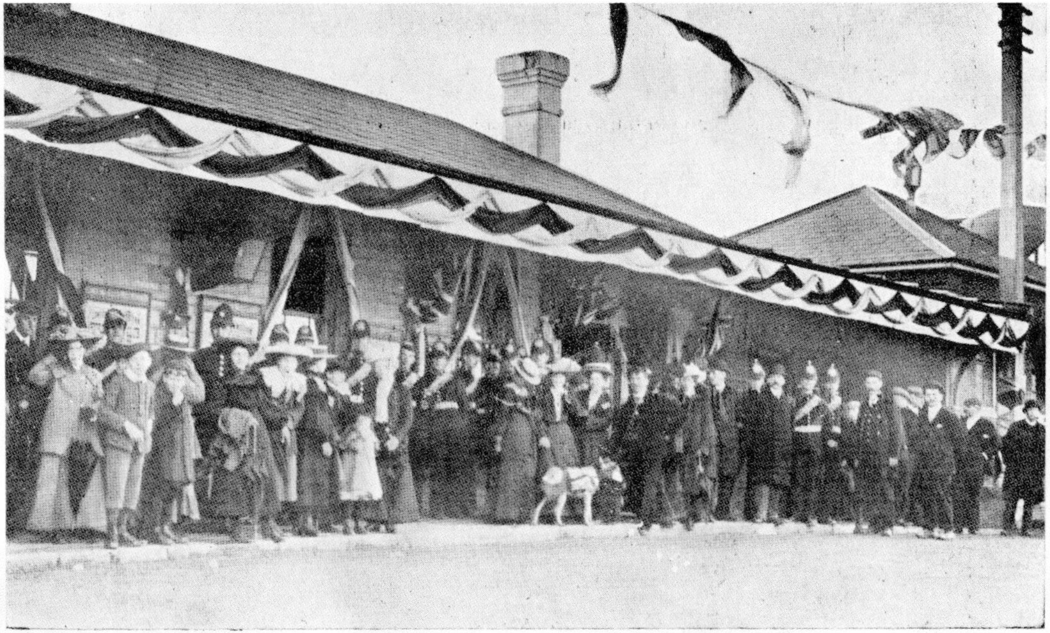

Waiting for Princess Henry at Fareham Railway Station.

67. For many years Fareham had seen members of the royal family passing through Fareham Station, usually en route to or from the Isle of Wight. Osborne House on the Island having been the favourite residence of Queen Victoria and Prince Albert. It was in Osborne House in 1901 that the old queen died and Fareham Station witnessed the sombre sight of her funeral train passing through on its way back to London. Now at last, in October 1905, a member of the royal family was to step off the train at Fareham for an official visit. This long overdue royal visitor was Princess Henry of Battenburg who was at that time the Governor of the Isle of Wight. This history making day saw the railway platform crowded with an excited reception committee. Amongst those waiting at the gaily decorated station were local dignitories, railway staff, several finely dressed ladies and some members of the army complete with regimental mascot.

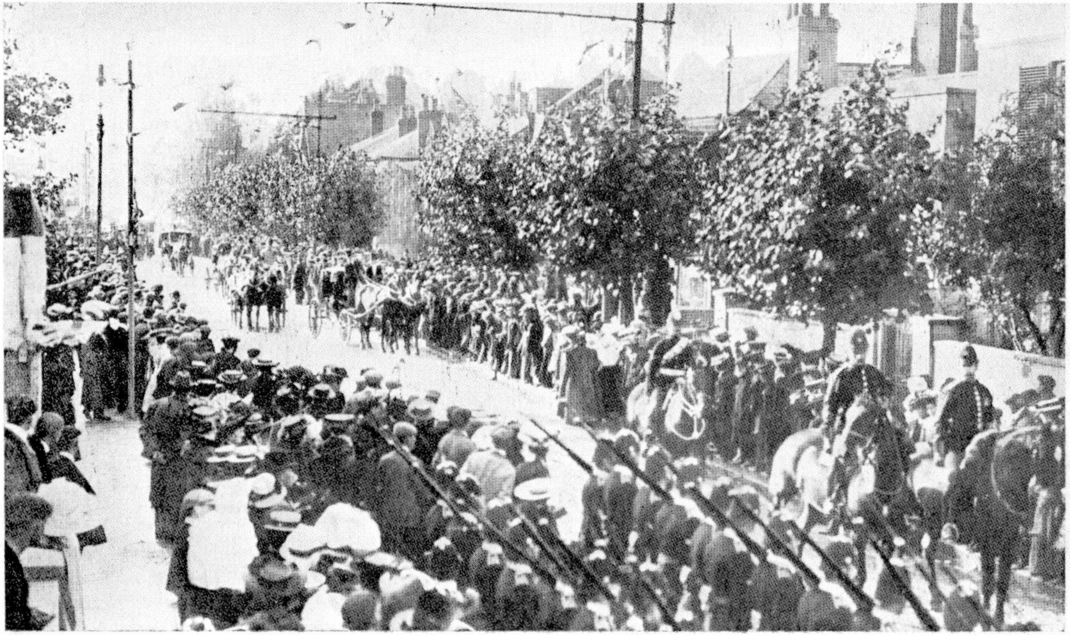

Royal Visit to Fareham : Procession in West Street.

68. Fareham had never witnessed scenes like this before as people came from miles around to see the royal procession passing along a tree-lined West Street in 1905. The royal visitor had become Princess Henry on her marriage to Prince Henry of Battenburg in 1885. Prior to that, this youngest daughter of Queen Victoria and Prince Albert was called Princess Beatrice. As a close companion of the queen before her marriage, the princess had also spent much time on the Isle of Wight, and it was there in the little church at Whippingham that she had been married. Her husband was later made Captain and Governor of the Isle of Wight and they lived there happily, being blessed with four children. Then in 1896, whilst with an expeditionary force in Africa, Prince Henry contracted malaria from which he died. Bravely putting the death of her husband, and five years later that of her mother aside, the Princess took up the threads again carrying out countless royal engagements like this one at Fareham in 1905 and at neighbouring Gosport in 1907.

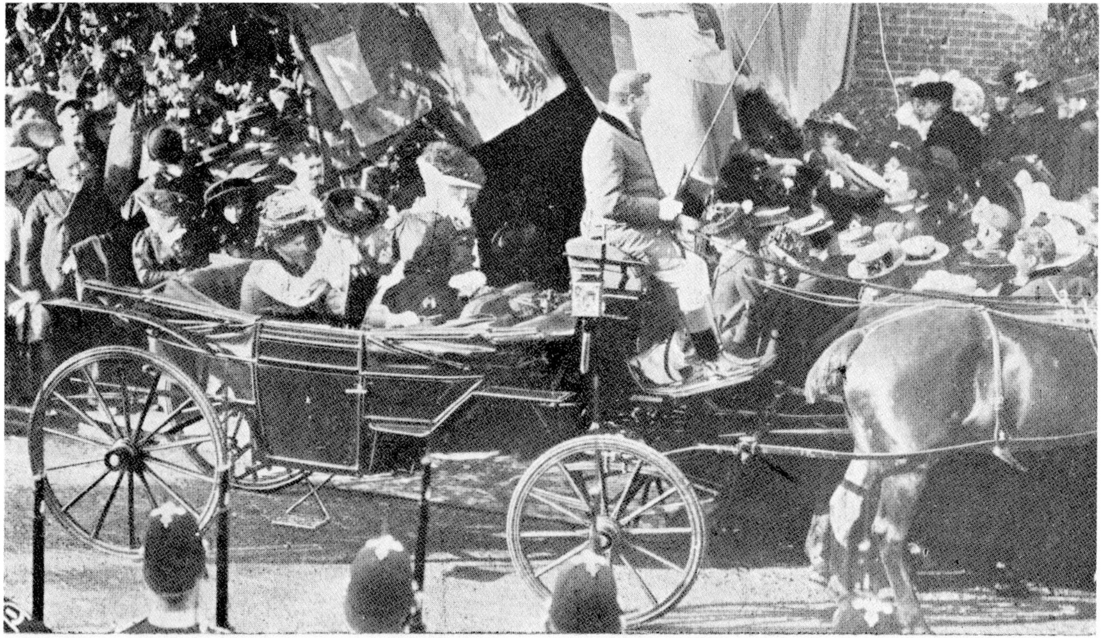

Princess Henry arriving at Fareham Drill Hall.

69. In this close up picture of the royal carriage, Princess Henry is seen arriving at the Connaught Drill Hall for the official reception. After the death of her husband the Princess had been pleased to be appointed to succeed him as Captain and Governor of the Isle of Wight. She had always been a popular member of the royal family, and a busy one, with her engagements taking her not just on the Island, but all over the country. Her daughter became the Queen of Spain, her brother-in-law was the Ruler of Bulgaria and her godchild became the last Tzarina of Russia. This grand lady was eighty-seven years old when she died in 1944, and Fareham had good reason to feel honoured by her visit back in 1905.

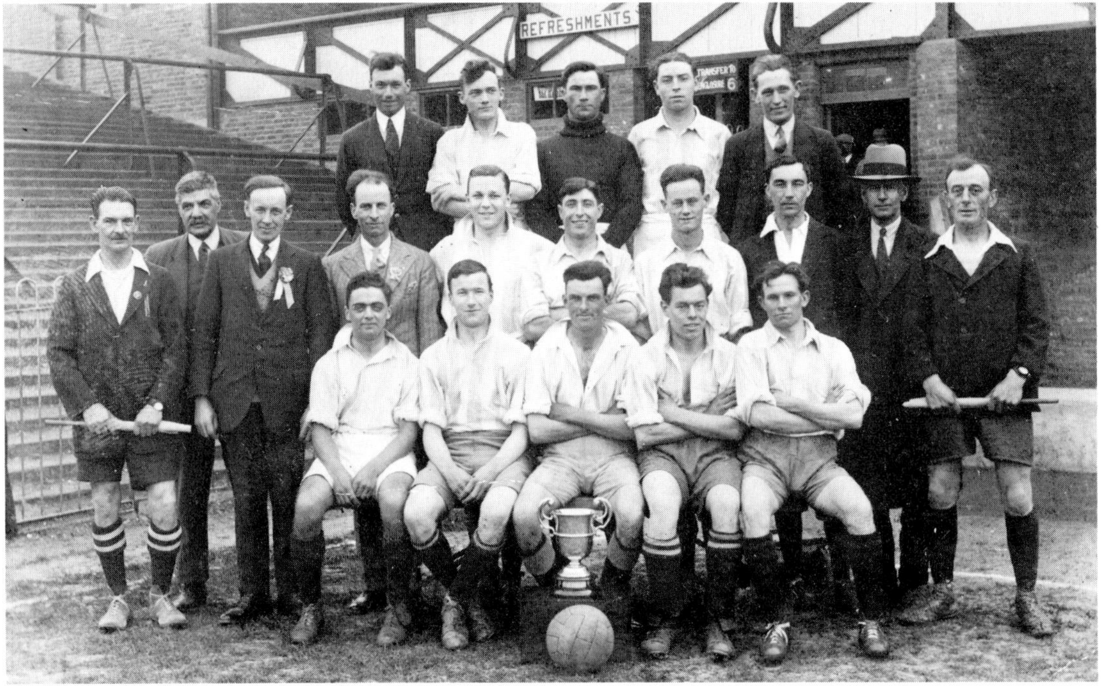

70. Pictured here at the 'Dell', the famous home ground of Southampton Football Club, is the Fareham Brotherhood football team at the end of the 1927-28 football season. They had just defeated the Southampton Brotherhood team in the final of the Sir William Portal Cup. The Brotherhoods were inter-denominational and Fareham held their meetings in the local Wesleyan Church. The gentleman wearing the trilby hat is Mr. Yeo who was the District Secretary of the Brotherhoods. Seen standing fifth from the left in the centre row is Len Goodall who was later to become the Treasurer of Fareham Council.

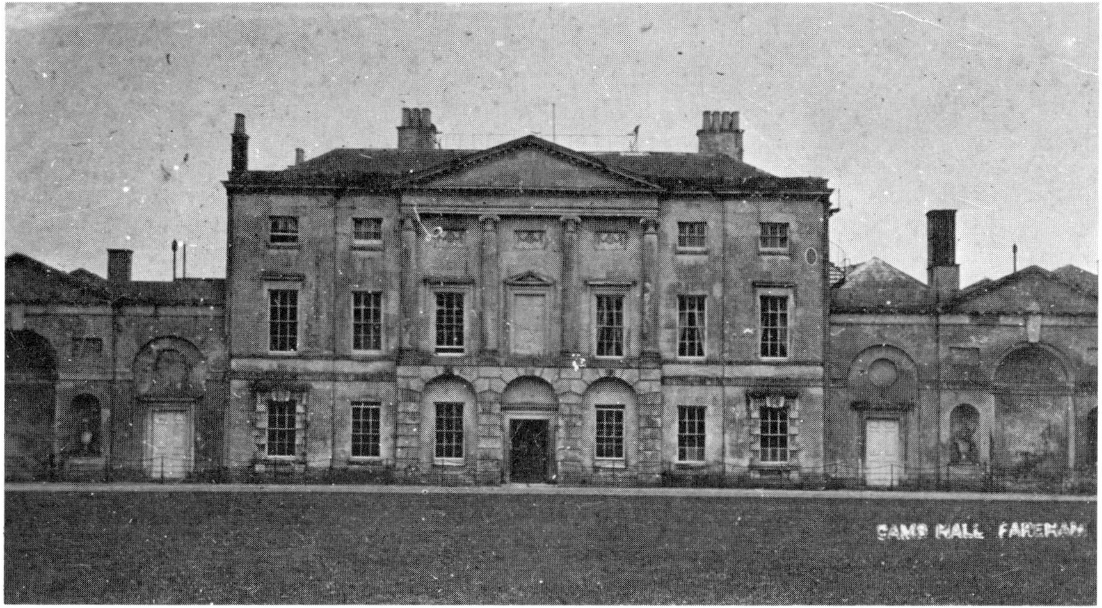

71. Cams Hall was for centuries one of Fareham's most stately residences. A manor house is recorded at Cams as far back as the 13th century. In the early 18th century a new building was erected on the site and this was purchased by the Delme family in 1781. The Delmes moved across Fareham from Place House to occupy the mansion and then proceeded to spend a small fortune on a part re-building and enlarging operation. The superb mansion that resulted became known locally as Cams Hall and remained in the hands of the Delme family for over one hundred years. It stood in a superb setting with views to Portsmouth Harbour and was approached up an impressively long drive passing through extensive and immaculate grounds. Since it was sold in 1895 it has had several owners and was used by the Admiralty in the Second World War. The shell of a building that remains today is the regrettable result of many years of decay and neglect. This postcard view shows the Hall as it was in 1908.

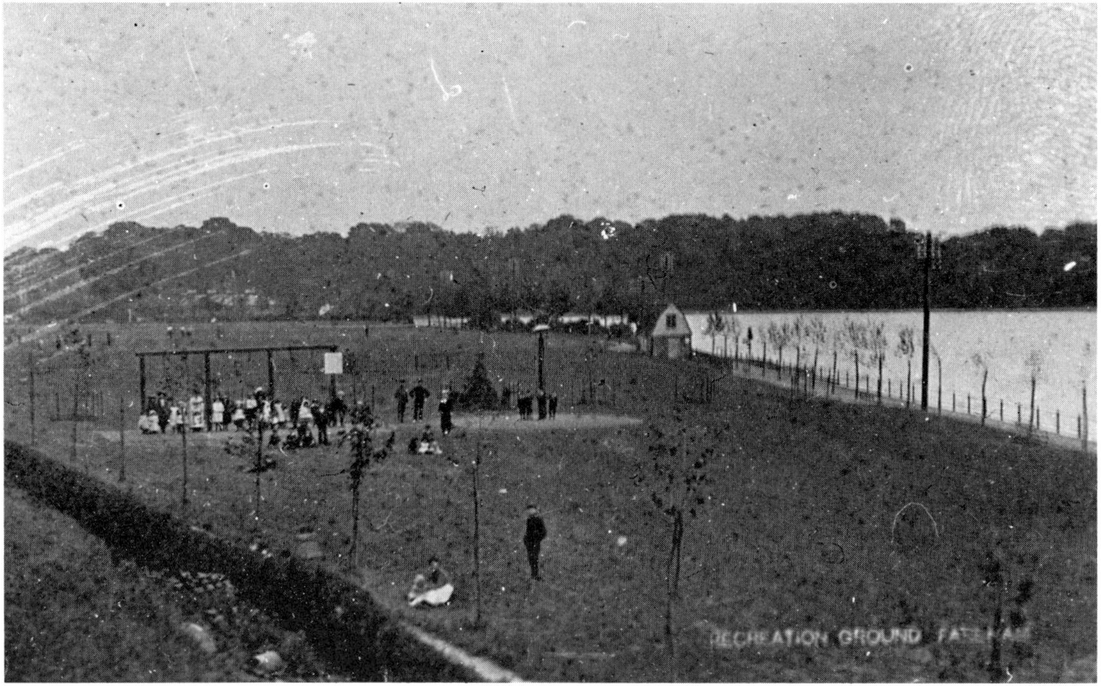

72. Considering its lovely setting, it is suprising that views of Fareham's old recreation ground are so difficult to find on old postcards. The waters of the Creek adjoin its southern boundary, whilst to the north it is sheltered by the high, tree-screened railway enbankment that carries the Fareham to Portsmouth line. This was the town's only recreation ground until shortly before the last war when a growing population necessitated a new ground being laid out opposite Price's school. This was called Park Lane recreation ground, the old ground then taking the name of its approach road and becoming Bath Lane recreation ground. For many years Bath Lane recreation ground was the home of Fareham Football Club, and partly because of its well-drained soil was acknowledged to be one of the finest playing surfaces in the county. This 1908 view shows the children's swings in the same spot as they are today.

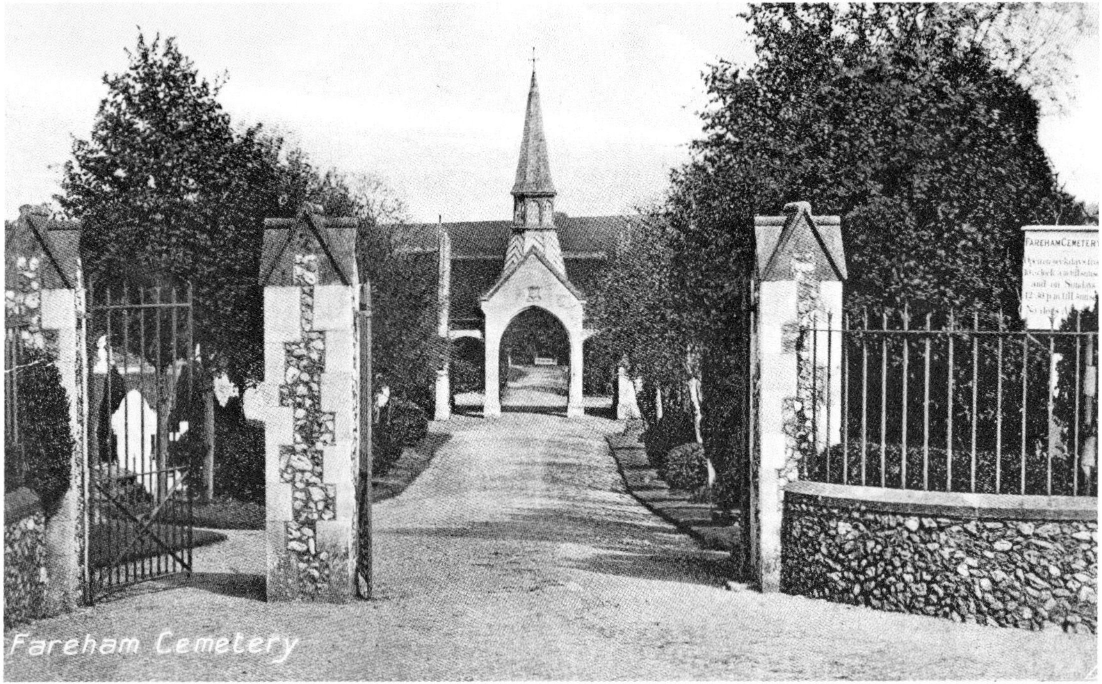

73. In 1848 sanitary conditions in Fareham were so bad that some of the inhabitants sent a petition to the General Board of Health requesting an inquiry. Later that year an inquiry was held, and at the same time an official carried out a thorough inspection of the town. Amongst the many things listed in his report, as needing attention, was the provision of a cemetery in Fareham. The only burial ground being the Parish churchyard which was completely full. The following year the Fareham Local Board of Health came in to being and started work to improve the general situation. One of their actions was to purchase some land off the Wickham Road, just north of the old workhouse, where a cemetery was laid out. The site had a pleasant aspect looking across to the Western slopes of Portsdown hill. The memorial archway in the middle of the cemetery was erected in 1889.

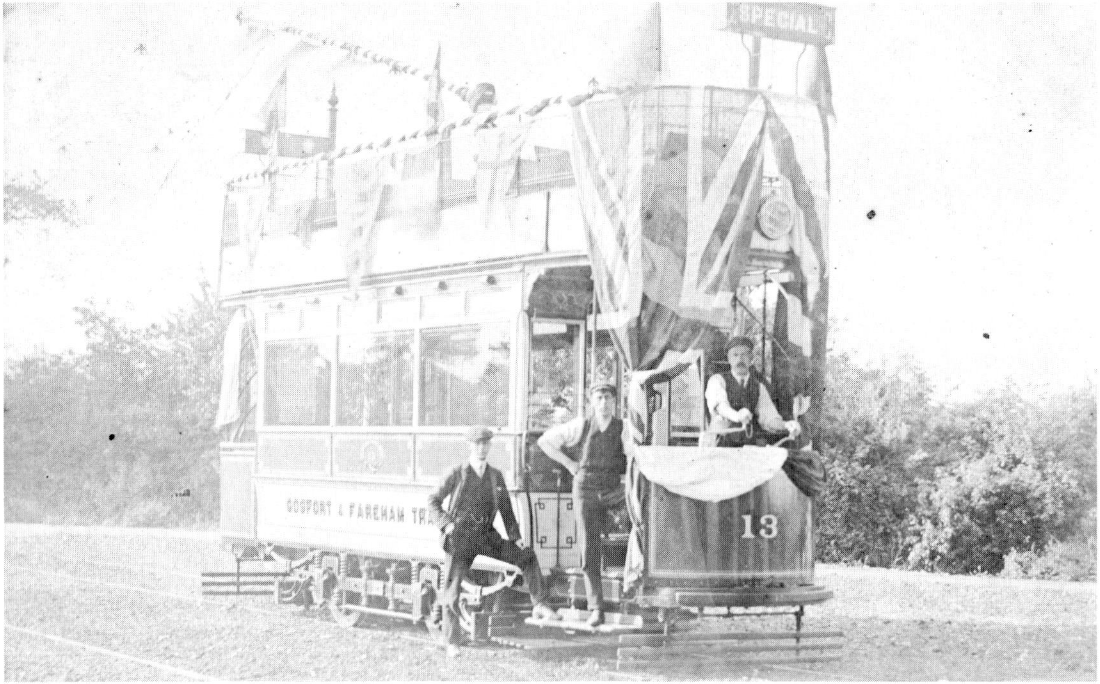

74. The three men pictured here pause in their labours to pose for the photographer. They have been busy festooning a vehicle of the Gosport and Fareham Tramways with flags and bunting. This was to prepare it for its part in the celebrations to be held in Fareham to mark the coronation of King George V and Queen Mary on 6th May 1910. As the main type of road transport in the country at that time, tramcars played a prominent part in the many galas and parades being held. Many of these vehicles with their splendid decorations were captured on old postcards. The number of the tram selected for the big occasion in Fareham suggests that superstition was at a low ebb in 1910.

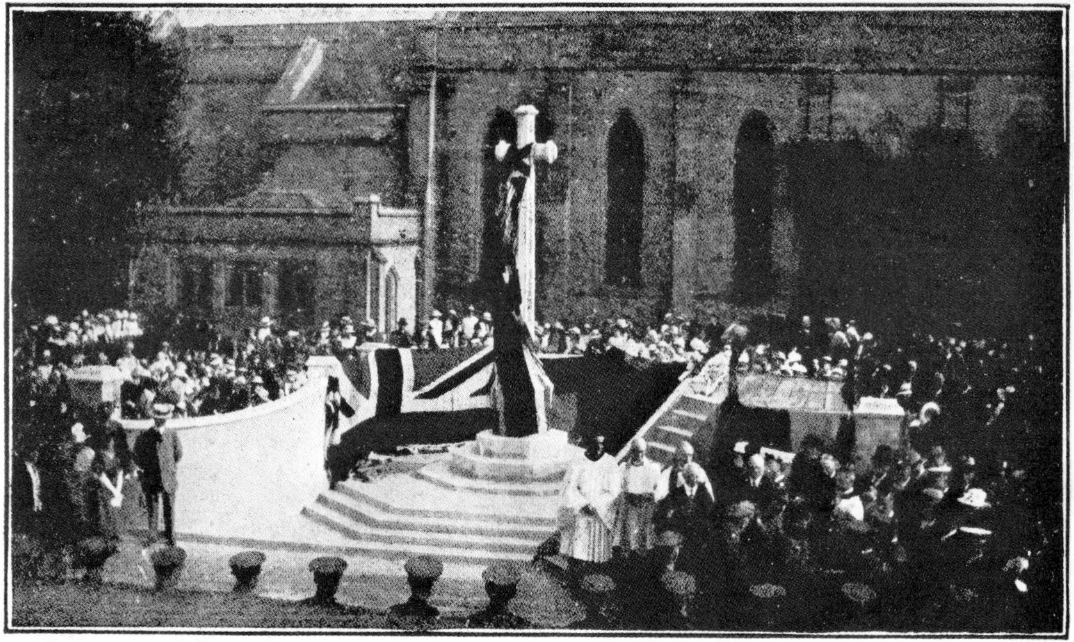

FAREHAM WAR MEMORIAL, UNVEILED BY EARL HAIG, 2ND JULY, 1921

75. Fareham's War Memorial stands in the West Street at the bottom of Trinity Street. The unveiling ceremony took place on 2nd July 1921 and was performed by Earl Haig. This photograph of the event appears to have been taken from the balcony of Pyle's Hotel. This building stood across the West Street from the Memorial and is now the site of the Gas Company Showrooms. In the foreground can just be seen the military guard of honour. Members of the clergy and local dignitories greet the Earl as he arrives on the scene. The large crowd gathered for the occasion has overflowed into the grounds of Trinity Church. The church itself forming the background to the proceedings.

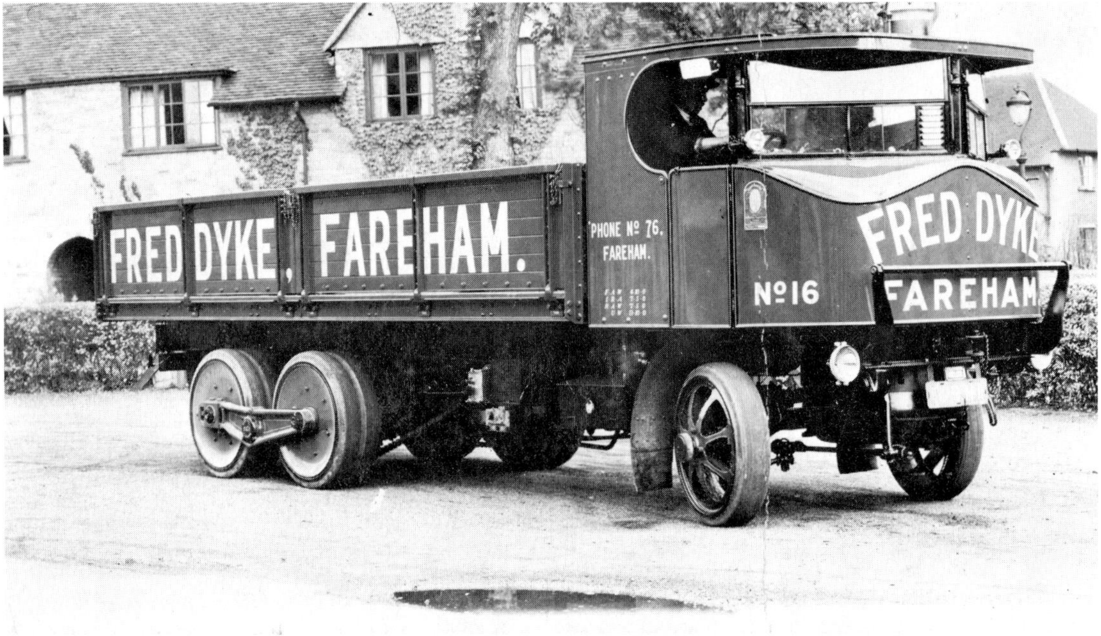

76. This superb example of an old Steam Lorry was one of the earliest of a growing fleet of lorries built up by Mr. Fred Dyke. In the years after the First World War Mr. Dyke's growing business in Fareham encompassed refuse collection, gravel and general haulage and furniture removals. He had a fine house built in Osborn Road, close to where the local gravel pits once were. His wife Mrs. Blanche Ruth Dyke worked very hard for various charities in the area. She was later to join Fareham Urban District Council and become Chairman twice before eventually retiring in 1965. When Fareham became a Borough in 1974 it was considered most fitting that this grand old lady should be one of the first people to be granted the 'Freedom of the Town'.

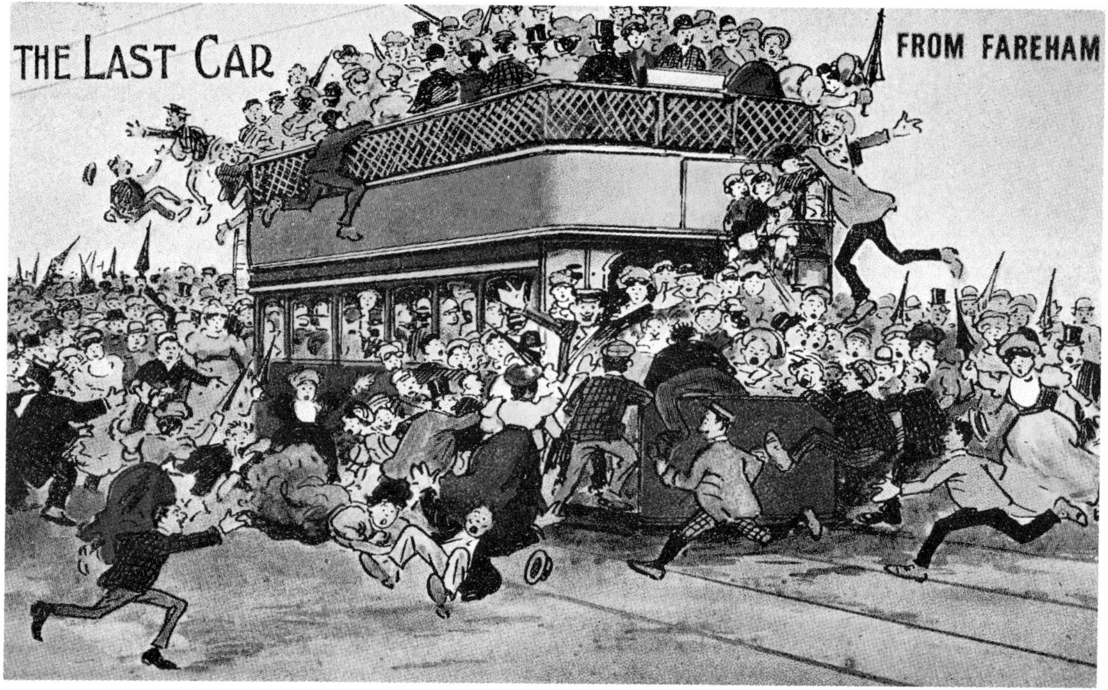

77. There was a vast range of comic postcards issued in this country during the 'Golden Age' of collecting. These cards drawn by a long list of artists portrayed typical British humour at its best and touched upon every aspect of Edwardian life. Amongst the most popular of those depicting the transport of the day were the series captioned 'The Last Train from' or 'The Last Tramcar from' just about every town in the country. 'The Last Car from Fareham' pictured here was issued very much with tongue in cheek. With the local Fareham to Gosport service operating every fifteen minutes scenes like this on the last scheduled tram would seem to have been unlikely. Nevertheless, the purchasers of these cards must have been well pleased with the amount of action they were receiving for their money.

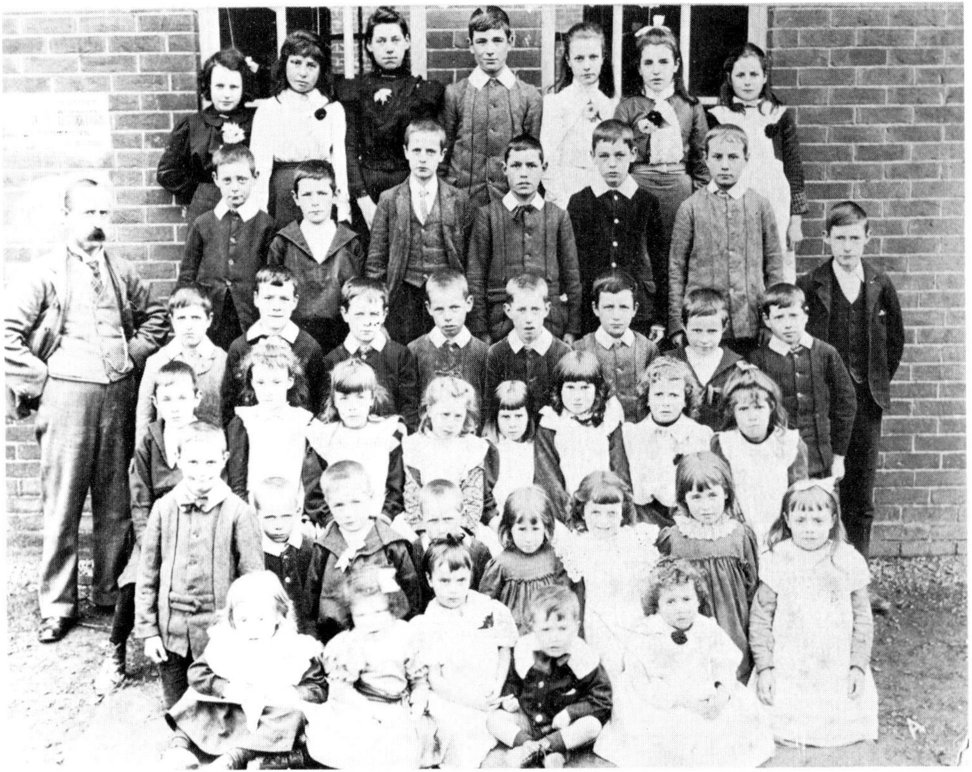

78. This photograph features pupils of the village school at Fontley in 1905. The taking of such a photograph was an important event in those days and the boys and girls were obviously instructed to wear their best clothes to school that day. The youngsters, who appear to be of all ages, have scarcely a smile amongst them, presumably Edwardian photographers did not know about 'cheese'. The schoolmaster in particular looks as though he really begrudges every minute that his pupils have to spend away from their books of learning. The old Fontley school stands on the lower slopes of Fontley Hill and was extended in 1926.

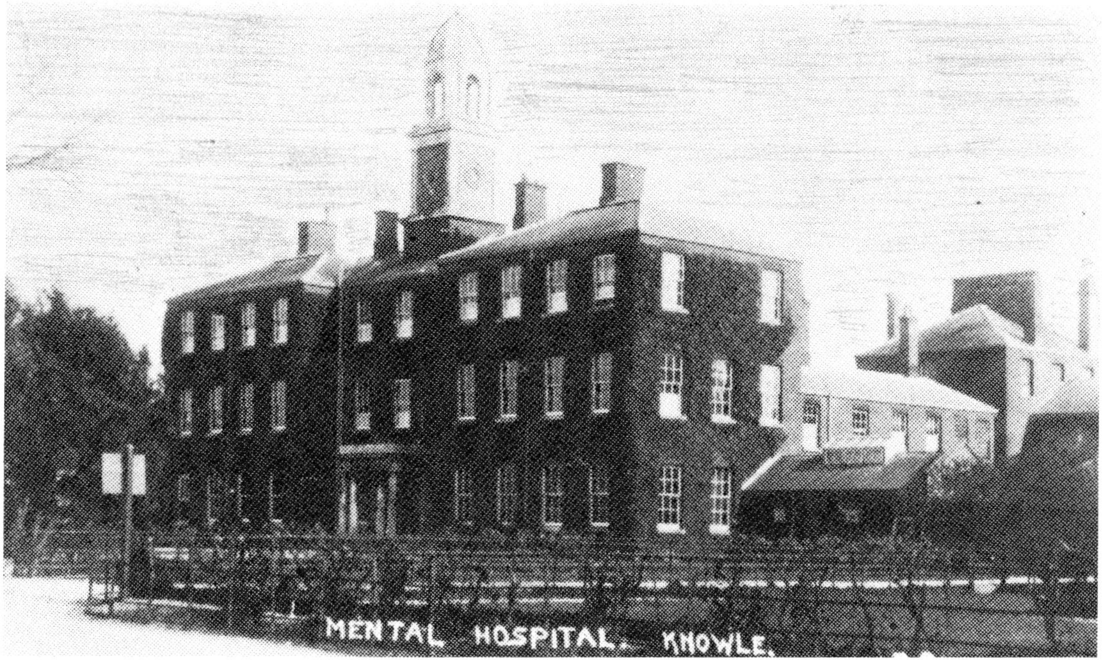

79. Knowle Farm stood on the northern outskirts of Fareham and covered an area of some one hundred acres. It was bought by the County in 1852 and became the site of the Hants County Lunatic Asylum. The Institution thus built in such splendid isolation, did present travelling problems for visitors and ingoing and outgoing patients. These were relieved to some extent by the opening of the Meon Valley Railway when the hospital was given its own stopping place at Knowle Halt. Knowle Mental Hospital, as it is known today, was built to cater for five hundred patients and has since been considerably enlarged. Male and female patients were admitted from any part of Hampshire by an Institute recognised as being forward looking for its time. The wards were spacious and the inmates were allowed considerable freedom. Many were employed on simple duties in the kitchens or in the extensive grounds and gardens. There was too, a varied programme of leisure activities. All the facilities at Knowle have been enlarged and improved upon up to the present day.

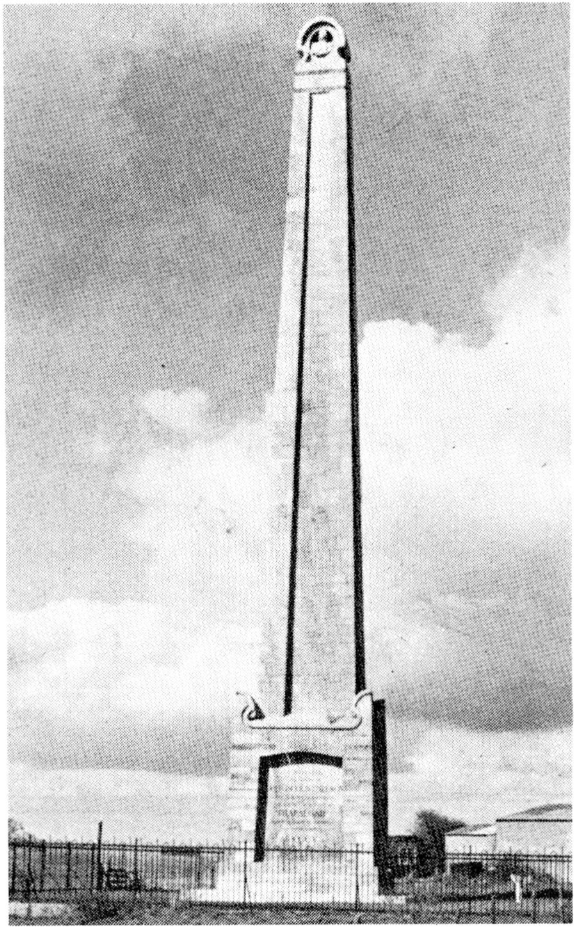

80. Standing on the top of Portsdown Hill in what is now called Monument Lane is this simple monument, the foundation stone of which was laid in 1807. The monument was erected from subscriptions raised by the officers and men of the Fleet who had served under Lord Nelson at the battle of Trafalgar. It was in honour of Lord Nelson and in celebration of that famous victory over the French on 21st October 1805. It was to be some thirty years later before Nelson's Column was raised in London's Trafalgar Square.

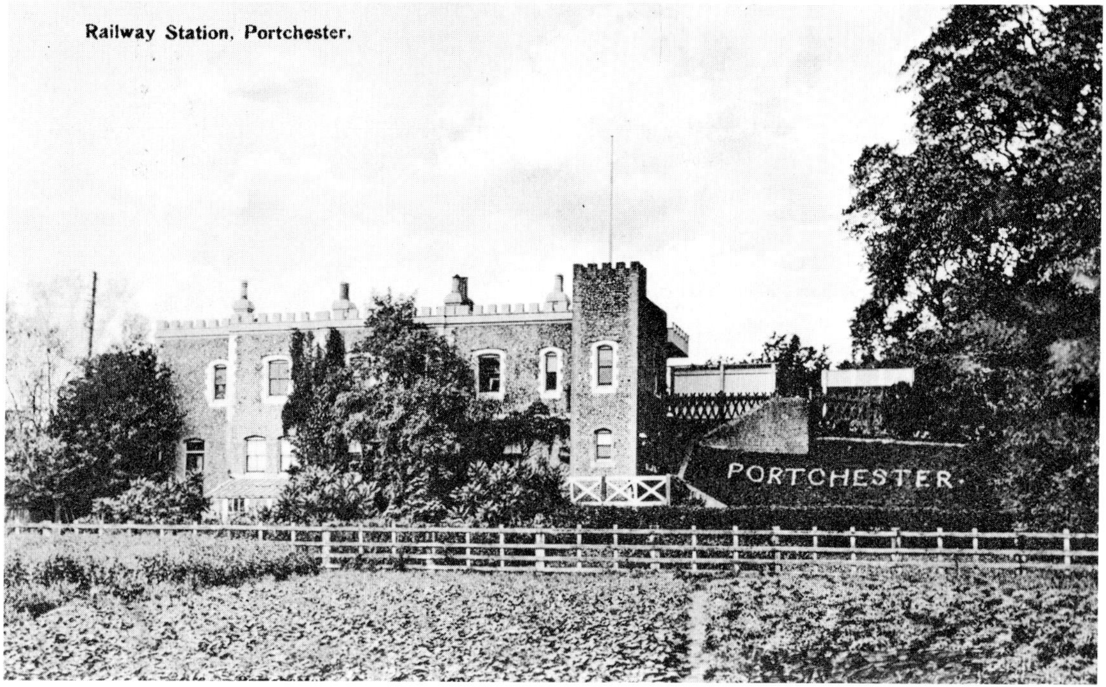

81. Porchester Railway Station is situated just north of the village. It was opened in 1848 when the railway line was extended from Fareham to Portcreek junction to give Portsmouth direct access to the Fareham to Eastleigh line. The exterior view shown here is from a postcard published by J. Cushen of Porchester Post Office in 1908. It shows the unique appearance of the station building, built of brick and flint in the design of a castle. Before the 20th century brought drastic improvements to roads and road transport, long distance travellers usually used the railway. No doubt the authorities thought the station's castle – like architecture would be in keeping, and would impress the many visitors passing through the station on their way to view the famous Roman fortress nearby.

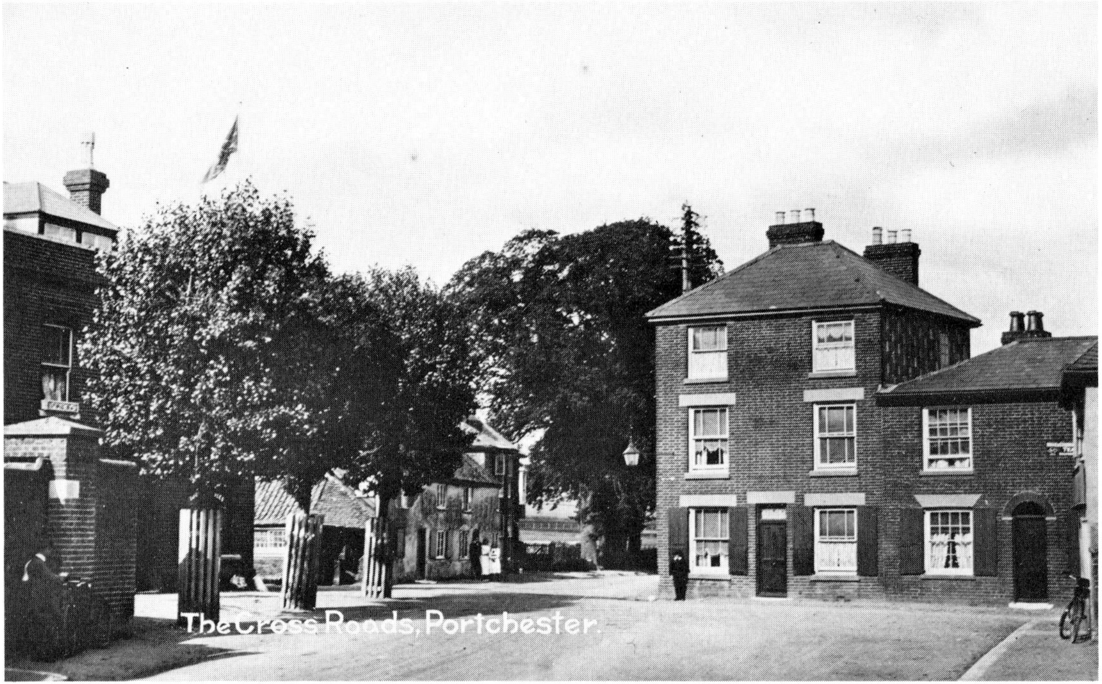

82. Coming out of the Railway Station and travelling south down Station Road one arrives at the Porchester Crossroads. This was the scene there as pictured by A.H. Sweasey in 1923. Opposite Station Road was Castle Street which led to the old village and the Castle. Making up the crossroads was the main Fareham to Portsmouth road. Many changes have taken place here over the years and especially since the last war. The construction of a new road by-passing part of the old Porchester West Street and a large roundabout at the foot of Castle Street became desperately needed to cope with the modern day volume of traffic. Even with these road improvements and the building of the new south coast motorway to the north of Porchester, traffic along this road through Porchester is still very heavy.

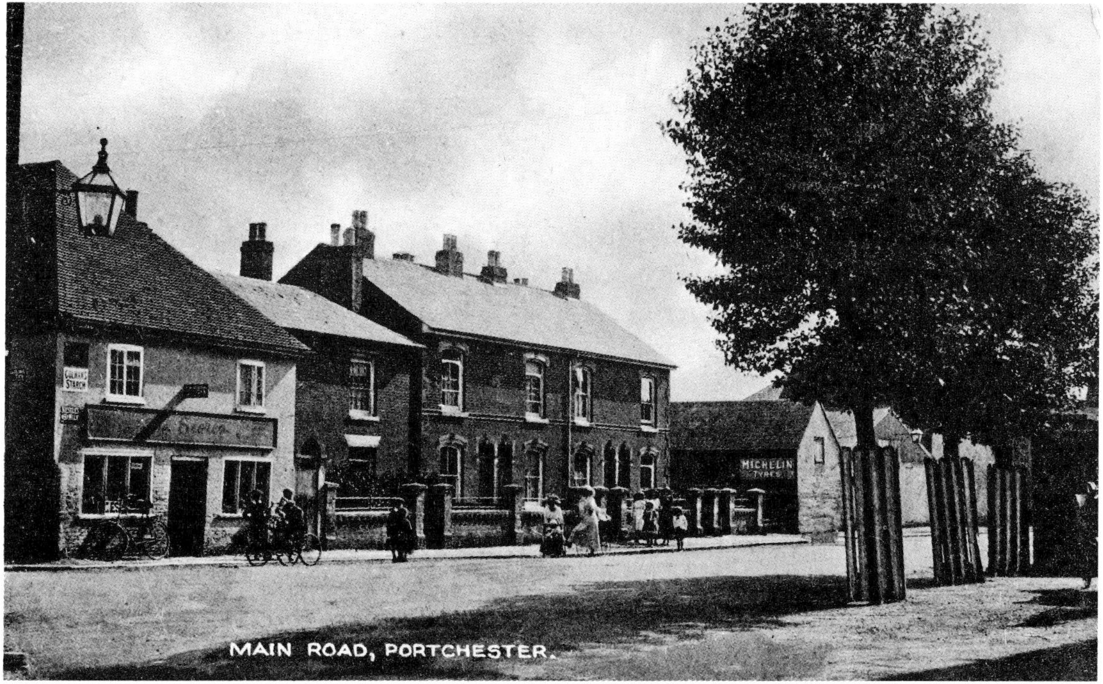

83. The centre of life in this part of the main road at Porchester was the village shop named 'The Stores'. Here was sold every conceivable item of general grocery, all of which could be delivered free to your door by first class carrier bike. Also stocked was ice-cream, together with a marvellous range of loose confectionery, which no doubt accounted for all the children in the picture. Porchester main road without a car in sight was not uncommon in 1910, but the advertising sign for Michelin Tyres gives an indication of the shape of things to come. In recent years the construction of a shopping precinct has diverted traffic from this part of the main road. Here the local residents can once again shop in peace, although with the pressures of modern living things are not quite as sedate as they were in the old days.

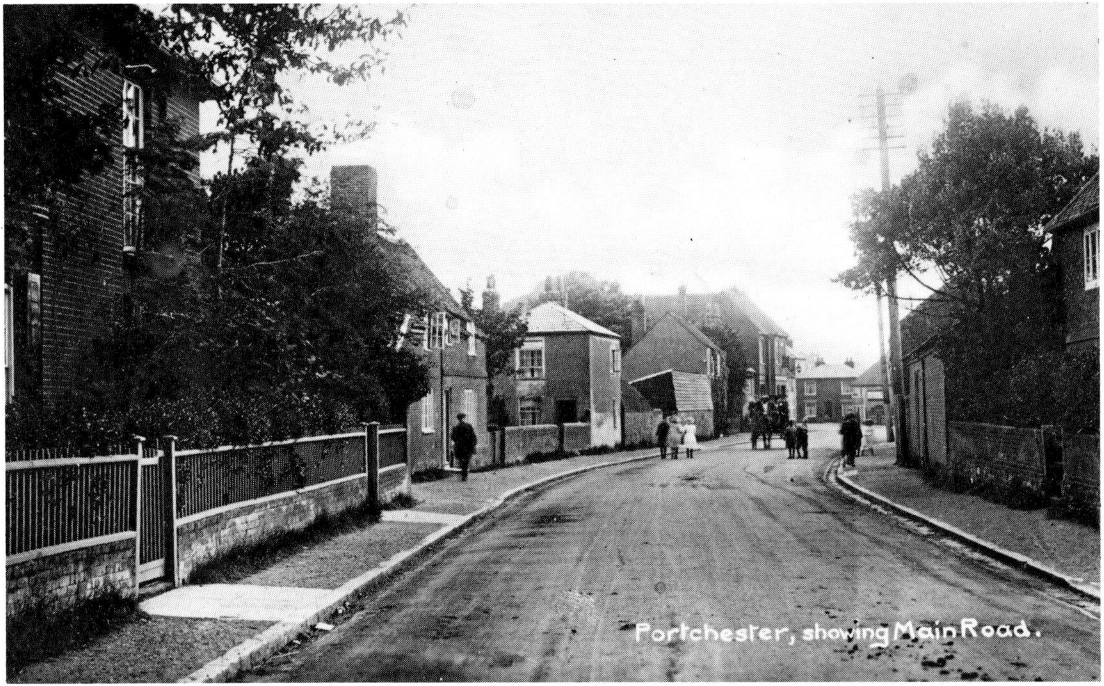

84. The photographer must have been standing about level with where the Community Centre is now when he pointed his camera eastwards down the main road at Porchester in 1918. The only transport in sight is the horse and cart with five passengers on board, being watched with great interest by two groups of people standing in the road. In the background can be seen the houses standing at Porchester crossroads. The picture here is much altered today with the buildings on each side of the main road having long since disappeared in the cause of repeated road widening. The main road itself has now been re-routed and bears off to the left to avoid the shopping precinct.

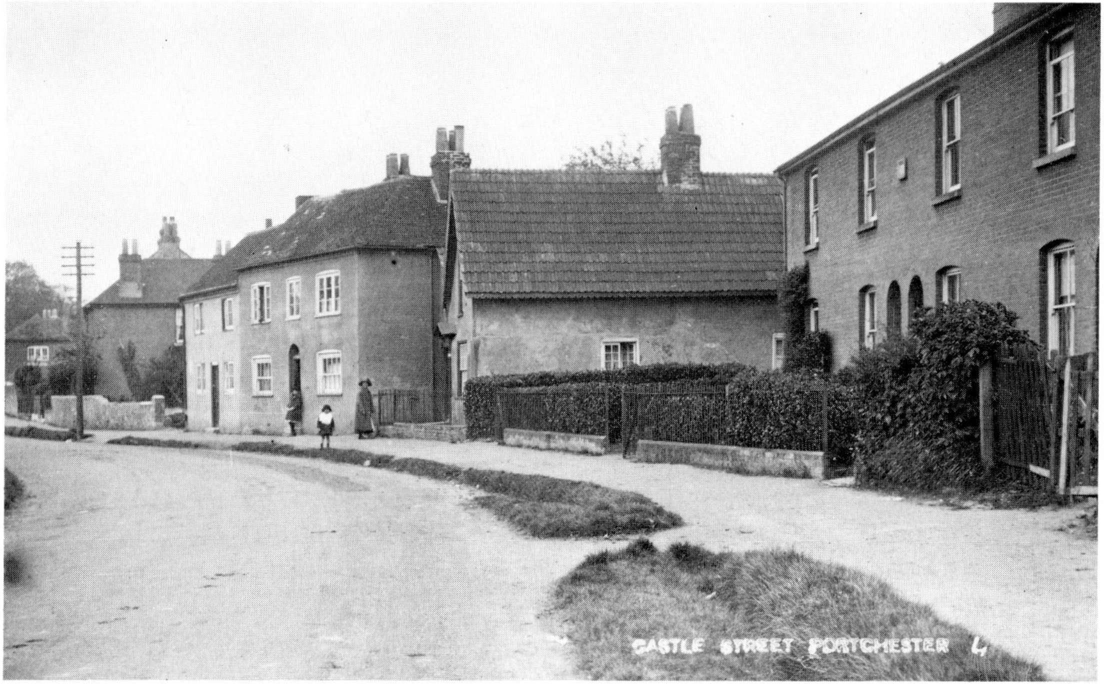

85. This photograph of Castle Street was taken in 1912. It is the view facing towards the Castle end of the street from a point just south of the White Hart public house and the junction of White Hart Lane and Castle Street. From this bend in the road on southwards time appears to have stood still for many years, thanks to the conservation order that protects this part of the old village.

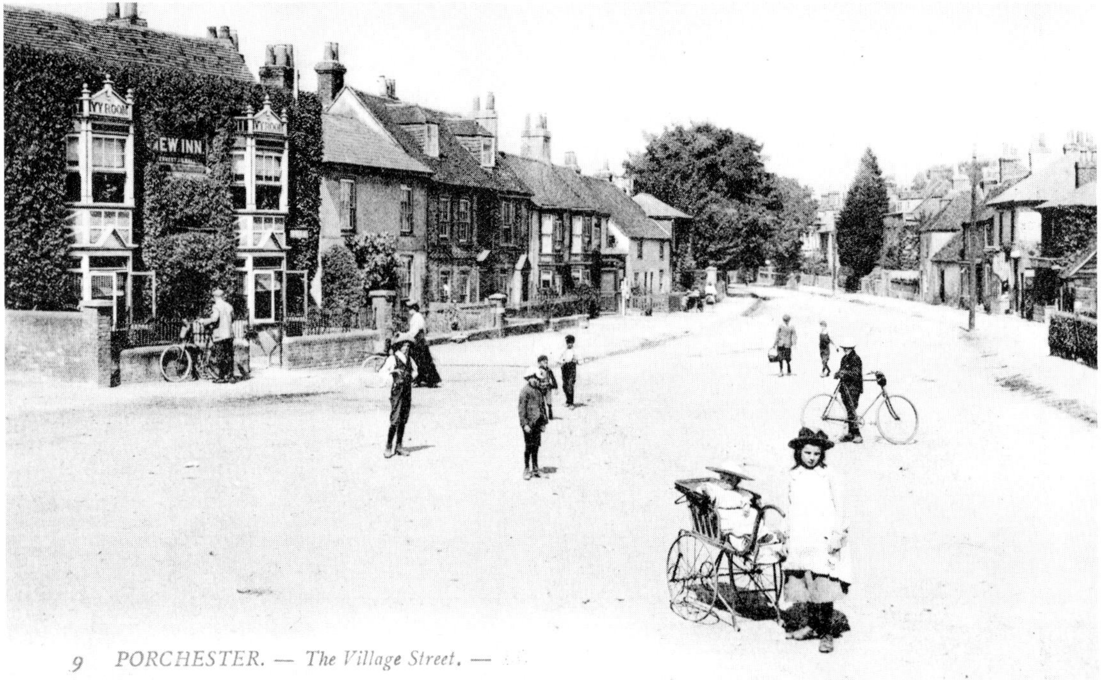

86. This photograph of the south end of Castle Street was taken in 1910. The New Inn on the left of the picture was a famous old public house once owned by Lion Breweries of Winchester. In those days parties of visitors came from far and wide to sample the ale and wonder at the ivy growing in profusion on the walls. This was one of six public houses that the village street boasted at one time. A few doors down from the New Inn stands the 'Cormorant' which dates from around 1815 and is the only public house of the six that still survives today. The photographer has also captured on film a nice example of a pushchair of the era and a glimpse of what the well-dressed Edwardian toddler wore.

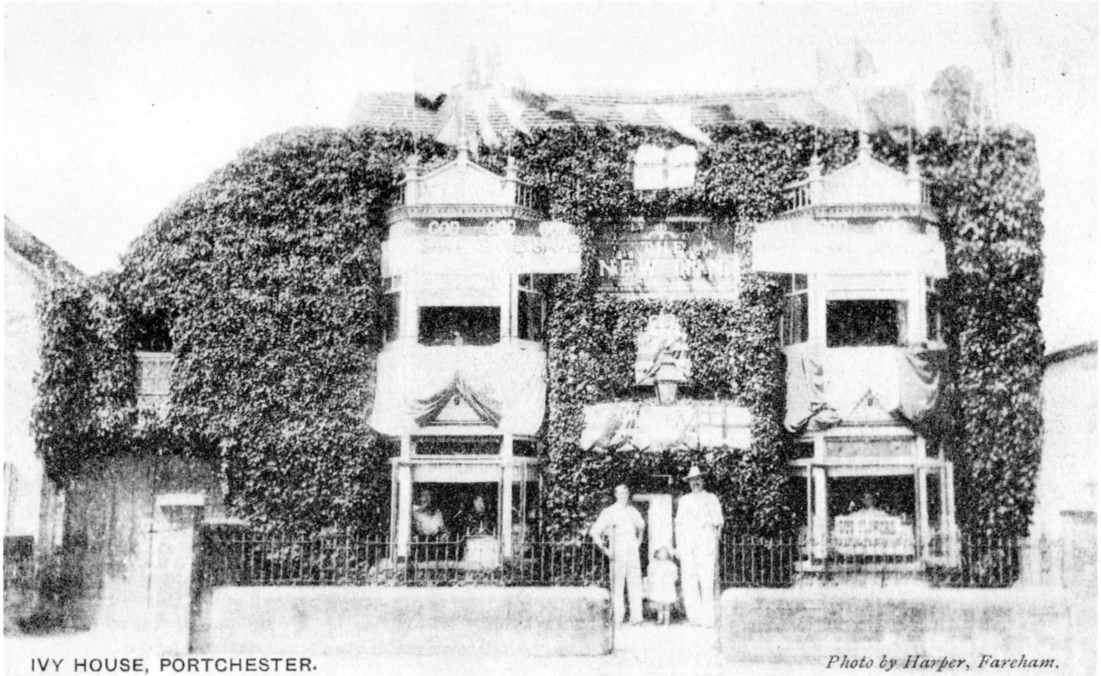

87. The splendour of the ivy on the walls of the old New Inn is pictured here by photographer Harper of Fareham. For years artists attracted to Porchester by the famous castle had stayed on to paint the old Ivy House. At one time the ivy having actually penetrated the thick walls of the house had been encouraged to grow all round the inside walls of the famous 'Ivy Room'. After closing down as a public house it became a private residence for a time before being opened up as tea-rooms in the mid-1920's. Years later it again became a private house and the owners then decided to have all the ivy removed. It is said that this decision considerably upset some of the older villagers. Today the old New Inn building appears as one of a row of attractive Georgian-styled houses.

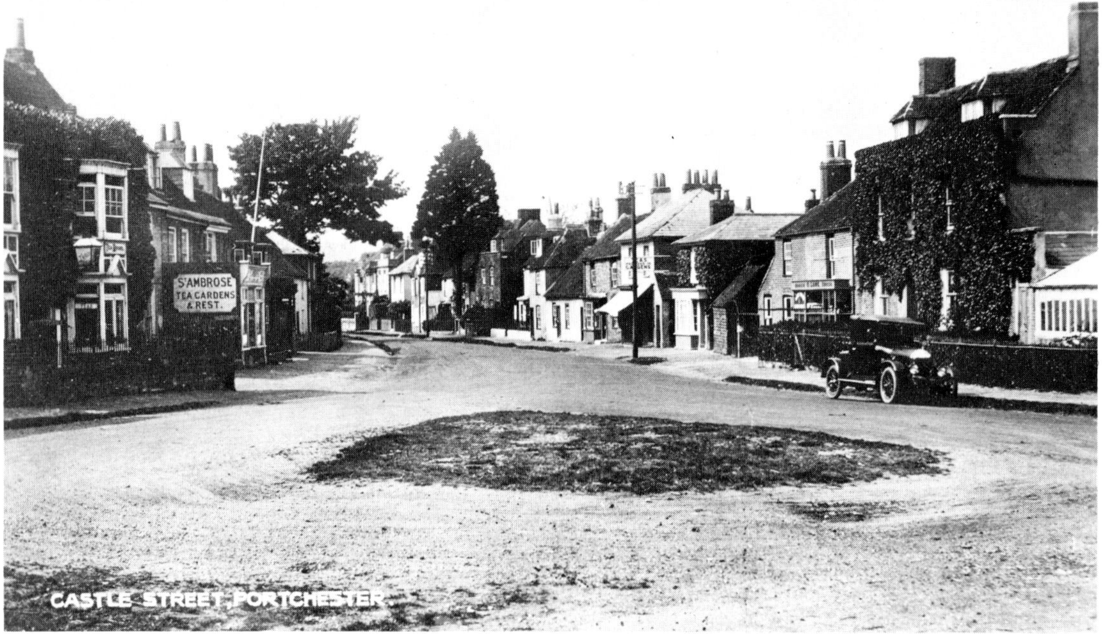

88. This photograph of what was once the old Porchester village square was taken by A.H. Sweasey in 1928. The old New Inn on the left of the picture can here be seen operating as tea-rooms. It also appears to be encountering considerable opposition from the premises across the road. The patch of green showing in the forefront of the picture was once the village green. To commemorate the Silver Jubilee of King George V in 1935 an oak tree was planted there. Today it has grown to be the centre piece of the scene, adding serenity and a welcome patch of shade.

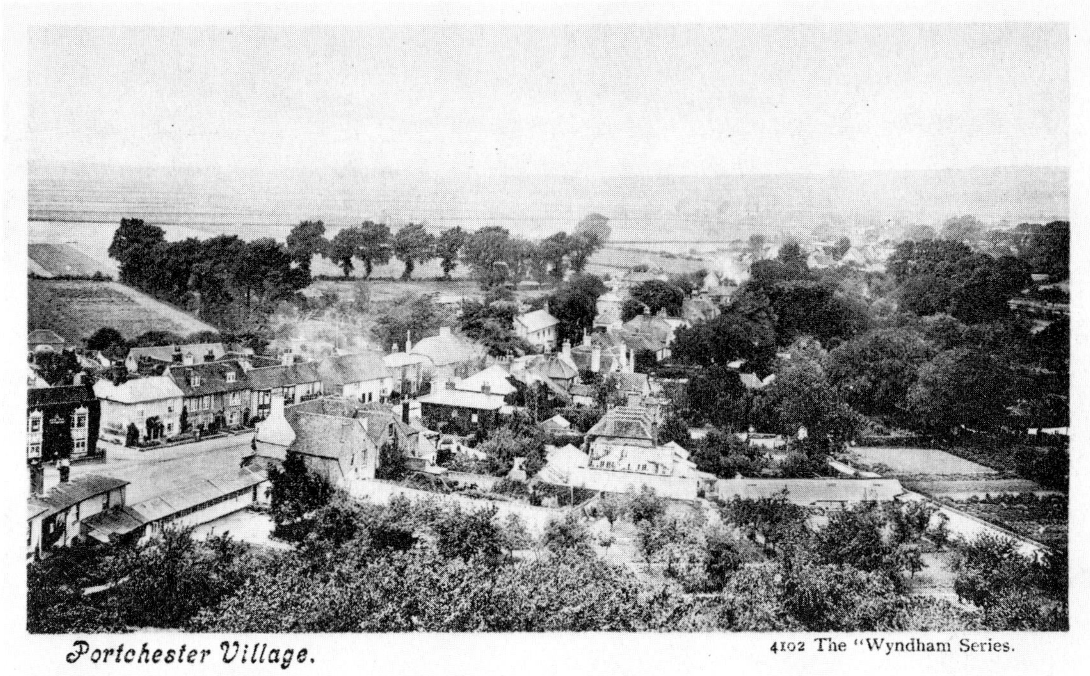

89. This was the view looking north from the top of Porchester Castle in 1909. The village is in the foreground and the slopes of Portsdown Hill run right across the background. Despite its sleepy appearance there was considerable activity in the area. There were several large farms and market gardens situated around the village. Then too, there was the constant stream of visitors from far and wide attracted to the Castle. Porchester had also been the scene of a successful pottery industry for many centuries. Then in 1840 Henry Leigh established a tobacco pipe, putty and whiting concern at the northern end of Castle Street. This business prospered for close to one hundred years, at one time turning out some 7,000 pipes each week. Customers from a wide area were supplied with these high quality, hand made, clay pipes. Thus Porchester obviously saw more activity than is apparent from this picture.

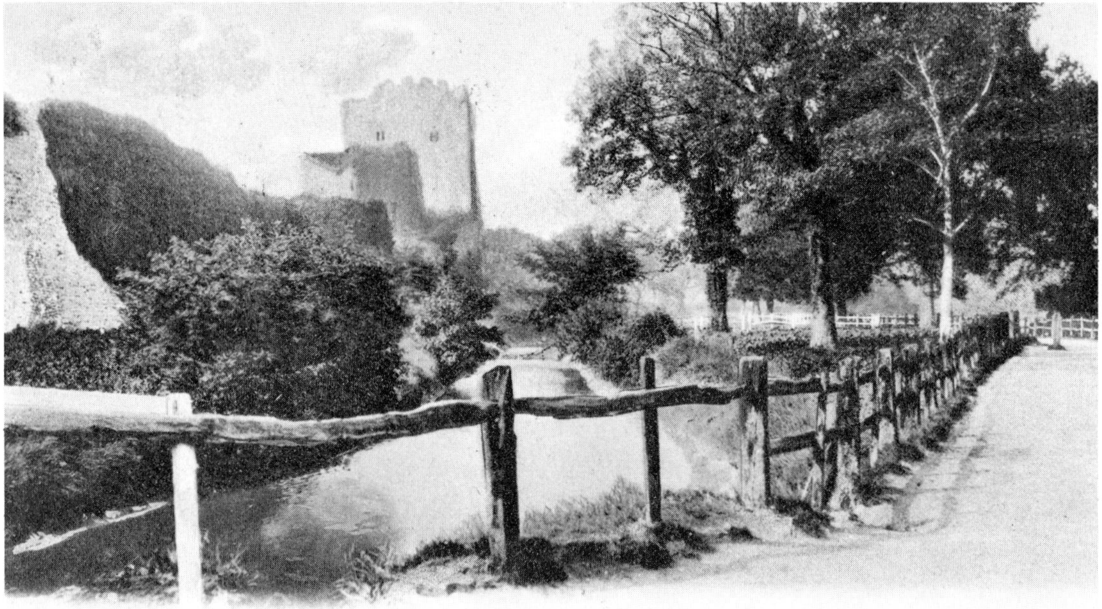

90. Moving south along Castle Street and passing through the old village centre, the road turning off to the left is Waterside Lane. This appears on the right of the F.G.O. Stuart picture taken here in 1906. On the grassy space between the lane and the moat once stood the wooden built barracks of the Military Guard. This was during the 18th century, when the Castle had been pressed into service as a military prison. At this time it was badly overcrowded with mostly French prisoners captured in the Napoleonic Wars. Their presence entailing the deployment of a large detachment of guards, at one time numbering two thousand. The sight of the moat filled with water makes this view considerably more attractive than it is today.

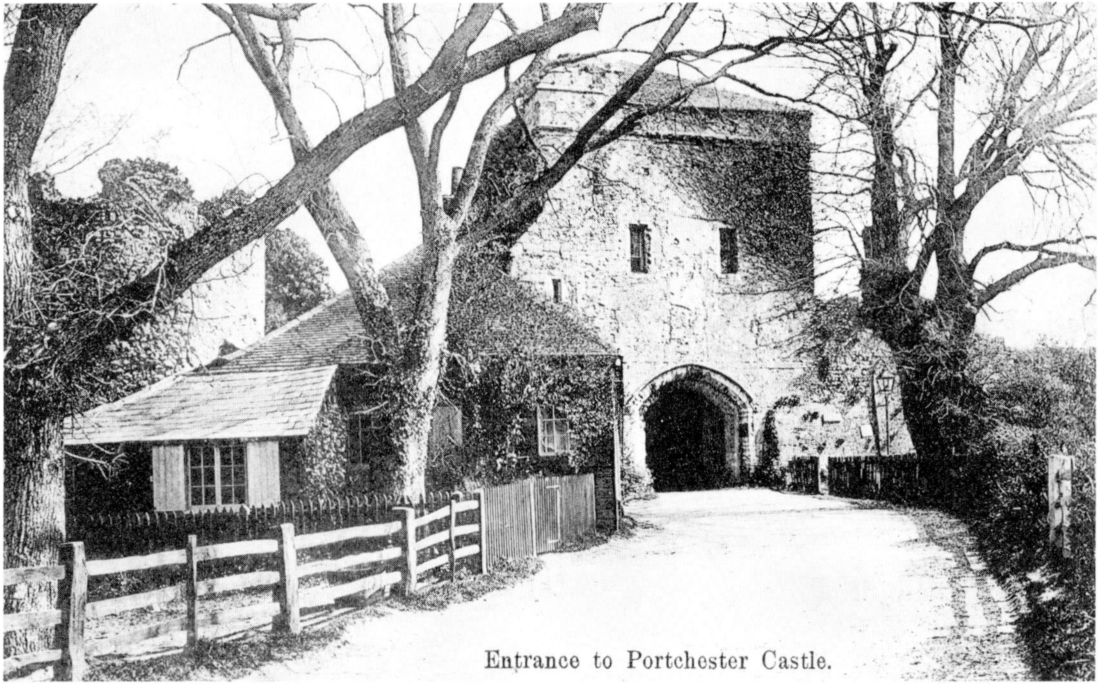

91. The approach road from the village leads up to the Landgate, which is the main entrance to Porchester Castle. The Romans built it almost twice this width and it was reduced to its present size by the Normans. Many members of the English Royalty have passed through this gate over the years. Henry II stayed at the Castle in 1163 and housed his treasure in the Keep. Both King John and Henry III are said to have visited on several occasions and Edward III used it as his headquarters whilst preparing for the battle of Crecy. Henry VIII and the ill-fated Ann Boleyn holidayed here in 1535. Good Queen Bess held Court here, and Charles I was another frequent visitor around 1626. In all an impressive list of royalty have passed through the Landgate that is pictured here on a postcard issued by J. Cushen of Porchester in 1912.

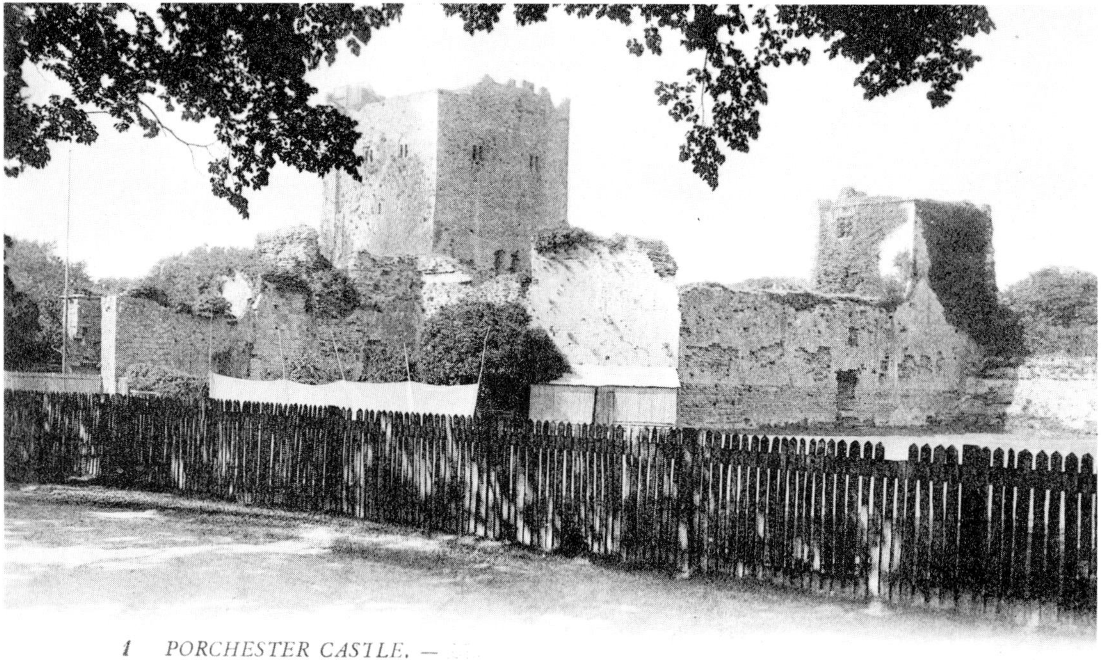

92. The Castle dates from the latter part of the 3rd century, when it was one of a series of such fortresses built by the Romans to counter the invasion threat posed by the Saxons. When the Romans retreated from British shores in the early part of the 5th century the Castle was to remain empty for many years. Later that century Saxons settled in the area, then occupying the Castle, they commenced to strengthen its defences to repel the Vikings. In the 12th century the Normans thoroughly restored the Castle, strengthening all the walls and building a new gate. A strong defensive building was also erected in the north-west corner of the old fortress. During the following centuries the Castle was used to varying degrees as a fortress, storehouse, hospital and prison. It stands today as one of the finest examples of a Roman Fortress still in existence. This picture was taken in 1910.

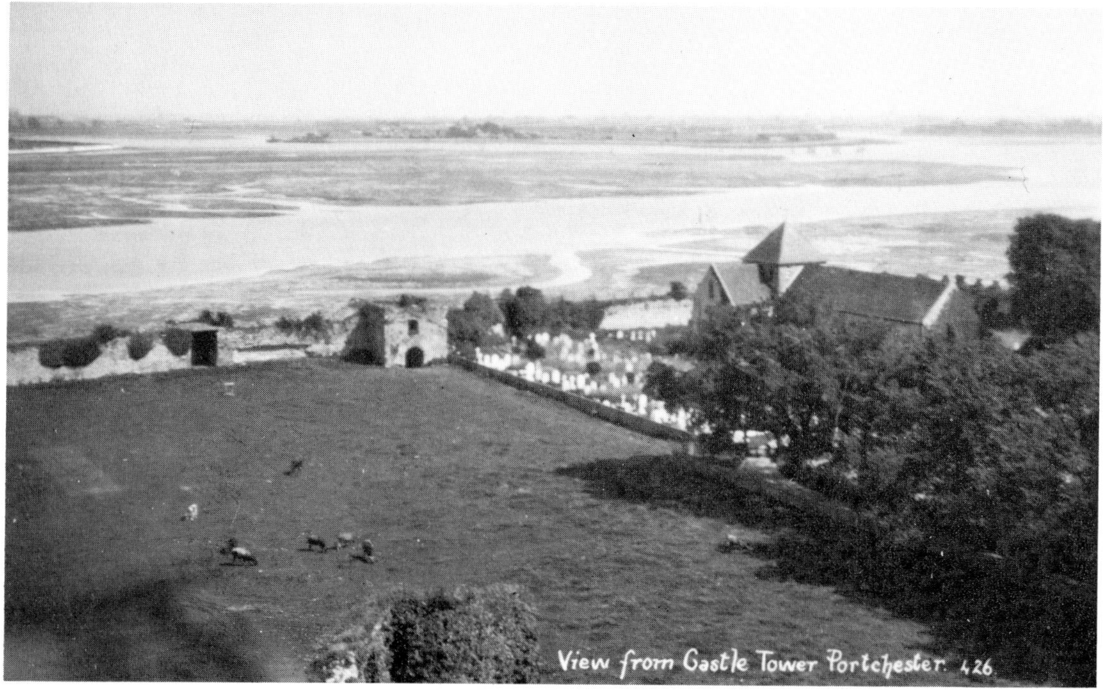

93. Taken from the Castle tower looking east towards Portsmouth, this view shows the upper reaches of Portsmouth Harbour. In the south-east corner of the area bounded by the castle walls is the Priory Church of St. Mary. Next to the graveyard, in the middle of the Castle's eastern wall, can be seen the Watergate. Ships bringing goods and men could tie up just a few feet away from this entrance to the Castle. In Norman times the original Watergate constructed by the Romans was extended outwards. With King Henry I having gained sovereignty over Normandy at this time, Porchester now assumed considerable importance. With its easily defensible position, and standing just across the Channel from Normandy, it became England's main south coast port for some years and the Watergate saw much use.

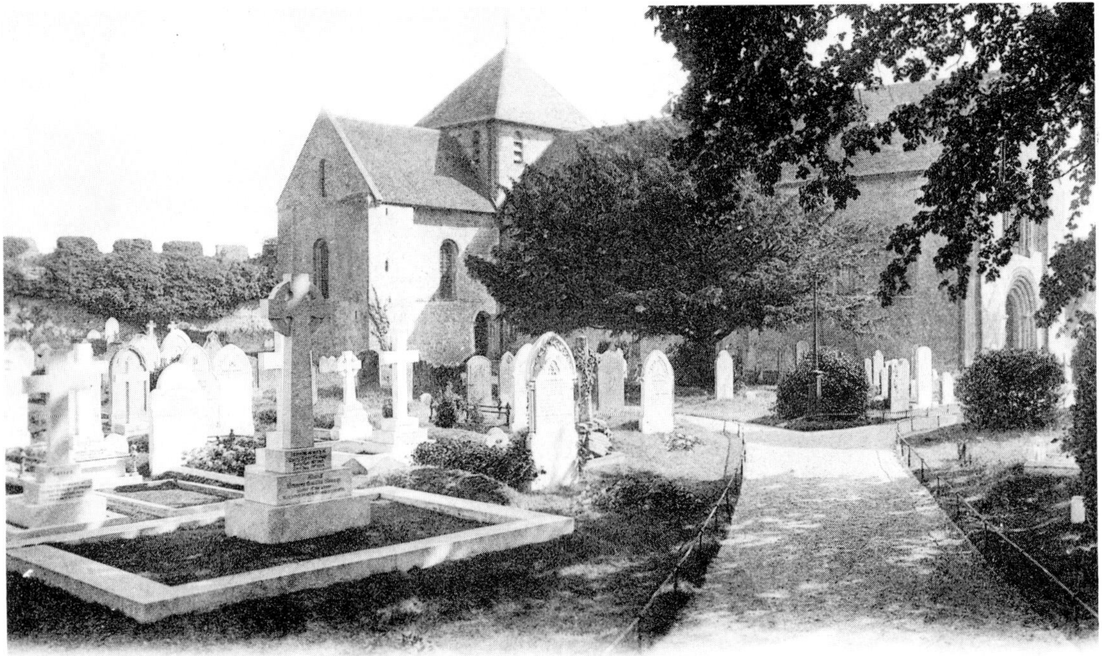

8 PORCHESTER. — The Church. —

94. The Priory Church of St. Mary stands within the walls of Porchester Castle. It is thought to have been built shortly before 1133. It was in this year that Henry I granted a charter to an Augustinian Order of Canons from Normandy. The Canons only remained in residence for a few years before moving to a new Priory at Southwick. Over the centuries the empty Priory was allowed to fall into a poor state of repair. Only restoration work in the reigns of Queen Elizabeth and Queen Anne enabling the buildings to survive. Towards the end of the last century the church was again in urgent need of attention. Thanks mainly to the efforts of the local population much work has been done since then, so that the old Priory Church was in fine condition to celebrate its 850th anniversary in 1983.

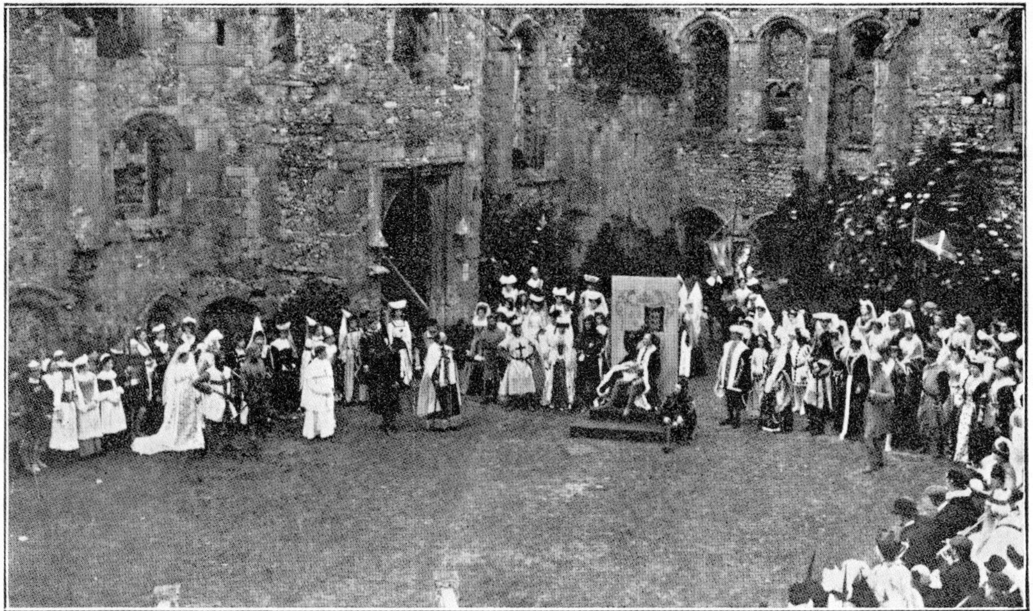

Portchester Pageant Series.] "HENRY V. AT PORTCHESTER, A.D. 1415." [*Copyright of F. A. Swaine, Southsea.*

95. Pageants were used as fine opportunities to stage extravagant historical and traditional exhibitions. They were a feature of the years making up the reign of King Edward VII. Many of the larger towns in England staged a pageant of some description at this time, some of the more famous being held locally at Romsey 1907. The Isle of Wight 1907 and Winchester 1908. Porchester was well known in this area for its galas and pageants, but the show put on in 1907 was something rather special, and joined the list of the most famous pageants held throughout the country. Pictured here is episode four of the 1907 Porchester pageant that was staged in the grounds of the Castle. It depicts Henry V at Porchester in 1415.

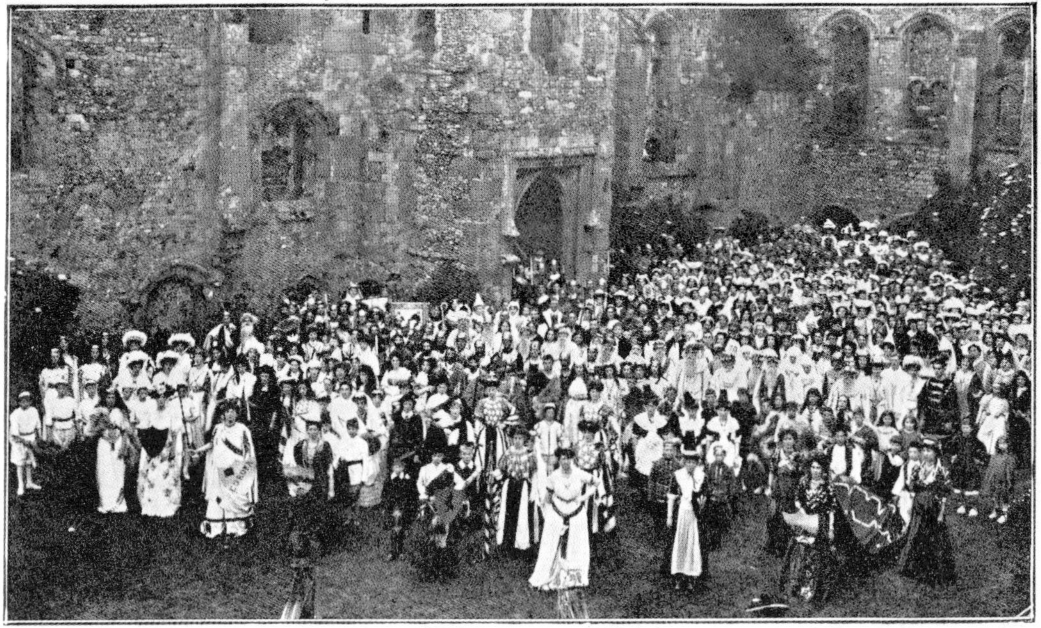

Portchester Pageant Series.] "THE GRAND SPECTACULAR FINALE." [*Copyright of F. A. Swaine, Southsea.*

96. The 1907 Porchester pageant was put on to celebrate the official birthday of King Edward VII. It was held on 28th and 29th June and was opened by Lady Bosanquet who was the wife of the Commander-in-Chief of Portsmouth. As was usually the case, the scenes of this pageant were all played out by local amateur performers. This production dramatised the story of Porchester through the ages in six episodes and was concluded by the 'Grand Spectacular Finale' pictured above. The whole performance was supported by the full band of the Royal Artillery and the Fareham and Titchfield Philharmonic Society. Records of the event state that the audience was packed to overflowing for each performance.

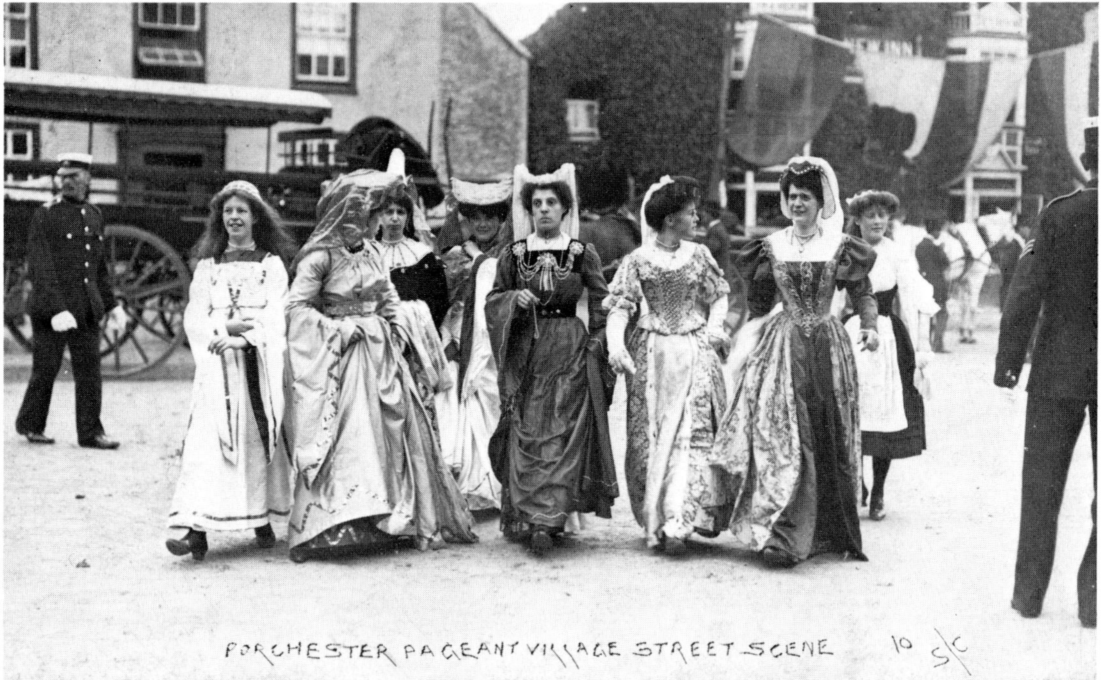

97. This group of gracious ladies are walking through Castle Street back to Porchester Castle, the scene of probably their greatest triumph. There is no doubt the 1907 Pageant was an outstanding success, and these ladies deserved to share in it, if only for the work that they had put in on their costumes. Each must have entailed many long hours of needlework, carried out with a fine eye to detail. In the background, partly hidden by flags, can be seen the New Inn public house. The horses and carriages that have brought the audience from near and far to view the pageant are lined up along the village street to await their return.

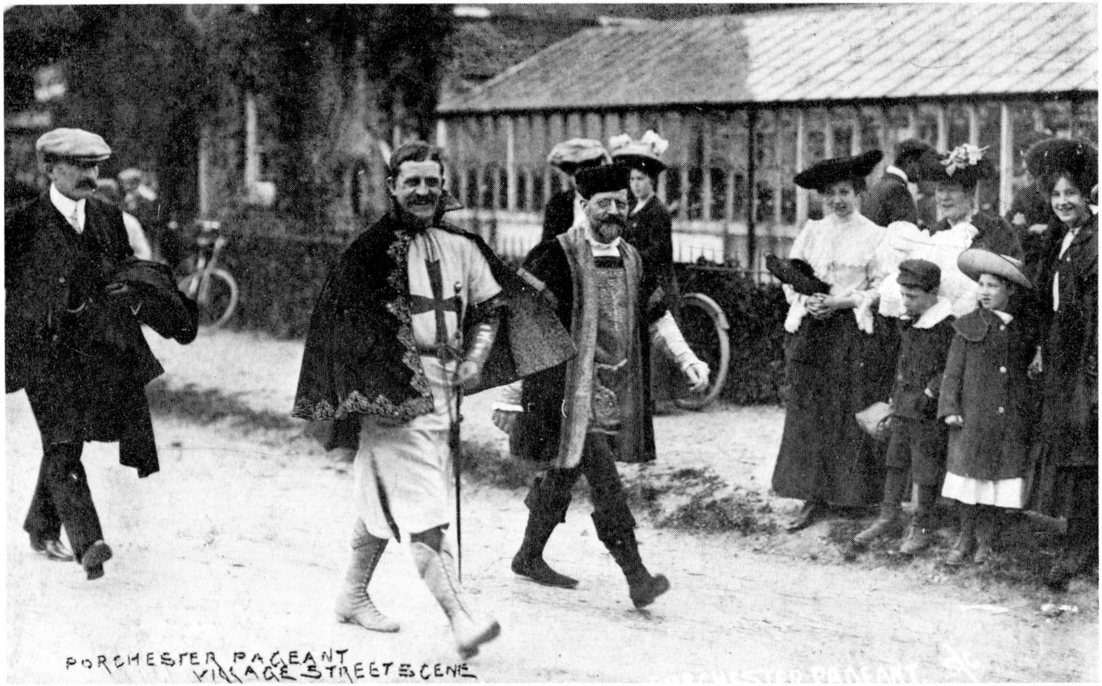

98. Taken between performances of the Porchester Pageant, this scene of the village was photographed from the 'New Inn' side of the street. The costumed gentleman smiling at the camera appears to be off to the Crusades as his part in the production. Some of the spectators in the street are wearing their coats on their arms which seems to indicate that the great event was blessed with warm, dry weather. The population of Porchester in 1907 was close to eight hundred people and it is reported that practically the whole village played some part in the historical production.

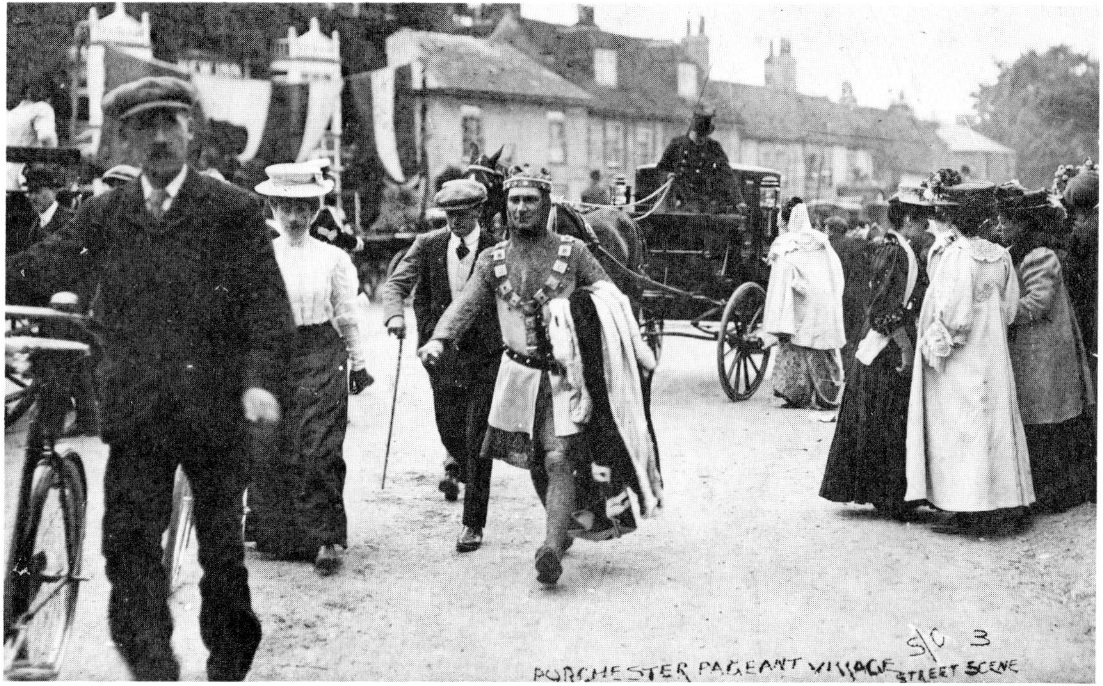

99. The first performance of the Pageant each day was from 3.00 p.m. until 5.00 p.m. and the second from 6.00 p.m. until 8.00 p.m. The very short space of time between showings must obviously have made the village square a scene of great activity, with one audience departing and the next arriving. This picture shows some of that activity in close-up. One performer strides purposefully through, while carriages with top-hatted coachmen stop to allow passengers to alight. To the right of the picture a group of grandly dressed ladies appear to be intensely discussing what they have just seen. What scenes the village saw in 1907, and how fortunate that this episode in the social history of the district was so clearly captured by the camera.

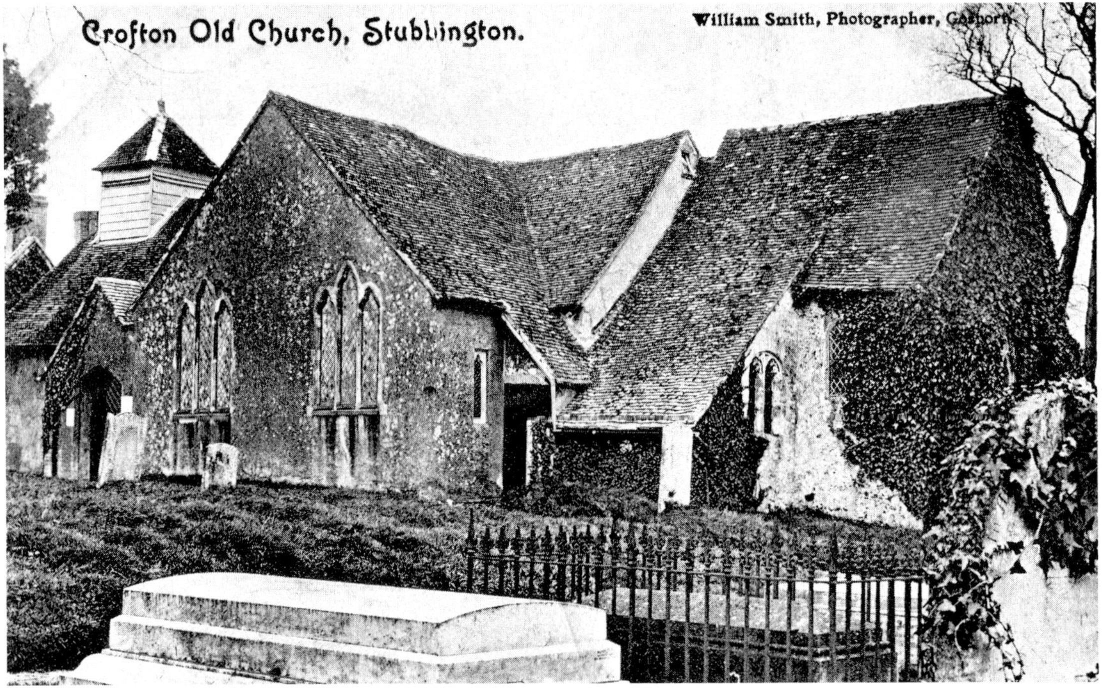

100. The old Holy Rood Church at Crofton is one of the oldest buildings in the area. It was mentioned in the Domesday Book and is believed to date back to the reign of King Arthur in the 9th century. This picturesque old church, which caught the eye of diarist Samuel Pepys in 1662, was extensively renovated in the 13th century. Periodic work on it since then has preserved it in reasonable condition to the present day. By the late 19th century it had become too small for the growing population of the district. A new church was built in Stubbington which took over the functions of the old Crofton Church in 1878. Now standing just off the Titchfield to Stubbington road and surrounded by its small beautifully kept graveyard it is a most attractive monument of the past.

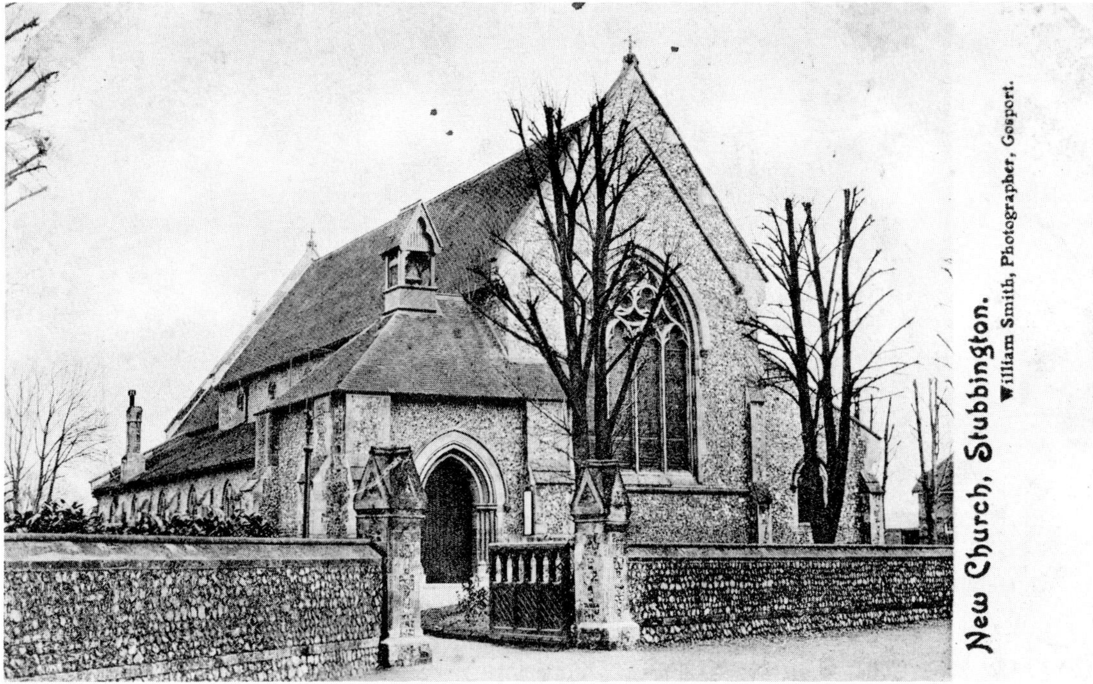

101. The new Holy Rood Church was built in the growing village of Stubbington in 1878. It was erected on ground donated by Mr. Montague Foster and the cost of the building, some £4,000, came from public subscription. The famous old church bell was originally at Place House, Titchfield. The Delme family took it from there to Cams Hall, Fareham when they moved. It later came into the possession of Mr. Foster when he purchased Cams Hall and he presented the bell to the new church. This 1908 view of the church by William Smith shows how the building appeared before the addition of the tower to the north-west corner.

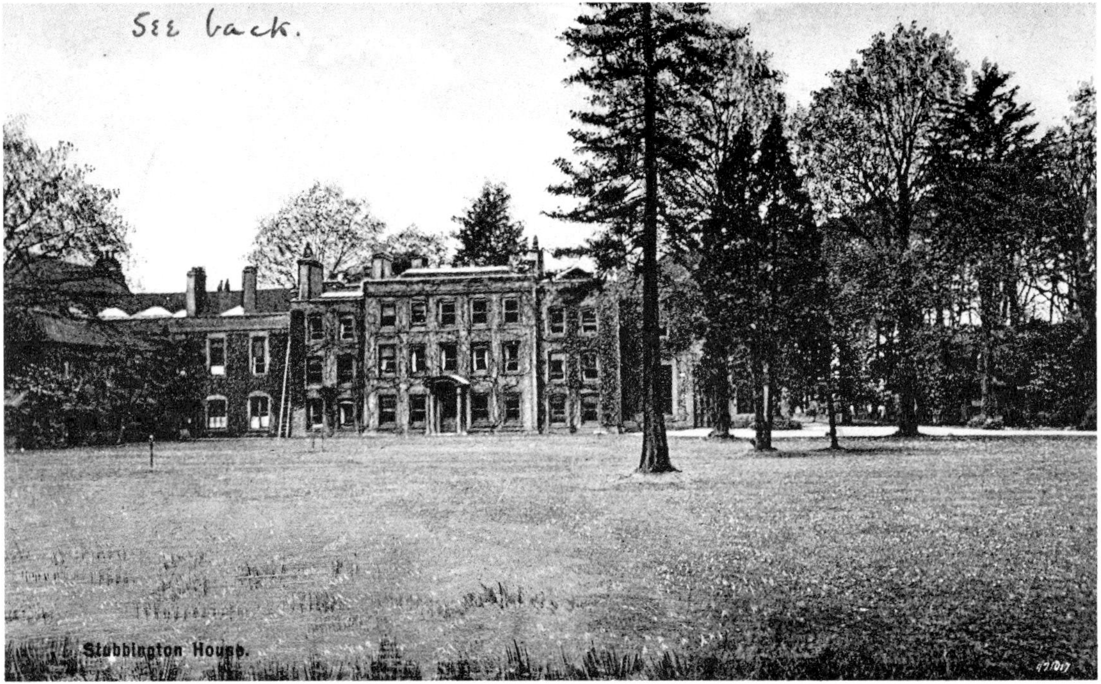

102. Stubbington House was an attractive Queen Anne building set in pleasant parkland. It became the home of the school founded by the Reverend William Foster in 1841. When he died in 1866 his wife kept the school running, and after her death seven years later their son Montague took charge. At the outset the school had just ten pupils and this total had risen to twenty-one boys and three teachers by 1871. Under Montague Foster's charge both the school buildings and the number of pupils were considerably enlarged. This postcard was sent by a pupil of the school in 1917. The message on the back reads 'This is only a tiny part of the school. Here Captain Scott and Lord Charles Beresford were educated under a former regime'. The school moved to Ascot some twenty years ago and the building was purchased by Fareham Council. Today it serves as the village Community Centre.

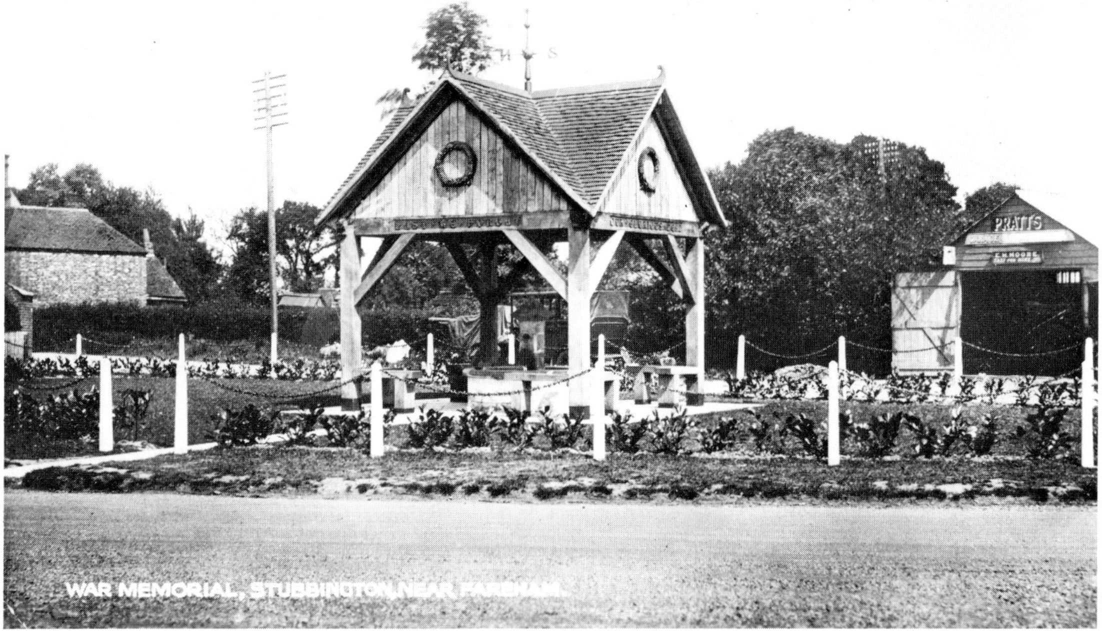

103. In the days when the fresh water supply came mostly from wells, the village pump was usually the focal point of village life. In Stubbington, as in many other villages, the pump was sited on the village green. In 1922 the wooden War Memorial pictured here was built by Arthur Tribbeck. It was constructed in the form of a shelter over the village pump. Because of war damage and re-development the memorial is now one of the very few pre-war erections still standing in the vicinity of Stubbington village centre. This 1929 postcard by A.H. Sweasey also shows Pratt's Garage facing the green. The building bears a sign advertising the taxi of E.H. Moore for hire. The vehicle itself, looking very much like an old London cab, is parked just behind the Memorial.

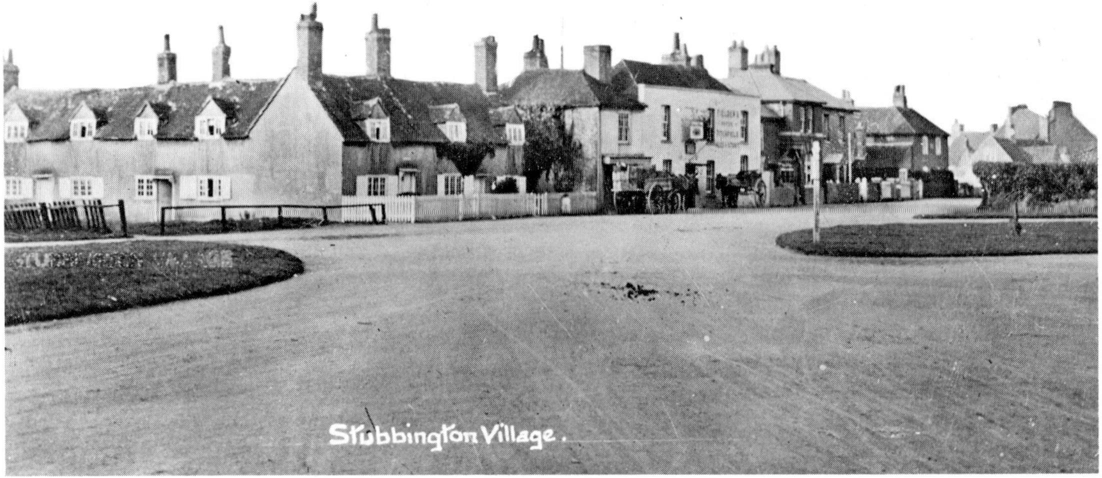

104. The postcard showing this view of the village was posted on 14th April 1913. The village green to the right looks strangely bare without the familiar War Memorial which, of course, was not to be erected for another nine years. What little activity there is seems to be centred around the old Sun Inn. The owners of the two horses and carts parked outside, no doubt in the company of a few locals, are inside busy sampling the Ales and Stout brewed by Fielders of Titchfield. The road past the old public house leads out of the village to Titchfield and Fareham. The row of cottages and the old inn are today replaced by a row of modern shops and a supermarket.

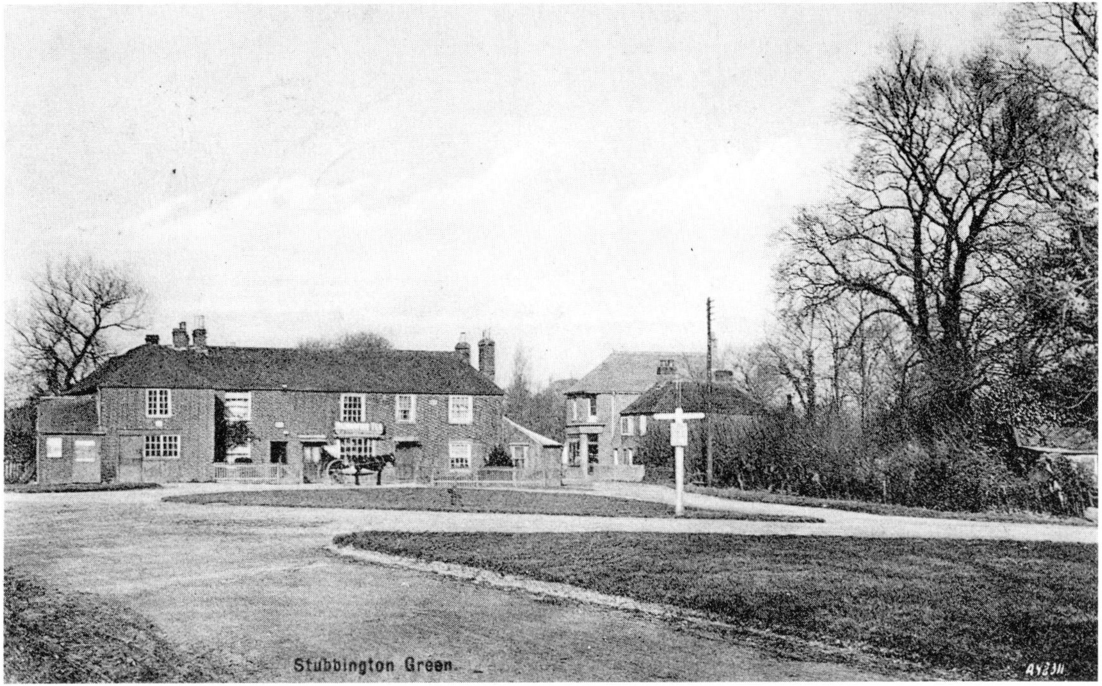

105. This row of cottages once stood on the northern side of the village green. The cottage on the extreme left of the row was the domain of the village blacksmith. Next door but one, seen with a large tea advertisement over the window and a customer's pony and trap outside, was the grocery store. The sign post on the green points the way to Titchfield and Fareham. This part of Stubbington survived up until the last war but was then badly damaged by a flying bomb in 1944. The site where these cottages once stood, and the tree filled ground on the right of the picture, are now occupied by some of the modern shops that face the green on three sides.

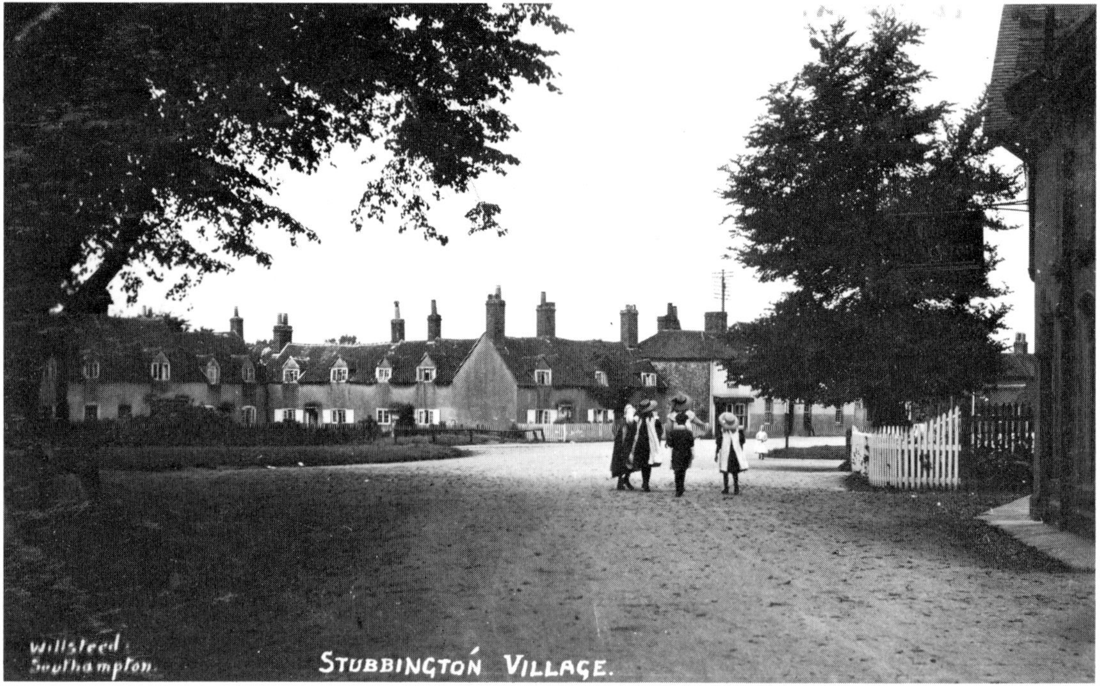

106. This is a 1906 view by Southampton photographer Willsteed showing the southern part of the village. Here the rows of cottages with their distinctive chimneys overlook a peaceful scene. Children play in the middle of the street and there is not a shop or any form of road transport in sight. Today the village offers the local historian a considerable challenge, for nowhere has seen more changes over the years than Stubbington. Partly because of enemy action, and partly because of the intensive building programme carried out in the area, the face of the village has undergone a complete transformation. The new shops and roads were obviously badly needed to give an expanded population the conditions and service expected in modern times. The older inhabitants, however, must surely view today's village with mixed feelings.

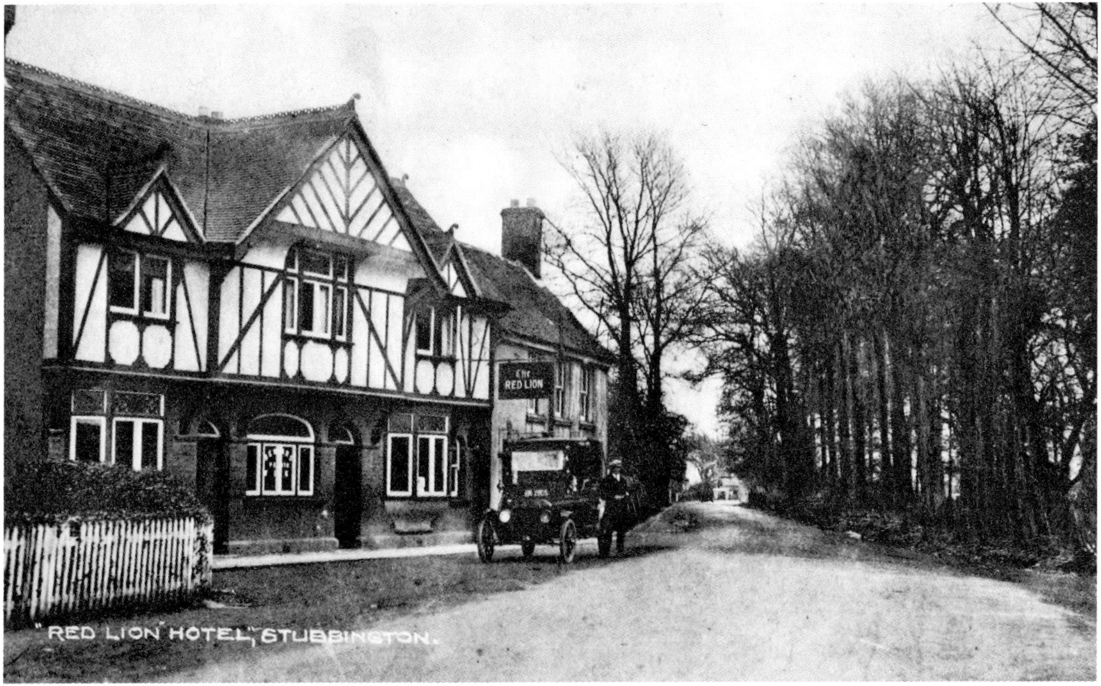

107. The Red Lion Hotel was the largest of the three public houses that served the village of Stubbington at the turn of the century. Standing just where the road from Gosport enters the village, this was always a popular calling place for the many parties of day trippers out from Gosport and Portsmouth to view the local countryside. As this picture indicates, it was also a calling place for the motor car in the pre-traffic jam and breathaliser test days. The Red Lion today stands adjacent to the busy village by-pass road and the tranquil scene pictured here is very much a thing of the past.

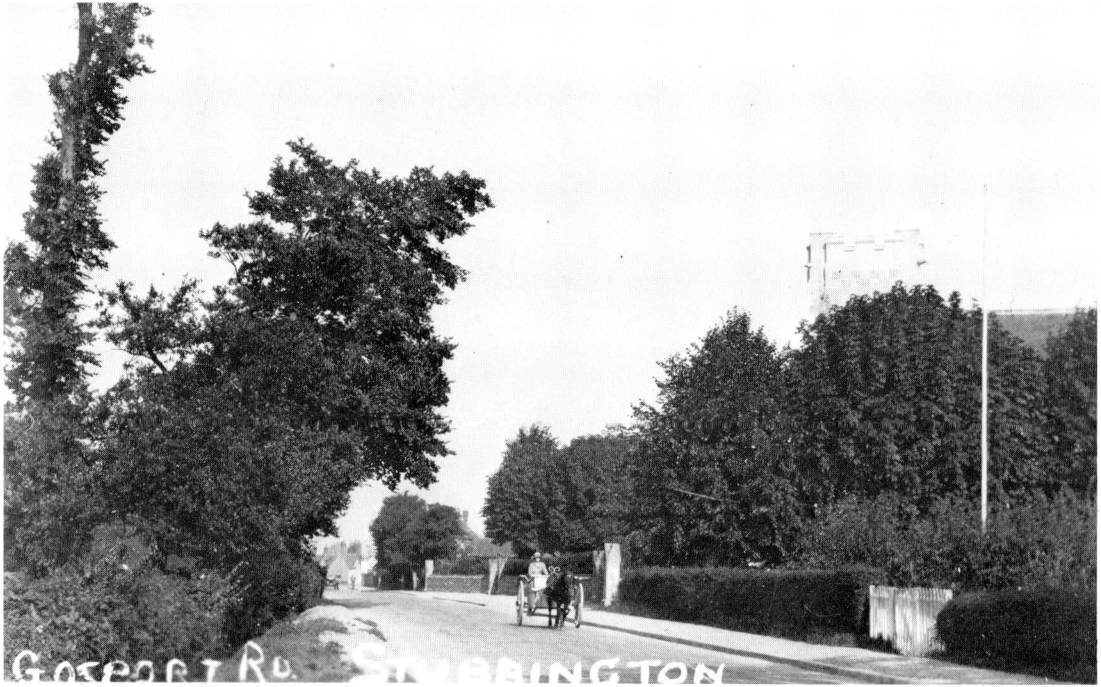

108. The pony and trap in the picture is seen heading out of Stubbington in the direction of Peel Common and Gosport. The village itself can just be seen in the background. Just behind the trees on the right of the picture is the Holy Rood Church. The distinctive square tower showing above the trees was built on to the church by Mr. Harry Tribbeck. It was completed in 1928, just one year before this picture was taken, as a memorial to the ex-pupils of Stubbington House School who lost their lives in the First World War. A large roundabout now stands towards the end of this stretch of road, where the Fareham to Lee-on-Solent road by-passes the village.

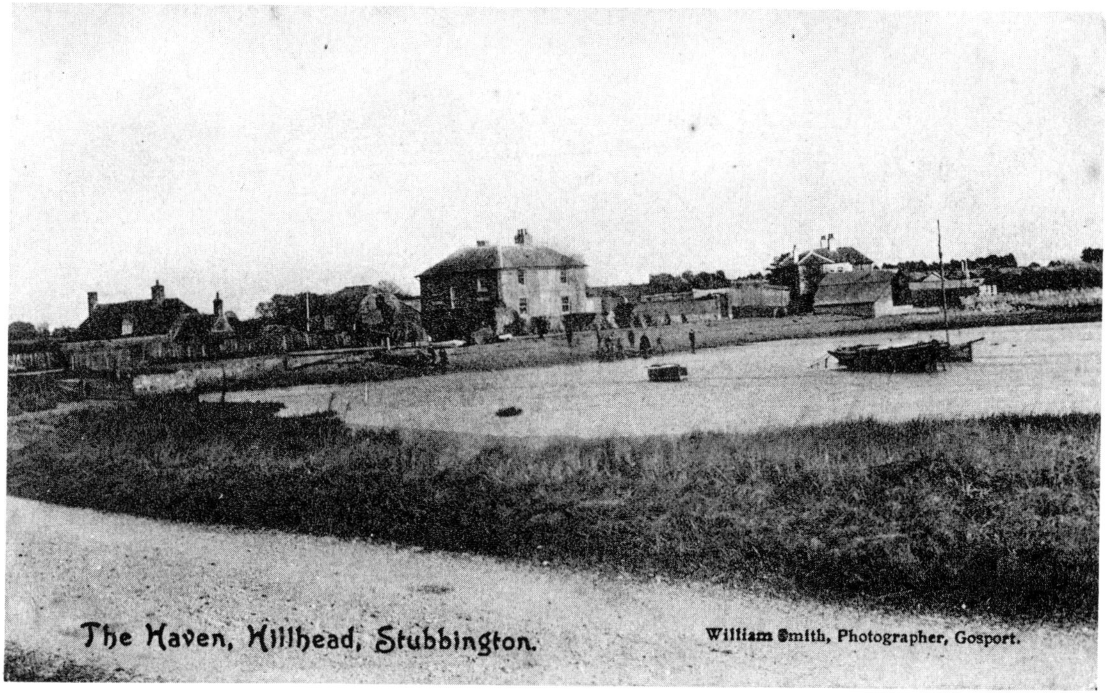

109. This sheltered part of the south coast has always seen considerable shipping activity. From the iron-age Celts who used the River Meon as a harbour, right through until the 17th century, there was a steady passage of craft up the river to the port of Titchfield. The dam built across the Meon to drain the marshes virtually closed Titchfield as a port, and eventually reduced the river mouth to a home for sailing boats. The Haven is where the River Meon reaches the sea just west of Hillhead village. It is not much changed from this 1906 picture by William Smith. Most of the buildings still survive, although the water is now packed with the boats of the Hillhead Sailing Club. Just to the left of the buildings lies the Titchfield Haven Nature Reserve which is now a fiercely protected area.

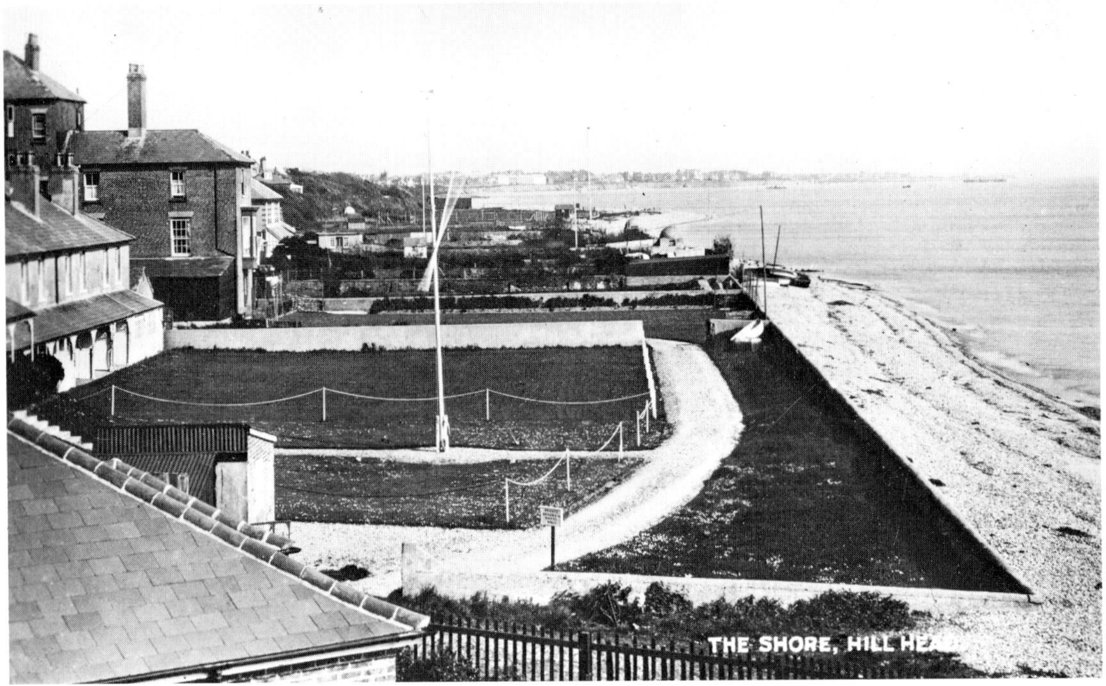

110. This photograph was taken from the bottom of the slip road leading down to the shore from Hillhead village. The view with the camera pointing east is virtually unchanged today. Only in the background, at neighbouring Lee-on-Solent, have drastic changes occurred. The pier just visible, stretching out to sea, is pictured here in 1927 before the erection of Lee Tower. Both have now long since disappeared. Whilst the Hillhead shoreline has remained the same, the village itself has grown enormously. Steady development since the 1920's, accelerated after the Second World War, has seen Hillhead and neighbouring Stubbington become one large unbroken residential area.

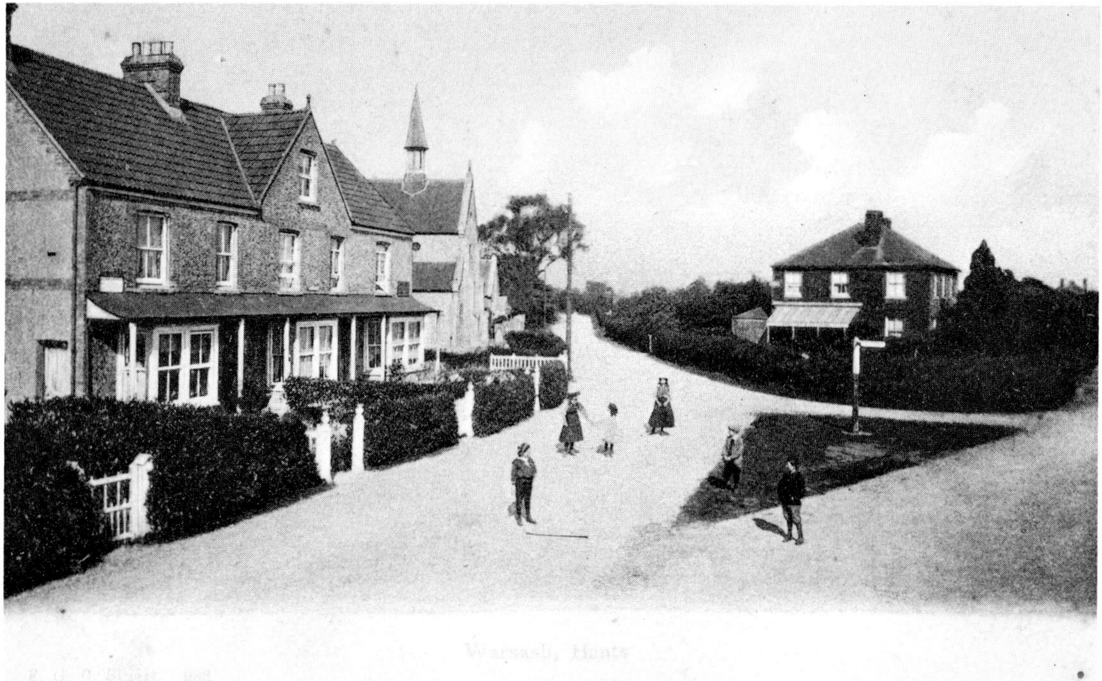

111. The gravels around Warsash left by the receding ancient seas have given up many flint axe heads and the like. Assorted implements from the Bronze Age have also been found locally. These finds indicating that the area has been inhabited since pre-historic times. In later years Warsash had become part of the Manor of Titchfield and at the time of the dissolution was spelt *Warishassefeld.* The village pictured here by F.G.O. Stuart in 1909 appears very small, quiet and countrified and gives no indication that the water is only yards away. It is that water, Warsash being at the mouth of the river Hamble, that has led it to become a centre for small craft. There is a large Sailing Club on the waterfront whilst at the nearby College of Nautical Studies merchant navy officers from all over the world receive training.

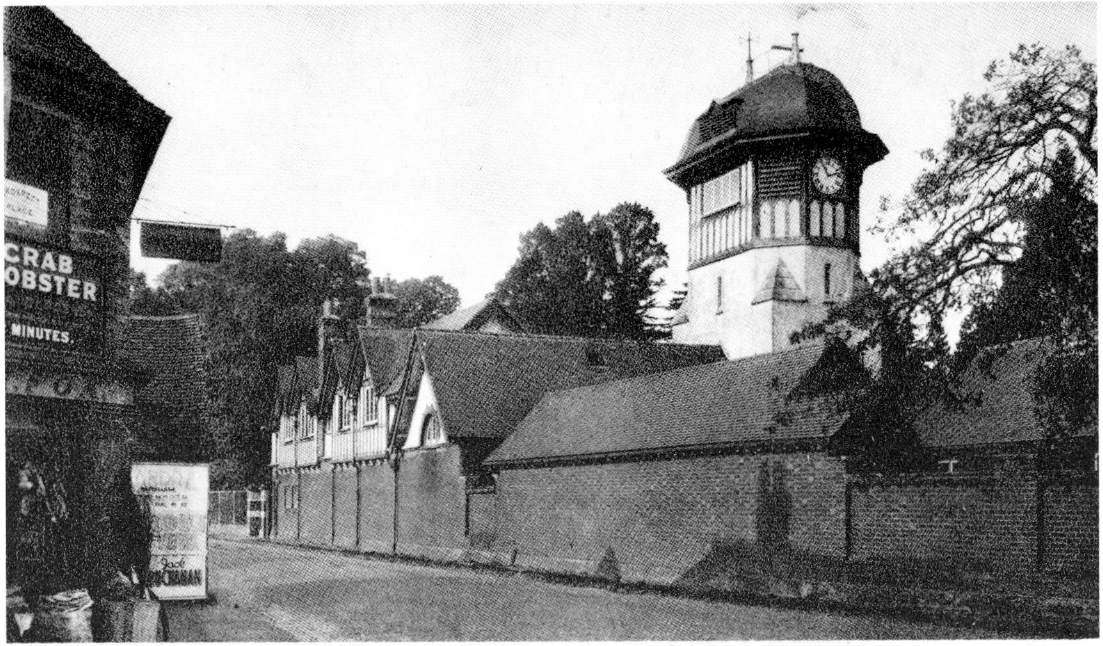

CLOCK TOWER, WARSASH

112. Mr. E.G. Fox of the Supply Stores, Warsash, published this view of the Clock Tower in 1922. The crab and lobster advert on the left of the picture draws attention to one of the main tourist attractions of the village. In the first half of this century coach parties would call regularly at Warsash to sample the delights of these freshly caught shellfish. In earlier days the area was better known as a place where salt was manufactured. In the Salterns at Hook and Warsash domestic and medicinal salt was produced in large quantities. It was transported by pack horse through Sarisbury Green, across the old Swanwick ferry and on to Winchester. This local industry was eventually transferred to the north of England on economic grounds. Whilst the Clock Tower building still remains, the lower structure in the foreground is now the site of car showrooms. The advertising hoarding across the road announces that a Jack Buchanan film is currently being shown at Fareham's Alexandra Cinema.

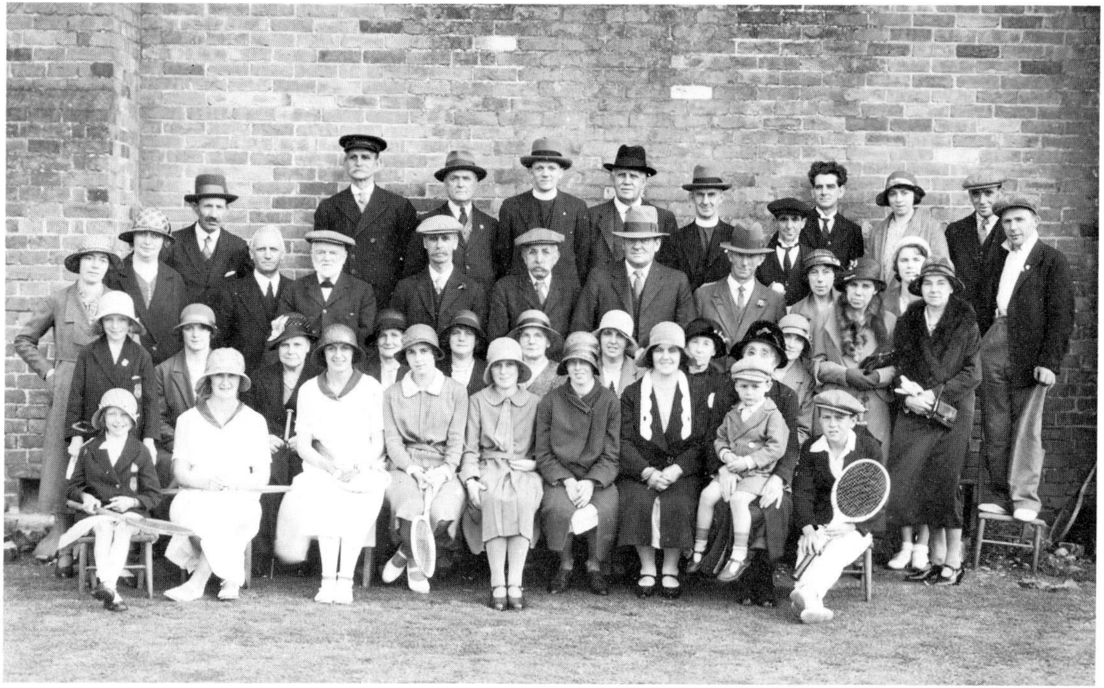

113. The group pictured here were all members of St. Mary's Church, Hook, Warsash. The church obviously had a tennis club in those days, and this photograph appears to have been taken before play commenced. It is a little unusual to see two gentlemen posing bare-headed for the camera in 1930. A steadily growing population in the latter part of the 19th century meant that the church of St. Pauls at Sarisbury Green was finding it difficult to cope with the increasing number of parishioners. To rectify this situation it was decided to create a new parish of Hook with Warsash in 1872. The church of St. Mary's was built in readiness for that date.

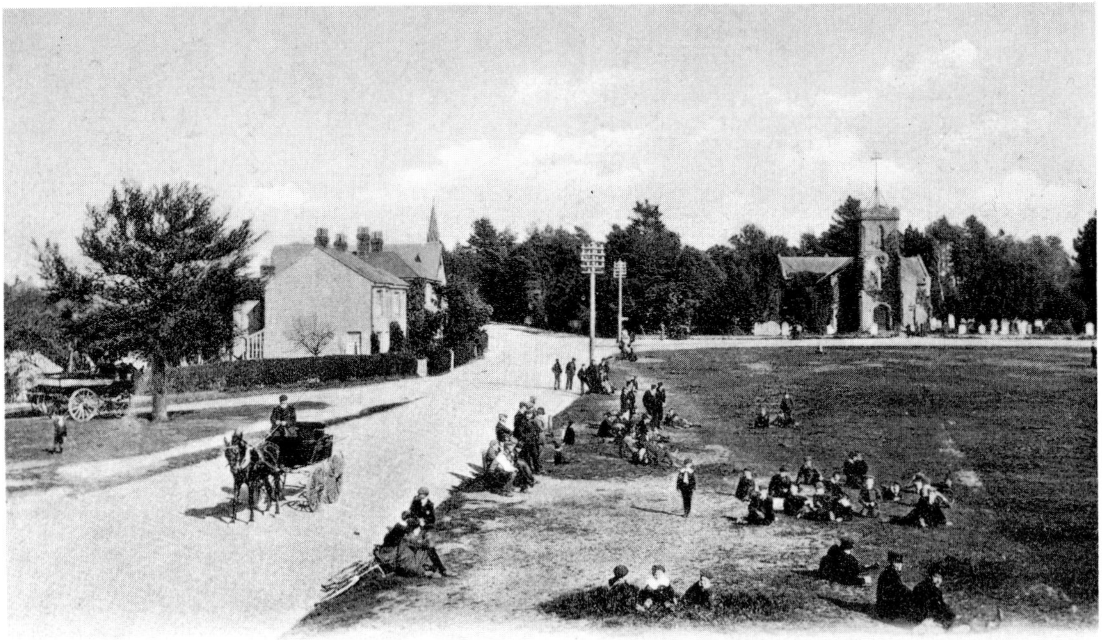

114. Sarisbury was once part of the Hundred and of the parish of Titchfield. The Green itself dates back to at least the middle of the 18th century, when there is a record of it being the venue for cricket matches. In the 1860's most of the common land in the area was effected by the Land Enclosure Act. The object being to fence all common land and bring it under cultivation. The continued casual use of this land was considered wasteful in view of the now rapidly increasing population needing to be fed. At the time there were fears for the future of the Green but happily it was never enclosed, being protected by another Act of Parliament preserving all village greens. This photograph taken by F.G.O. Stuart in 1907 shows the Green and St. Paul's Church before the erection of the lych gate.

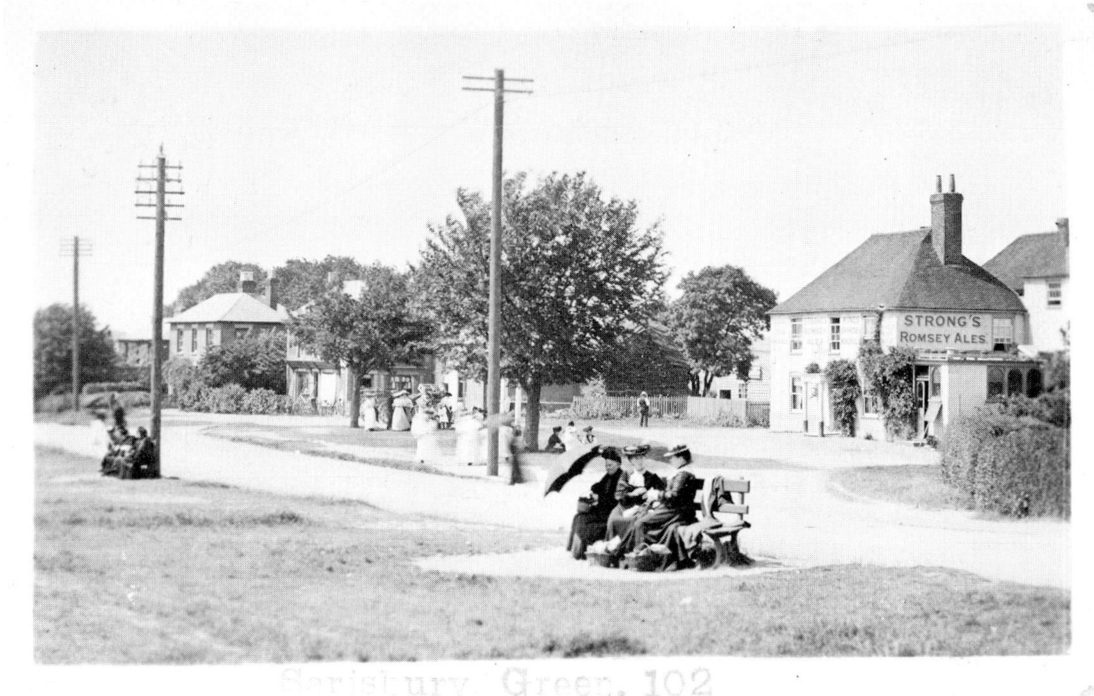

115. The village inn always played an important part in the social life of a village and the one at Sarisbury Green was no exception. This photograph dates from July 1905 and shows the New Inn, as it was then called, facing out across the Green. It occupied this site for at least one hundred and fifty years and is seen here ready to dispense Strong's Romsey Ales to the local inhabitants. In more recent times the old public house has been taken over by Whitbreads and its name changed to the 'Bat and Ball'. In the foreground one lady sits on the edge of the green with sunshade raised. Others in their long summer dresses seek the shade of the trees outside the New Inn. This providing a typical Edwardian English scene on a lovely summer's day.

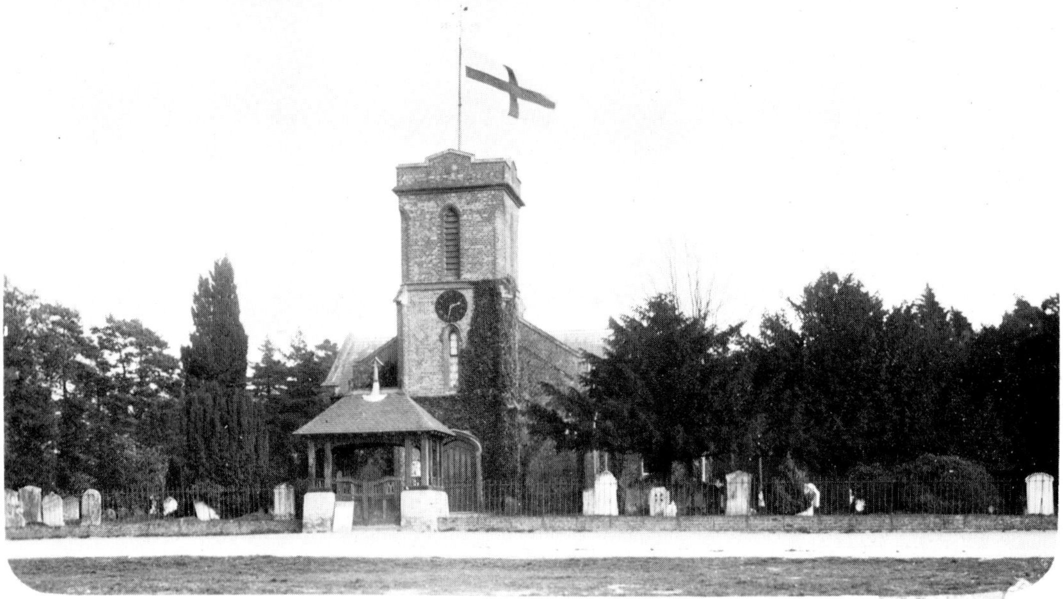

116. St. Paul's Church faces west across Sarisbury Green and is the parish church of Sarisbury and Swanwick. In 1833 Henry Peter Delme conveyed a sufficient plot of land to the Church Commissioners for a church and vicarage to be built. The parish church opened its doors for the first time three years later. Henry Peter Delme, a member of a prosperous and well-known Huguenot family, was at that time the Lord of the Manor of Titchfield, of which Sarisbury was once a part. The churchyard was consecrated in 1836, to be the burial place for all the parishioners and inhabitants of the hamlets of Newtown, Warsash, Sarisbury and Swanwick. The church was rebuilt and enlarged in 1888 and was pictured here in 1910.

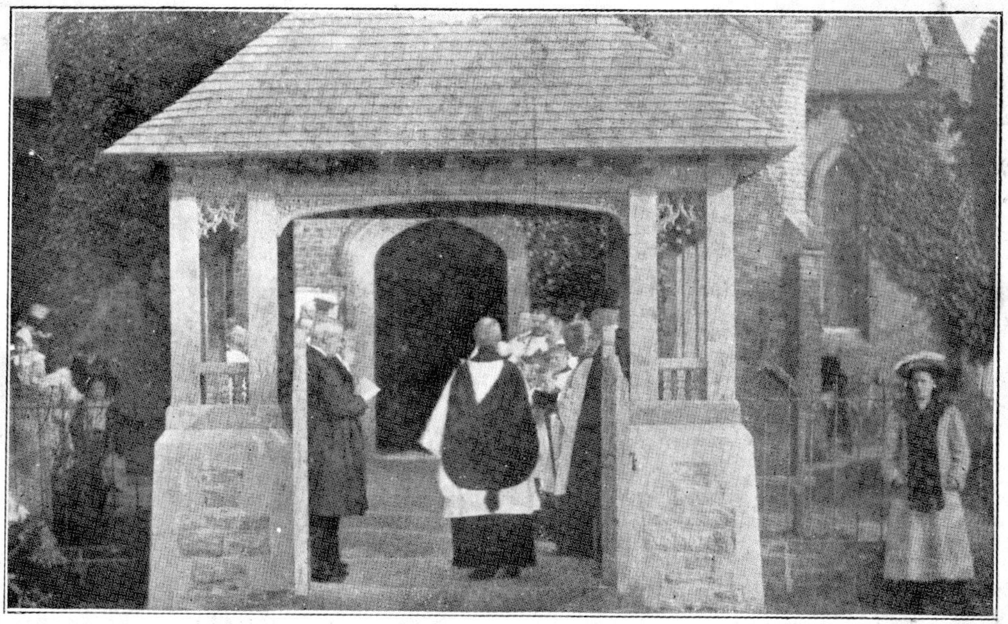

DEDICATION OF LYCH GATE, SARISBURY CHURCH, MARCH 12TH, 1908.
Photo. by F. Pannell, Fareham.

117. Mrs. Louisa Seymour was the sister of the Reverend Richard Harvey, who was the vicar of the parish of Sarisbury towards the end of the last century. She was responsible for many charitable acts in the district, one of which was the donation of a piece of land and buildings to the parish, to be used as a school. Following her death, the grateful parishioners enlarged the church organ, and erected a lych gate in the memory of the good lady and her brother. The lych gate was dedicated on 12th March 1908 and can still be seen today. This picture of the actual ceremony was taken by Fareham photographer Mr. F. Pannell.

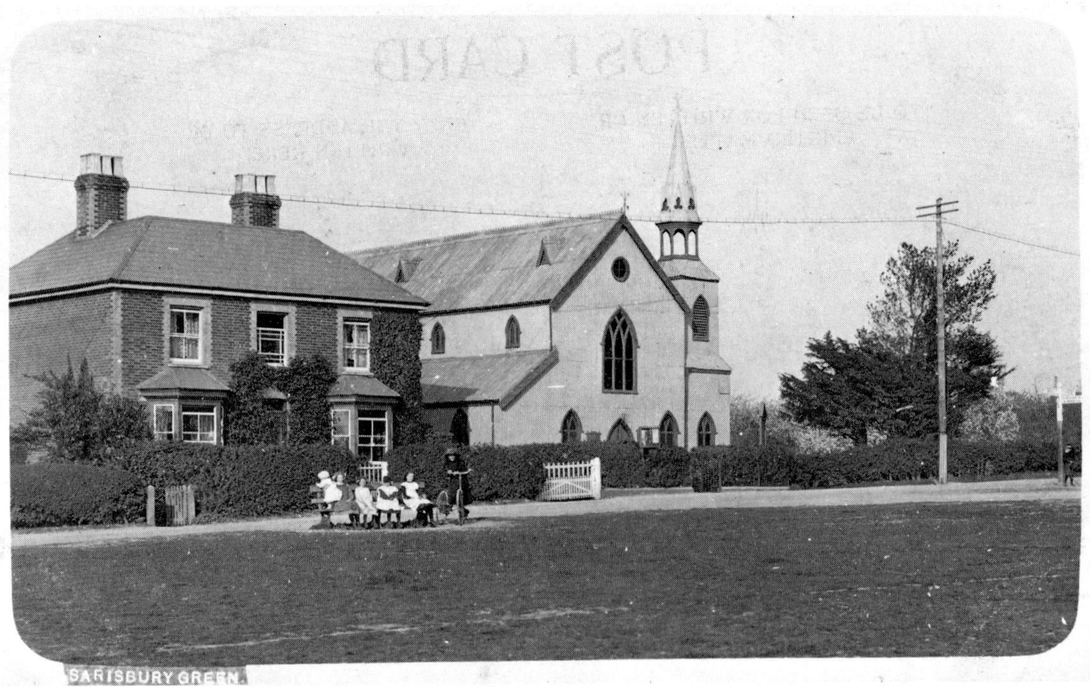

118. By the year 1800 the population of Sarisbury was increasing steadily. William Reed, a resident of the area, began to organise the local Noncomformists, and meetings were started in his home. The attendance at these meetings increased so much that a chapel was built in Swanwick Lane in 1802. Many years later, a new chapel was built in Holly Hill Lane, and then in 1886 a move was made to a new site opposite St. Paul's Church. The original church built there is shown in this 1914 picture. This building was replaced by the United Reform Church built at a cost of £4,000 and opened on 22nd July 1931. It is still referred to as the William Tidd Matson Memorial Church. Mr. Matson was the resident minister in 1887. He was a well-known writer of hymns, several of which are still included in the present day Congregational Hymn Book.

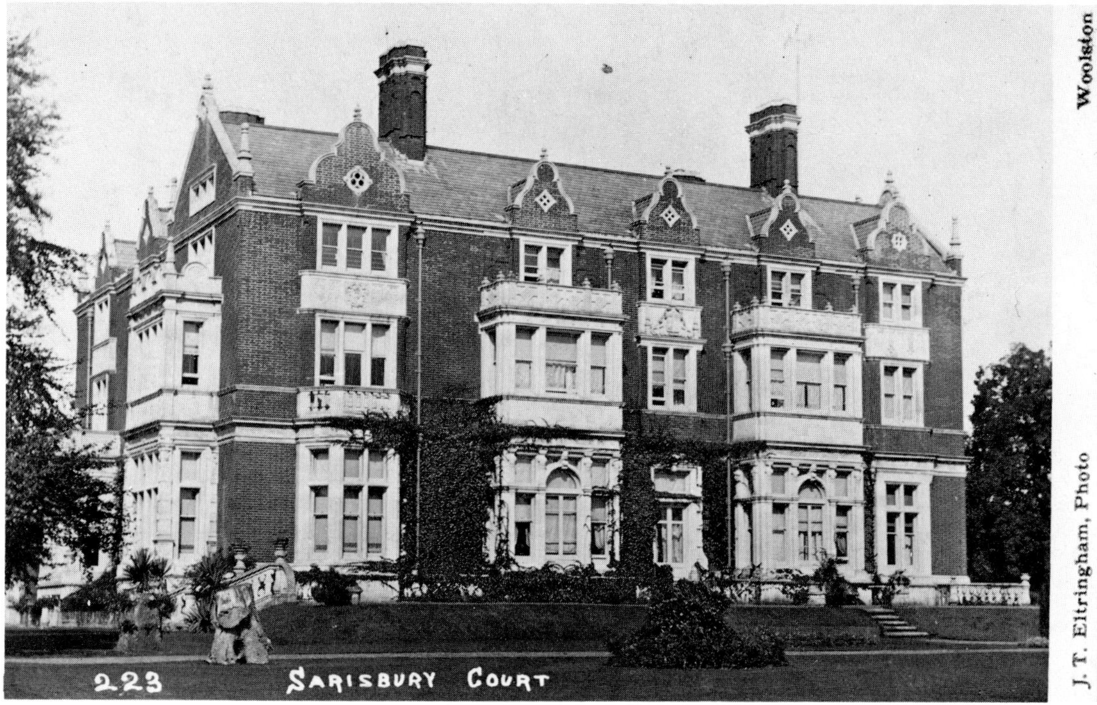

119. Holly Hill House, later known as Sarisbury Court, was one of the district's finest houses. Standing in impressive grounds in Holly Hill Lane, its everyday running required a small army of servants. Over the years it was the home of many well-known people and was eventually bought by Mr. Quinton Hogg. It was then used as a summer home for the boys of his London Institute. The house was later purchased by Sir Edward Walter K.C.B. who was connected with the Times newspaper. Moving into this century ownership had passed to William Garton who was the head of the H.P. Sauce Company and a leading figure in the world of early motor cars. Sarisbury Court, pictured here in 1905, has now been demolished, having become a victim of modern economics, like so many of the larger old houses throughout the country.

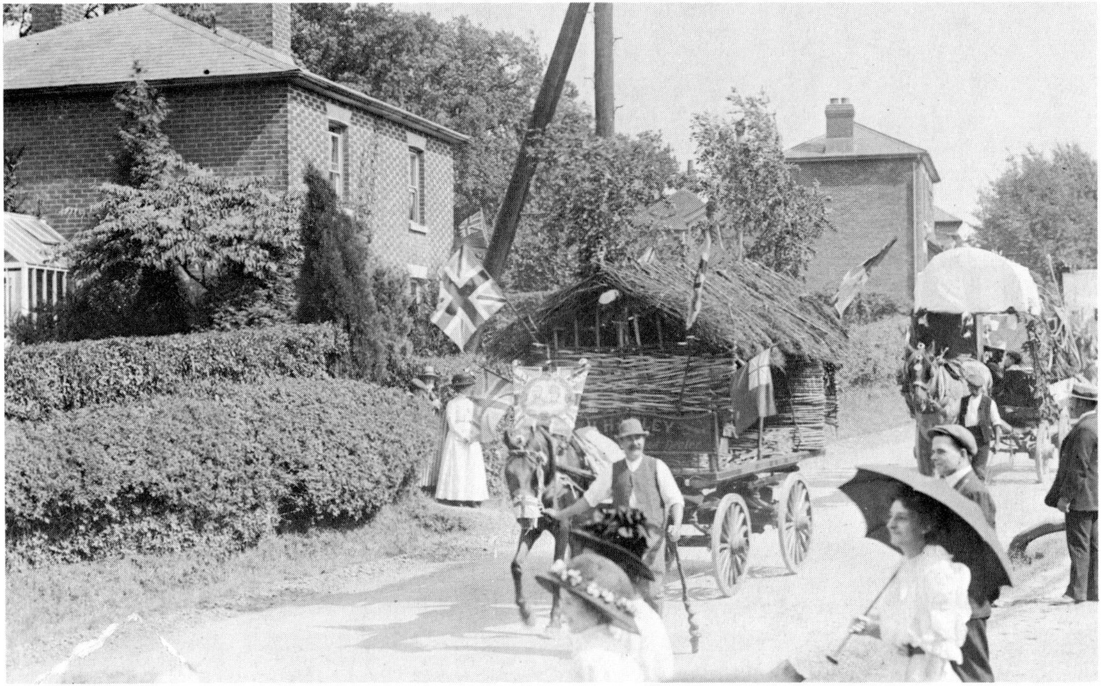

120. As has already been seen in the earlier pages of this book, the people in Edwardian times never wasted an opportunity to have some fun and put on a show. Life was hard in those days and people worked long hours for little reward, so the odd day off was much appreciated. Grand occasions, like the coronation of King George V and Queen Mary in 1910, were just too good to miss. This is part of the carnival parade to celebrate this event passing through Sarisbury, and no doubt ending up on the village green. It looks a fine hot day for the occasion with sunshades in evidence as well as some splendid summer bonnets.

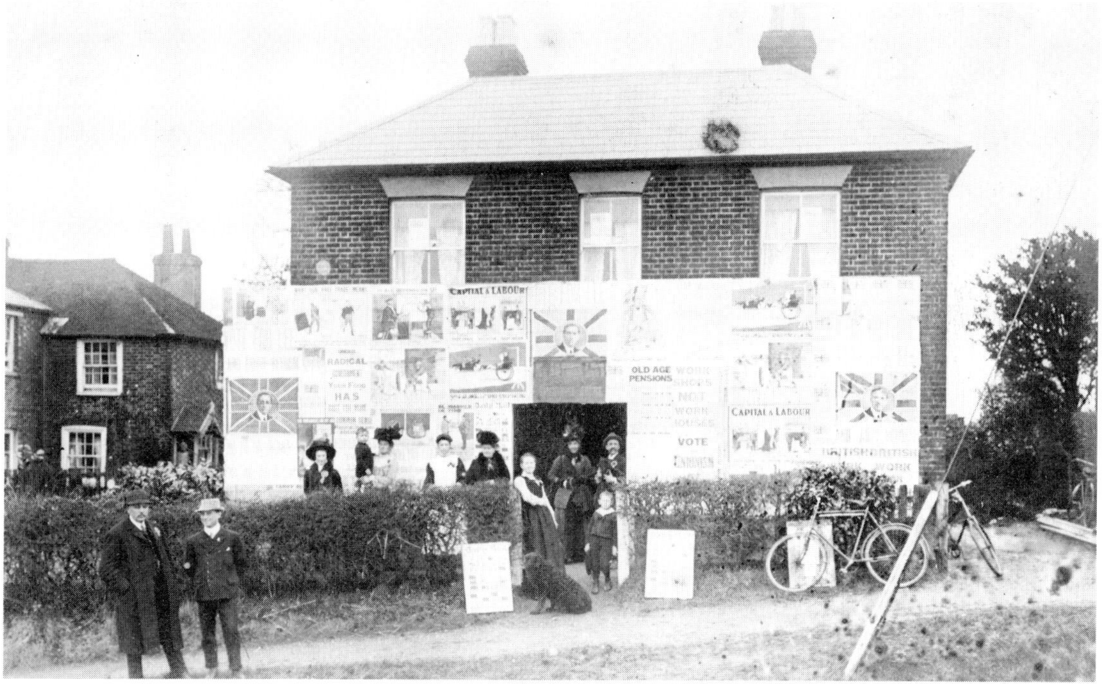

121. Even quiet little Sarisbury Green could not escape the election fever that gripped the country in January 1906. This house in Sarisbury has been transformed to serve as the Committee Rooms of the local candidate Mr. A.H. Lees. It leaves no one in any doubt of its political bias, with party members sporting large rosettes as they pose amid sheets of election literature and posters of Mr. Lees as the centre piece of Union Jacks. This election was brought about by the issue of Protection for home produced products versus Free Trade which had split the Conservative Government. As a result of the controversy the Balfour Government resigned in 1905 and the 1906 election was fought largely over the Tariff Reform issue. Mr. Lees was in favour of the reform of trading laws and was successful in his bid for re-election.

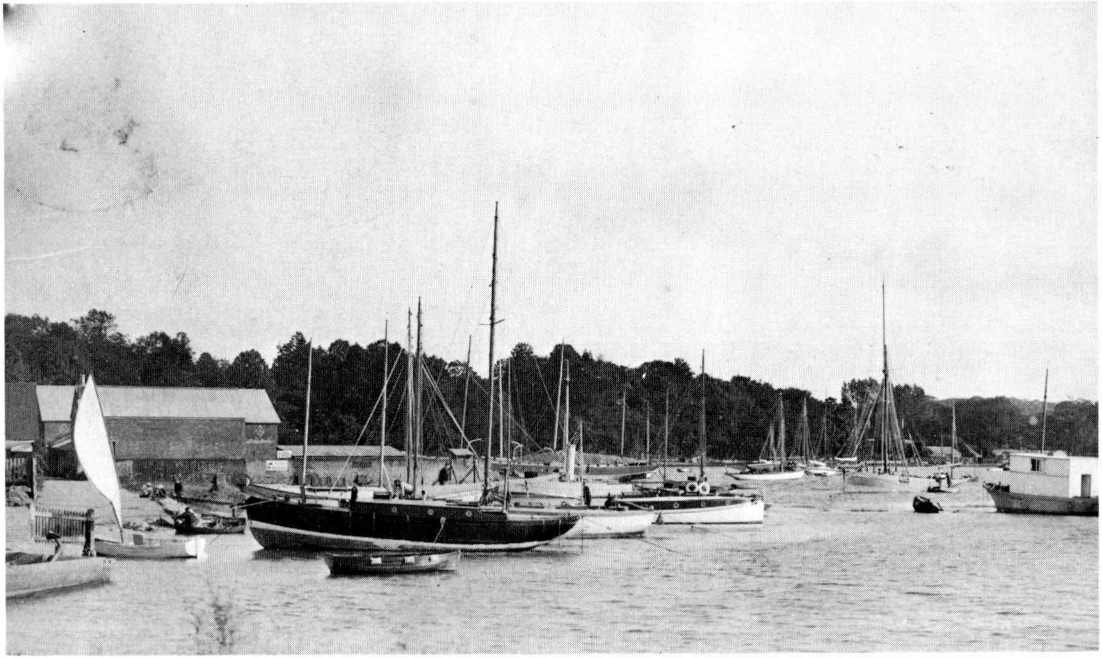

122. The river Hamble has long been a safe, sheltered anchorage for small boats. This view of the tree-lined Swanwick shore was taken in 1914. On view is a fine assortment of small craft from dinghies to houseboats and sea-going yachts. Today the picture is much the same except that there are many more boats, with not an empty berth in sight. It is also much more commercialised with a thriving boat building and repairing industry in operation. Moving on down the river between the village of Hamble on the right shore and Warsash on the left, one comes to Southampton Water leading into the Solent.

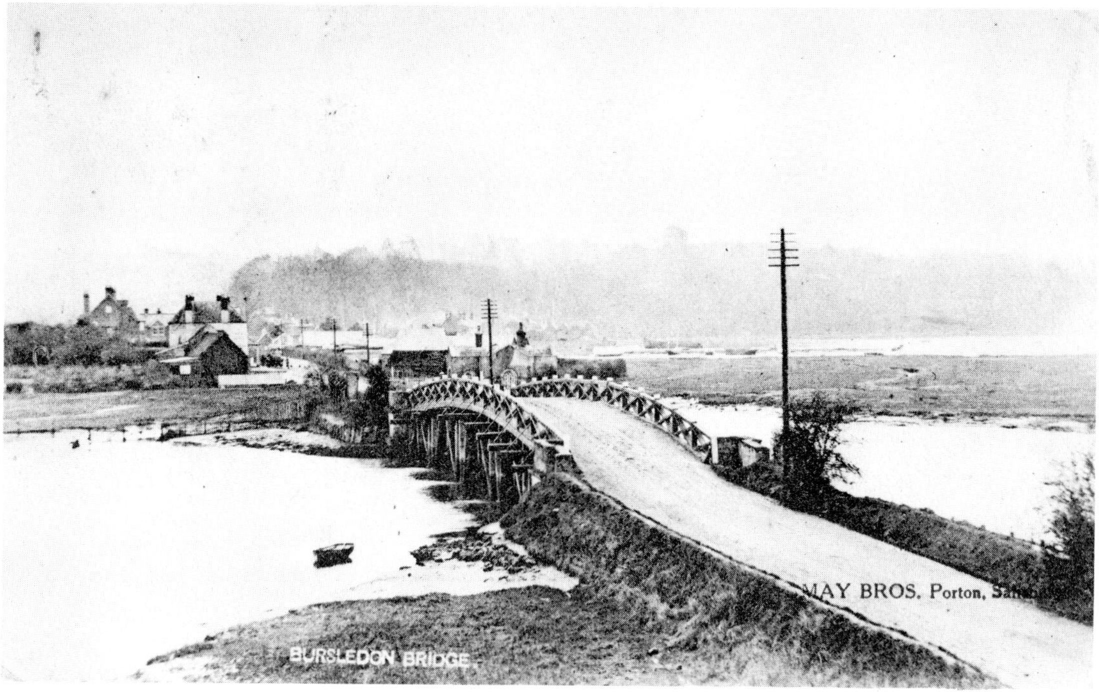

123. The river Hamble forms the western boundary line of the Borough of Fareham. This is the old Bursledon Bridge, crossing the river and leading to the village of old Bursledon to the left, or on up the hill in the direction of Southampton. This 1905 view was taken from the railway bridge on the Bursledon side of the river, looking back over the road bridge to Lower Swanwick. Sarisbury Green lies on up the hill behind the distant trees. This bridge was built of wood about 1800 and once had a tollgate on the Swanwick side. In the days before the bridge, a ferry used to operate across the river at this point. The old bridge was long ago replaced by a much larger structure to cope with the demands of modern day traffic along this stretch of the busy A27 road.

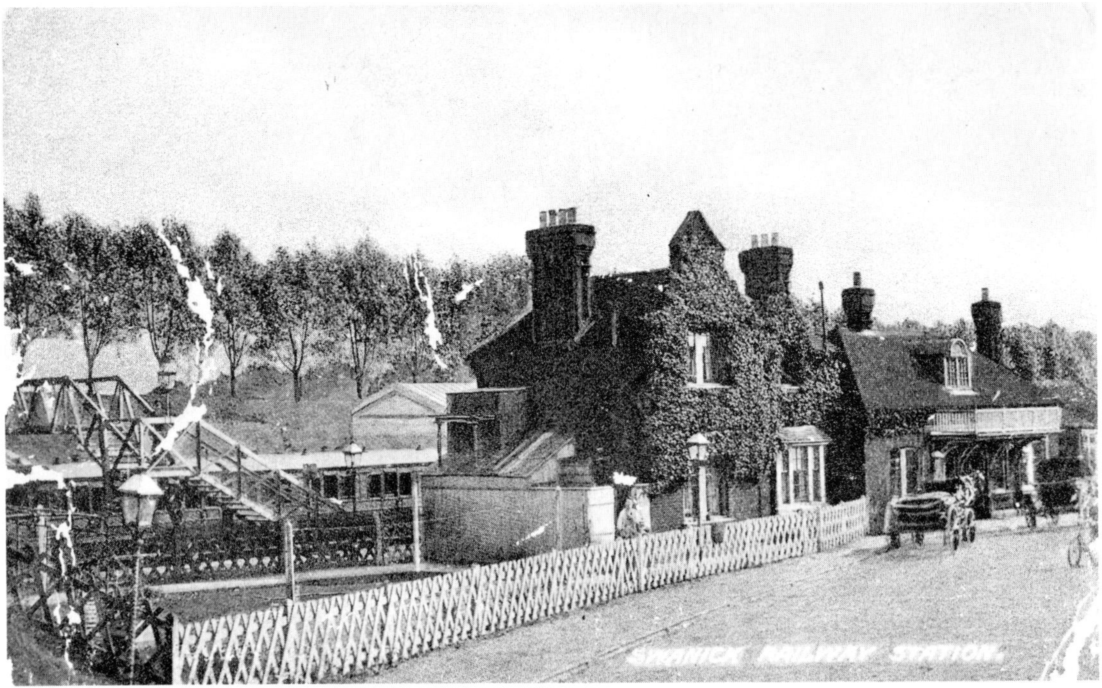

124. Swanwick Railway Station was opened in 1889 when a rail link was established between Fareham and Netley. For the best part of the year it was the sleepy country station pictured here in 1904. In the strawberry season however, it was the scene of great activity. Swanwick and Sarisbury were at the heart of the strawberry growing area in this part of Hampshire. In a good season in pre-war days close to three million baskets of strawberries were despatched by rail. This colossal output having to be loaded on to one hundred and sixty special trains. To cut heavy packaging costs the industry opened up and operated its own basket making factory in Swanwick. Today strawberry production in the area has fallen considerably, with many of the old fields now covered by housing developments. The resultant increase in population in the area at least allows Swanwick Station to continue to operate as a going concern.

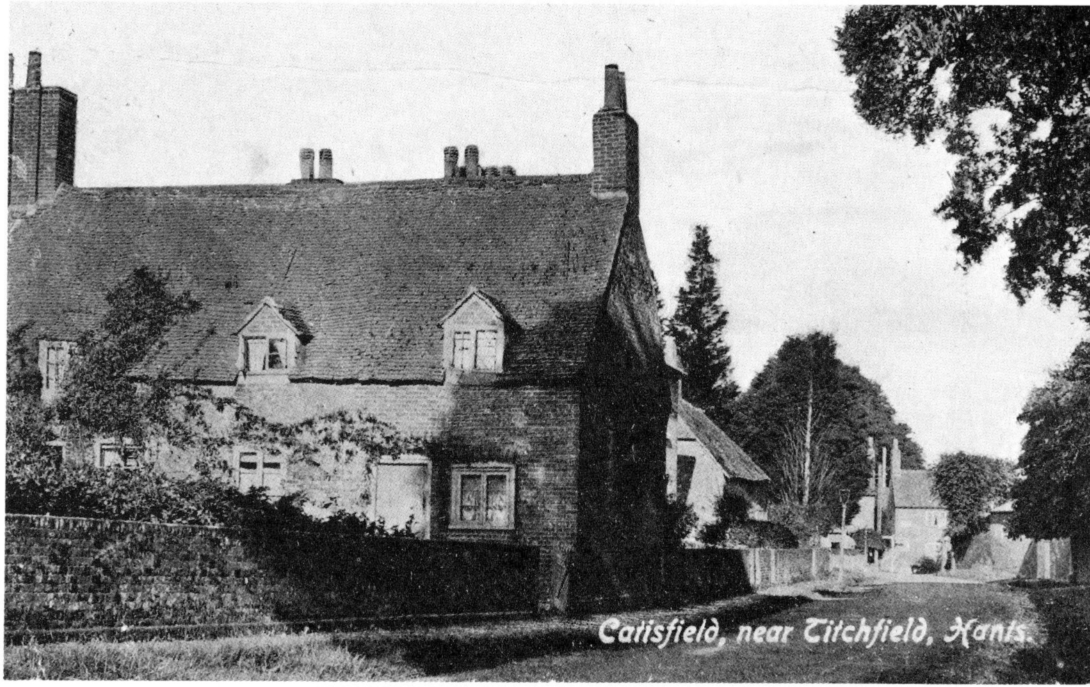

125. The village of Catisfield lies about a mile to the west of Fareham Town Centre. It stands on the eastern crest of Titchfield Hill overlooking the valley of the river Meon. Catisfield being just off the main highways, escaped any noticeable changes in the first half of this century. Only in recent years has any appreciable development taken place and this has been mainly on the edges of the village. Many old cottages like these photographed by A.H. Sweasey in 1919 still remain. The occupants once earned their livings by working in the surrounding fields and the old village still exudes an air of rural charm.

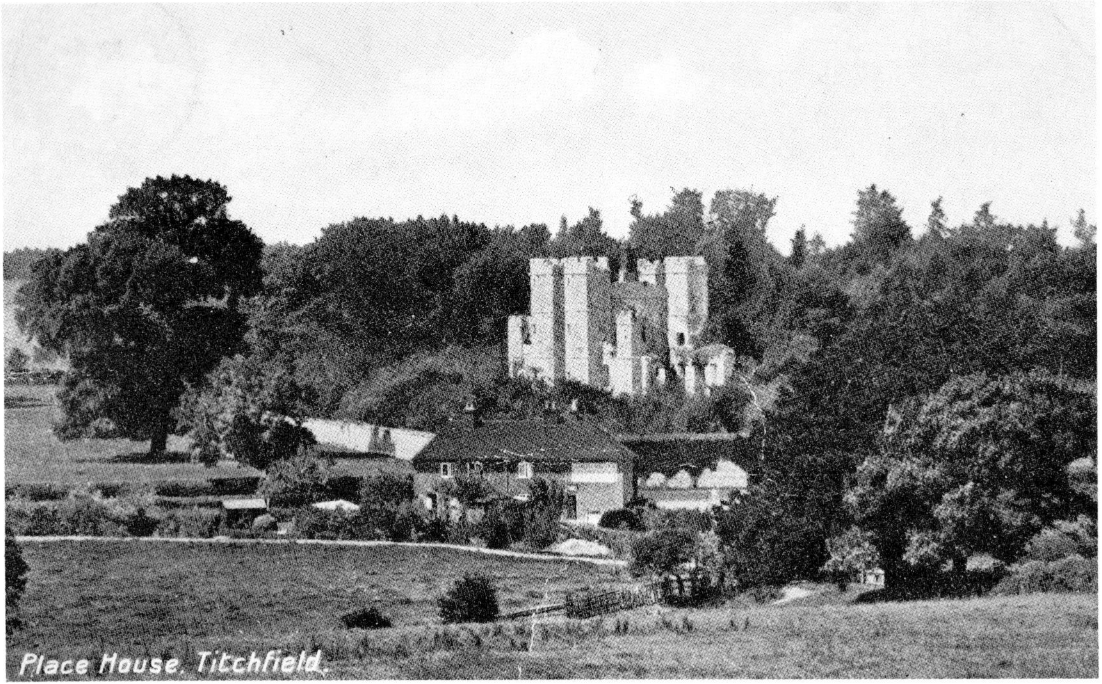

126. Moving down out of Catisfield village the photographer then took this view of Place House, Titchfield. In the foreground, standing on the banks of the river Meon, is the old Fisherman's Rest public house. Place House stands on the site of what was once Titchfield Abbey. The old Premonstratensian Abbey was founded for a colony of White Cannons in 1222. King Edward I granted the Abbott free warren in the Abbey lands in 1294 and this was later confirmed by King Henry VI. In 1537 the last Abbott of Titchfield surrendered the Abbey to King Henry VIII. The King later presented the old Abbey to one of his leading supporters, Thomas Wriothesley, who became Earl of Southampton in 1546 and was knighted in 1550. Titchfield became his home and he converted the Abbey to a stately, turretted home.

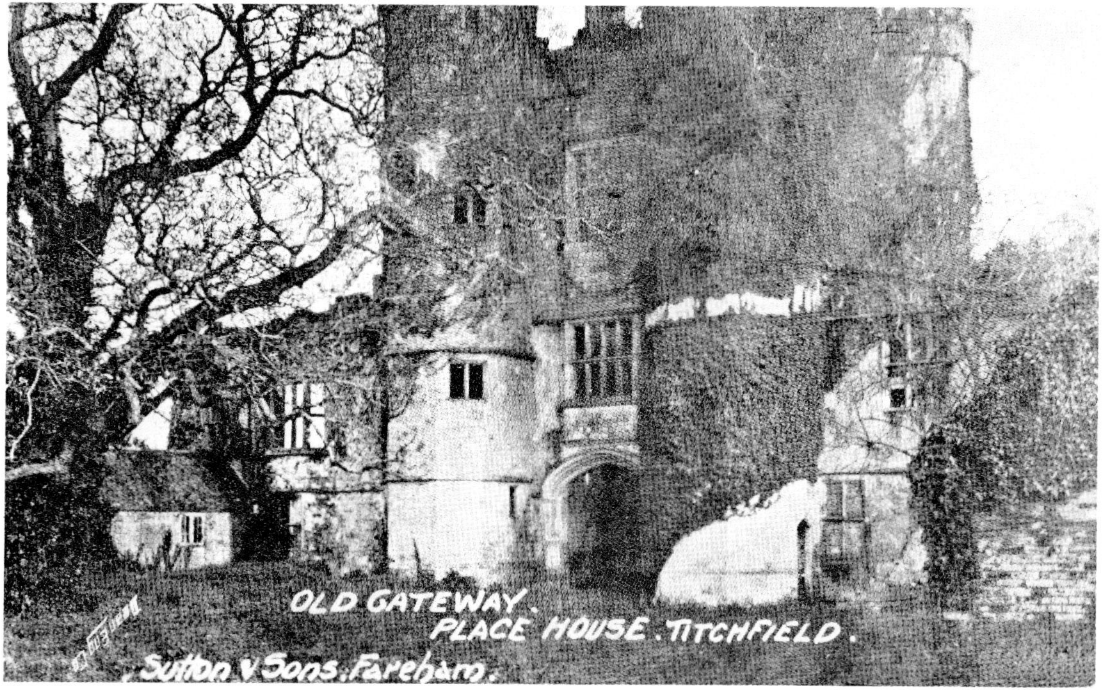

127. This is how Place House appeared to Fareham photographer Sutton in 1908. It is here that the second Earl of Southampton entertained Edward VI and Elizabeth. It is believed that Shakespeare later spent some time here as a guest of the third Earl of Southampton. The fourth and last Earl of Southampton was a fervent supporter of the Royalist cause. At his invitation King Charles I brought his young bride to stay at Place House. Then later when the Civil War was going badly for him, the King took refuge here, only to be arrested and taken to Carisbrooke. By 1711 the title of Place House had passed to the 3rd Duke of Beaufort and it was sold by the 5th Duke to Peter Delme in 1741. When the Delme's later moved to Cams Hall, they used some of the material from the House to improve their new residence. Place House is today scheduled as an Ancient Monument.

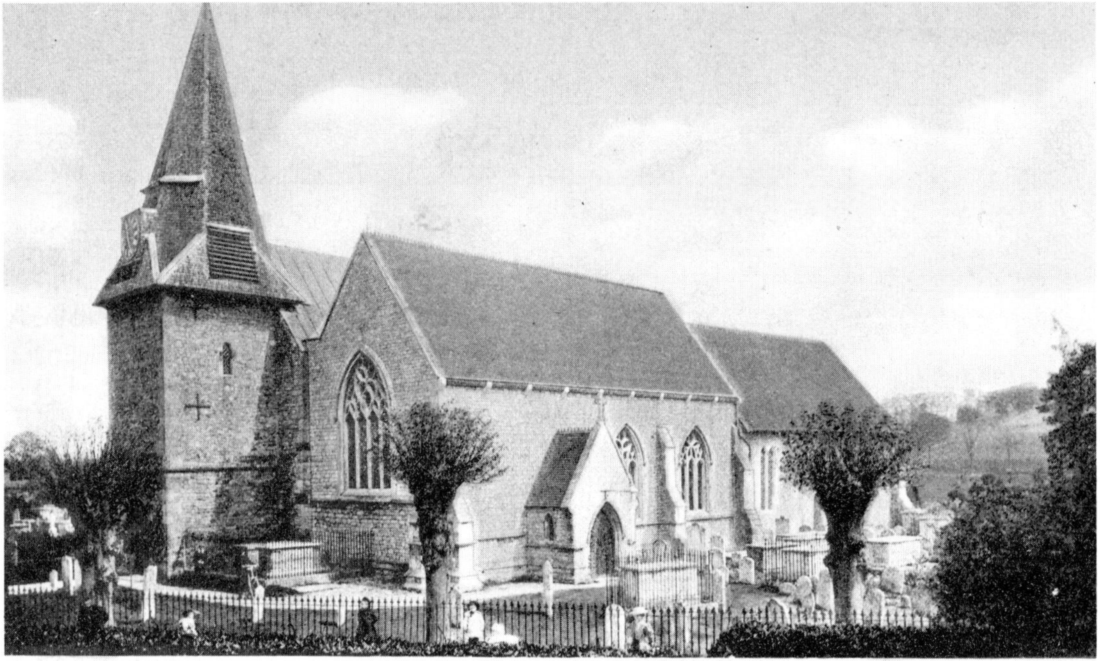

128. Church Street leads from the square at Titchfield to the lovely old church of St. Peters. This building is a fine example of early architecture with much of it being a mixture of Saxon and Norman work. The fine western doorway dates from the 12th century and the priest's door in the chancel is 13th century. The unusual spire and the north aisle were added in the 15th century. In the abbot's chapel stands an elegant marble and alabaster tomb. This is the monument to the first Earl of Southampton, Thomas Wriothesley and his wife and son.

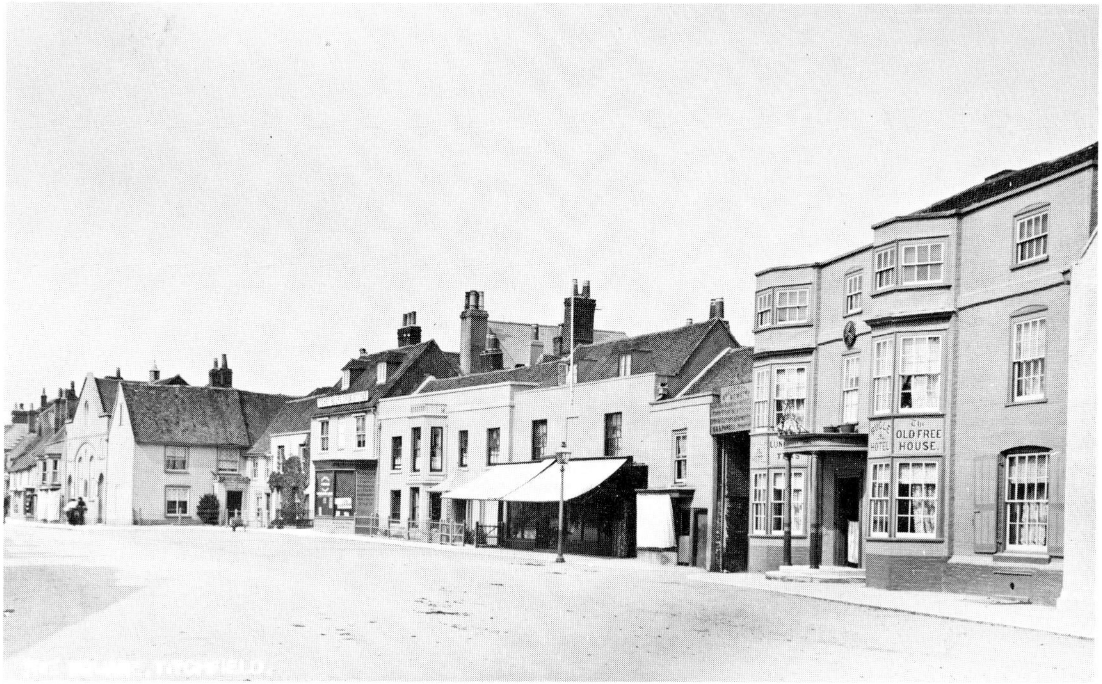

129. This side of Titchfield Square is dominated by the Bugle Hotel. This was once an old coaching inn and has changed very little in appearance since those days. When this picture was taken in 1905 the proprietors G. & A. Powell were engaged in other activities besides the dispensing of ales and spirits. Teas and luncheons were also served in the hotel whilst the Bugle Hotel Mews at the side of the building offered other services. Apart from good stabling facilities one could also hire a 'superior rubber-tyred cart' or make use of the General Carrier and Forwarding service on offer. A few doors along the Square was the Sidney House Drug Store. This filled the need in this largely farming community for an Agricultural Chemist. A large sign outside the shop proclaims that 'W.O. Smith's condition powders for horses are the best and cheapest that can be used'.

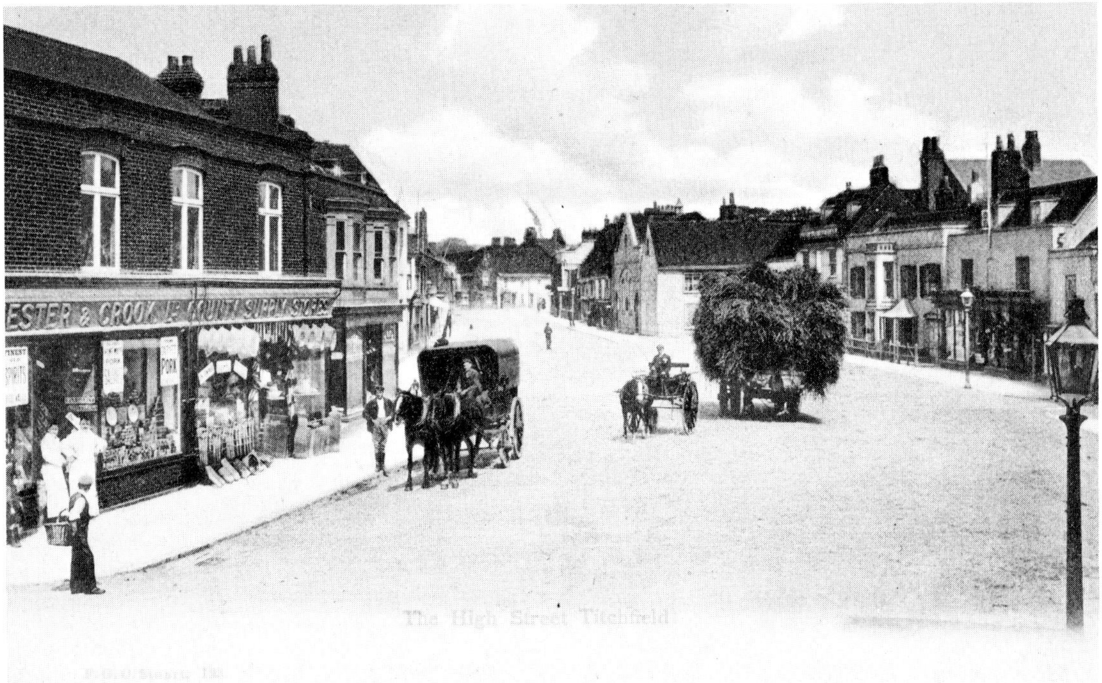

130. On the opposite side of the square to the Bugle Hotel once stood the large emporium of Lanchester and Crook Ltd., County Supply Stores. This F.G.O. Stuart card pictured the store on a summer's day in 1908. On sale was just about everything from wines and spirits and home made sausages to general groceries and hardware. Despite stocking such a range of commodities they were obviously not too busy to allow two smartly overalled staff to pose in the doorway for this photograph. Outside the store stands a delivery cart, whilst another horse and cart trundles across the square with the results of the day's haymaking.

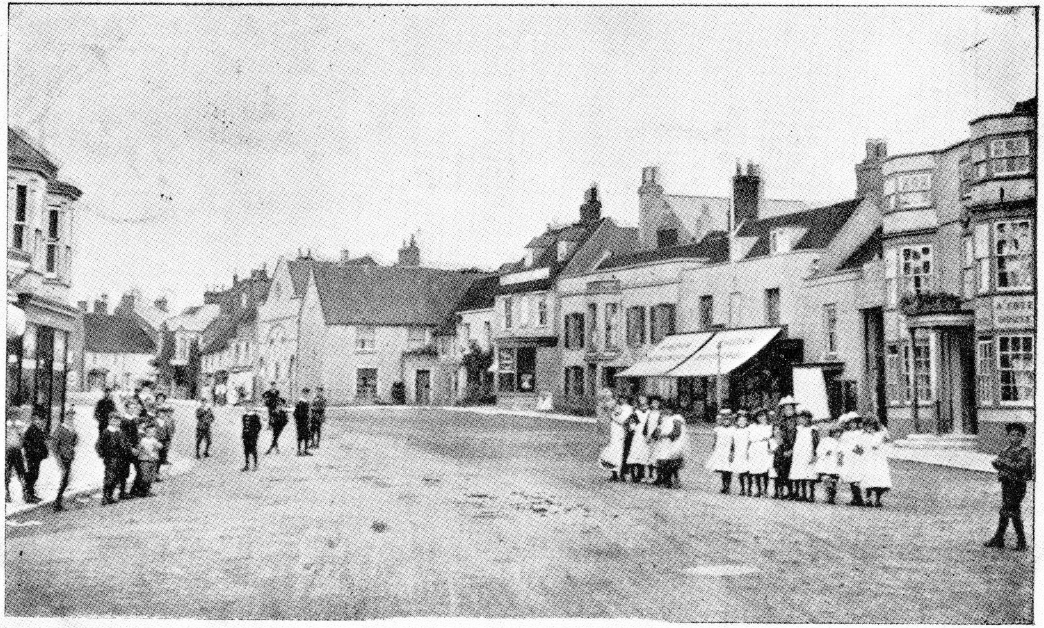

The Square, Titchfield

131. This general view of Titchfield Square dates from 1905. It shows a square full of the younger inhabitants of the village who all appear to be wearing their best clothes. Possibly the village school has just come out, or there is some kind of outing in the offing, although it is not clear why the boys and girls are in separate groups. The square has always been the centre of village life and a market, which received a mention in the Domesday Book, was held here for hundreds of years. A market hall was built in the square in the 16th century where it stood for some three hundred years. This was also where the five day fairs granted to the Abbot of Titchfield by King Henry VI were held.

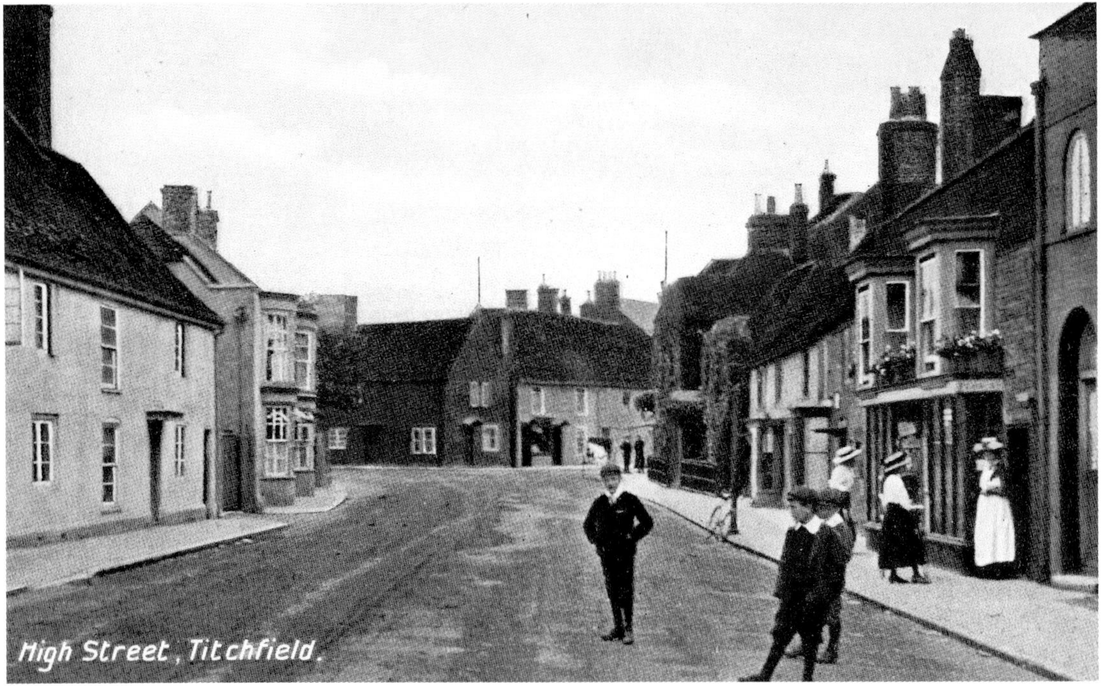

132. From this view of Titchfield High Street in 1905 it would appear that little had changed for hundreds of years. Titchfield has been a large village for centuries, with its streets lined with mostly two storeyed Stuart and Georgian type cottages. Since 1905 the village has successfully resisted change and remains a complete contrast to neighborouring Stubbington. The main Southampton to Fareham road was routed north of the village some years ago. More recently a new by-pass road has served to remove most of traffic bound for Stubbington and Lee-on-Solent from the village streets. All helping to make a visit to Titchfield today rather like stepping back in time.

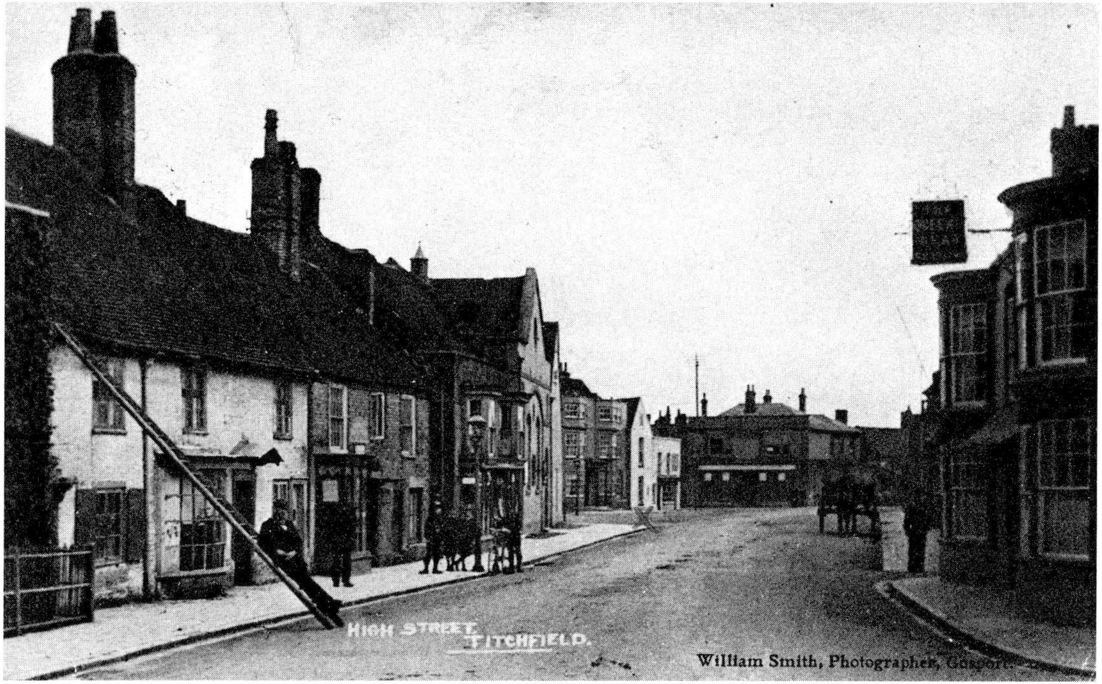

133. Looking back down the High Street towards the square another of Titchfield's famous old public houses 'The Queen's Head' is seen on the right. Like the Bugle Hotel in the square, this place of refreshment is also still going strong. When the old market hall was removed from the square in the last century it was rebuilt behind the Queens Head. Since that time the old building has again been on its travels, having been removed brick by brick to the open air museum at Singleton in Sussex, here to be preserved for posterity. This picture was taken by William Smith in 1910. It was not often that someone would adopt such an artistic pose for him as the gentleman on the ladder.

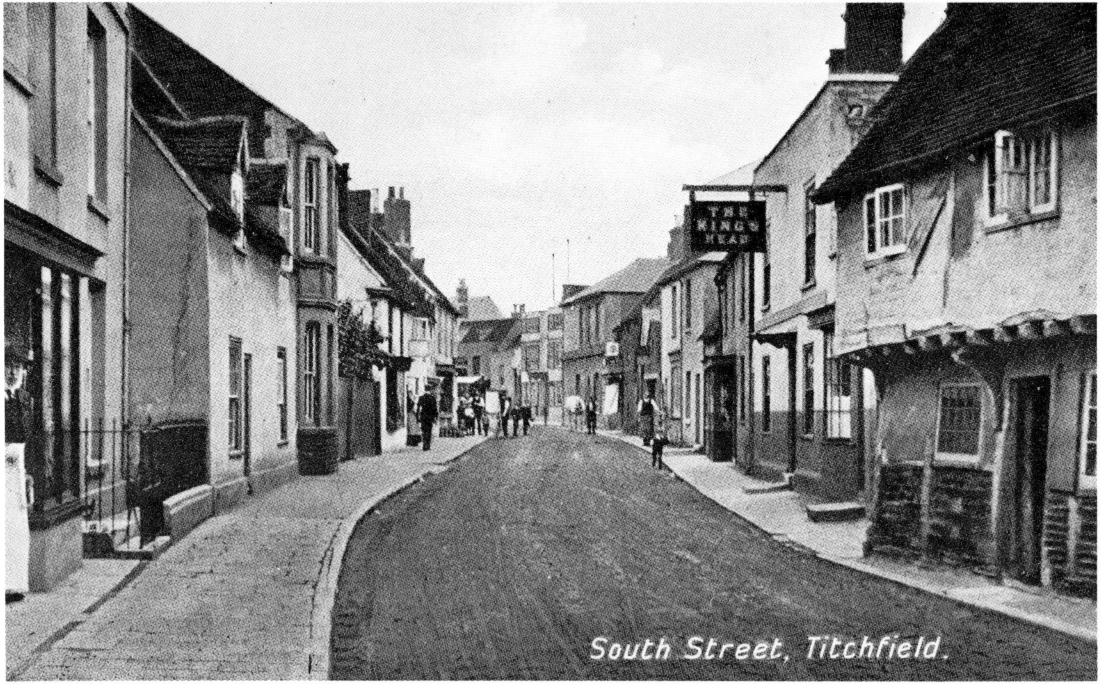

134. South Street is the road leading out of the Square to Warsash and Stubbington. This is how it appeared in 1910 and it has changed very little since then. The main casualty of the years is the King's Head public house which is now a private residence. Just around the bend of the road is the bridge over the river Meon. Looking at the river now it is hard to believe that from earliest times right up to the 17th century Titchfield was a thriving port. It was then that the Earl of Southampton ordered a dam to be built at Meon. Whilst this successfully drained the marshes, it also meant that no more could larger craft sail up to Titchfield. This unpopular action seriously affected the prosperity of the village.

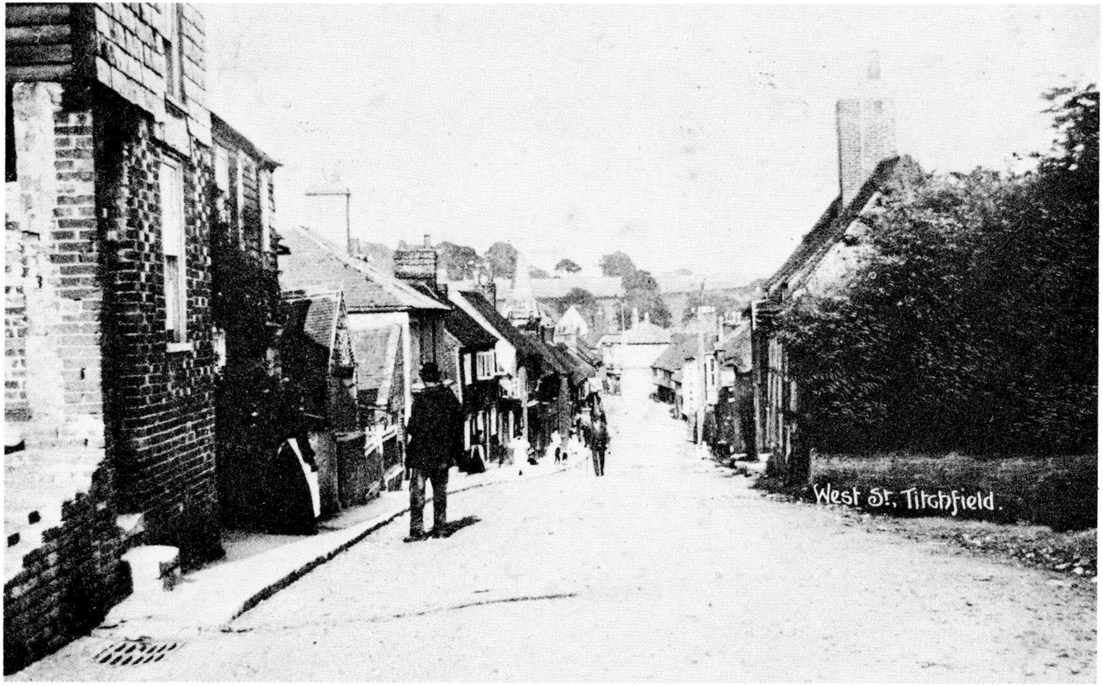

135. The lower part of West Street runs into Titchfield Square almost opposite Church Street. This picture was taken in 1925 from a position half way up West Street and looking back down to the square. In the distance can be seen the familiar shape of the church and steeple of St. Peter's. This is another long street, and when one considers how large the old village was, it is clear why in older times it was regarded as more important than Fareham. The parish boundaries once used to stretch from Warsash and Sarisbury in the west to Wickham in the north.

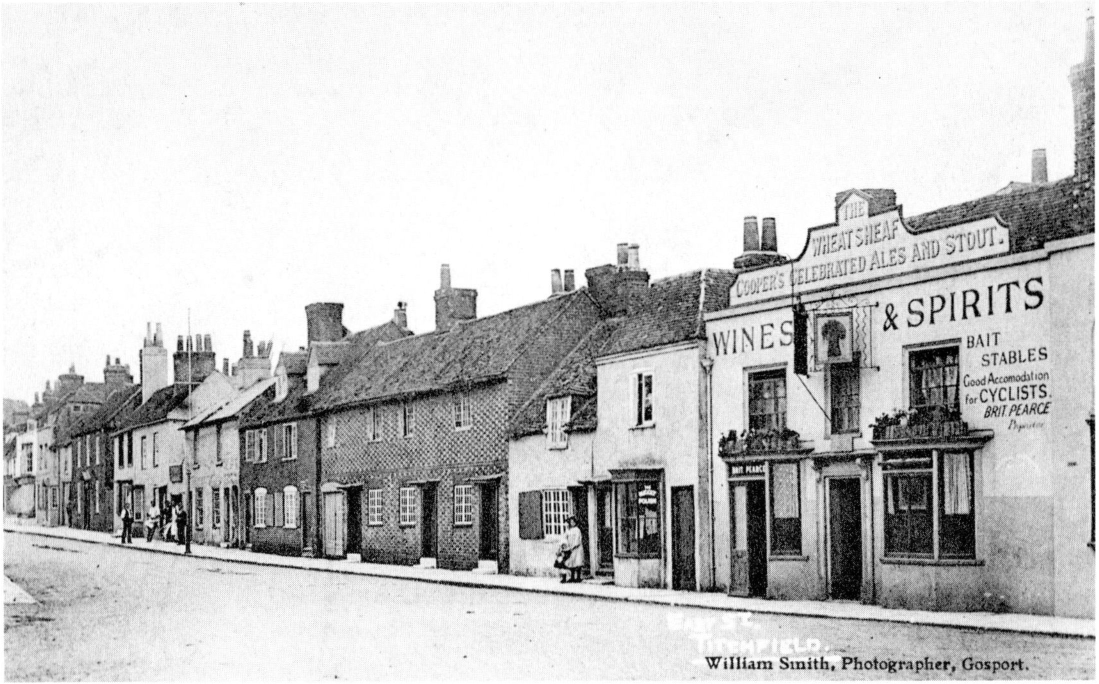

136. East Street leads from High Street on out of the village in the direction of Fareham. Taking pride of place in this William Smith photograph is the Wheatsheaf public house which is still in business today. An indication of the main forms of road transport of the day is given by the notice on the wall of the Wheatsheaf. Here the proprietor Brit Pearce advertises his stables and announces that he can offer good accommodation for cyclists. Half way down East Street is Mill Street. The latter now cut in half by the main Southampton to Fareham road leads to Place House. Before that is reached however, and only just over the A27, stands an old water mill. This mill, whose ancestor doubtless gave the street its name, is not now working, but is still in a good state of preservation.

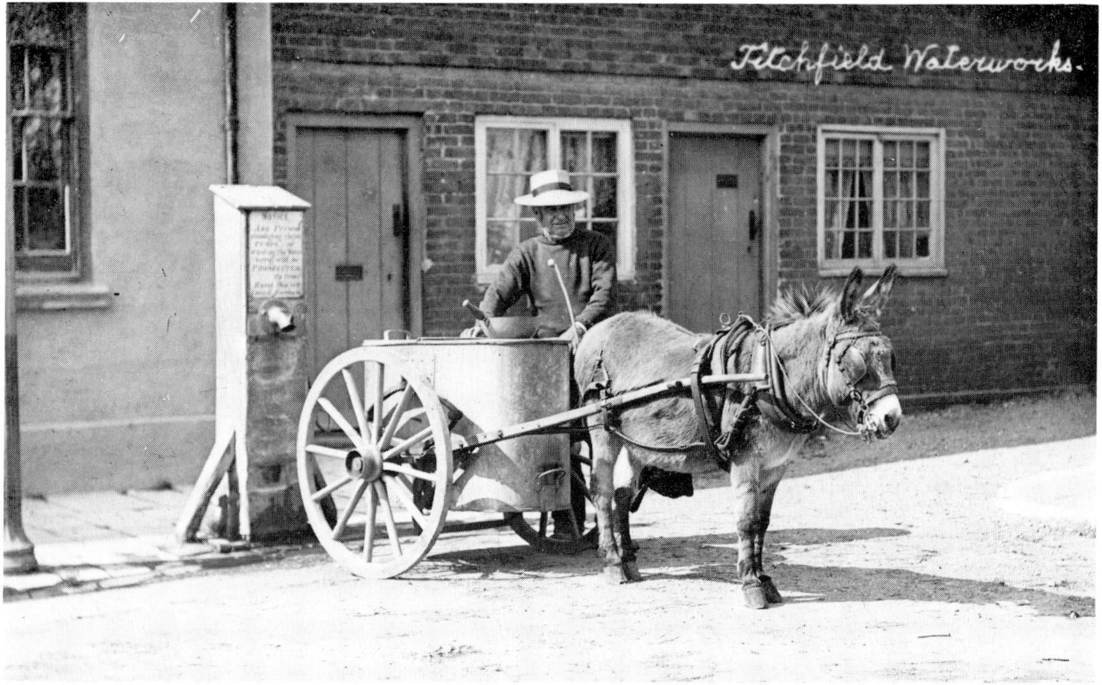

137. In the old days water, or rather the lack of it, was a perpetual problem in many parts of the country. For this reason the character pictured here with his donkey and water cart was one of the most important people in the community. The water problems facing the village population in those times are clearly illustrated by the message on the back of this postcard, obviously written by a visitor to Titchfield. It reads: 'The people have to pay dearly for their water in Titchfield. They are only allowed one bucketful before breakfast and one bucketful each afterwards. Sometimes milk is cheaper than water and people pour milk for a glass of water.'

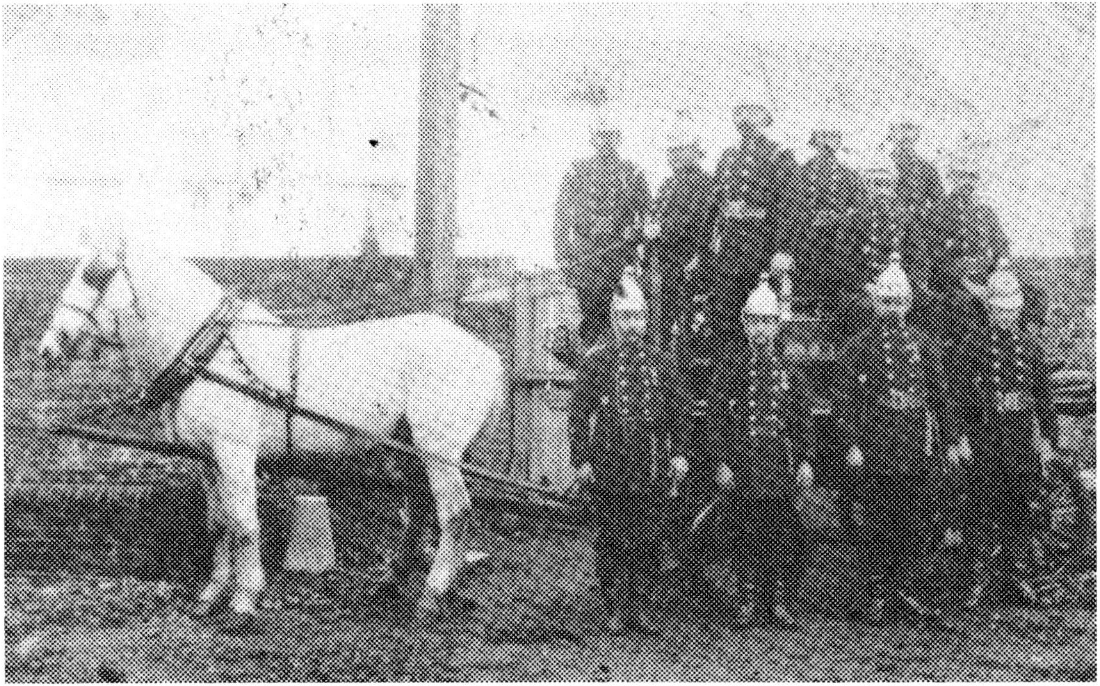

138. One fine body of men who were totally dependant on an adequate supply of water were the Titchfield Fire Brigade. Back through the centuries the population always lived in a real dread of fire. Often the best that could be managed to fight a blaze was a few bucketfuls of water drawn painstakingly from a nearby well. The high number of wooden dwelling places in existence also added to the danger. During the last century, many local fire brigades were formed, made up of volunteers. Although the early equipment was very primitive and needed a horse to make it mobile, at least it was a large step in the right direction. Stories abound of the exploits of those brave early firemen who started a tradition carried forward to the super-efficient fire fighting services of today.

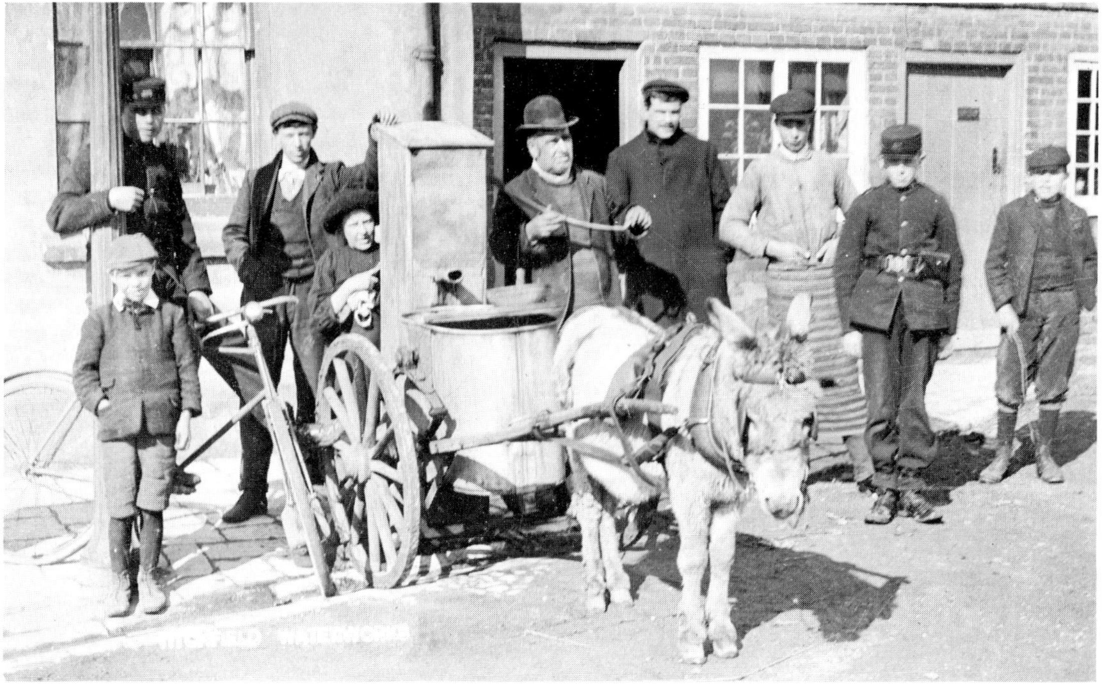

139. This interesting assortment of village characters were grouped around the Titchfield Waterworks in June 1906. With the exception of the man working the pump, everyone appears to be transfixed by the camera, including the donkey. The notice on the pump reads 'Any person damaging the pump or wasting the water thereof will be prosecuted – by order of Rural District Council, Fareham'. This again accentuates the importance attached to the village pump water supply. It was not until after the First World War that a piped supply of water reached Titchfield. In these modern times a ready supply of water both hot and cold is so taken for granted. It certainly makes one think to see how things were in this respect in the so-called 'good old days'.

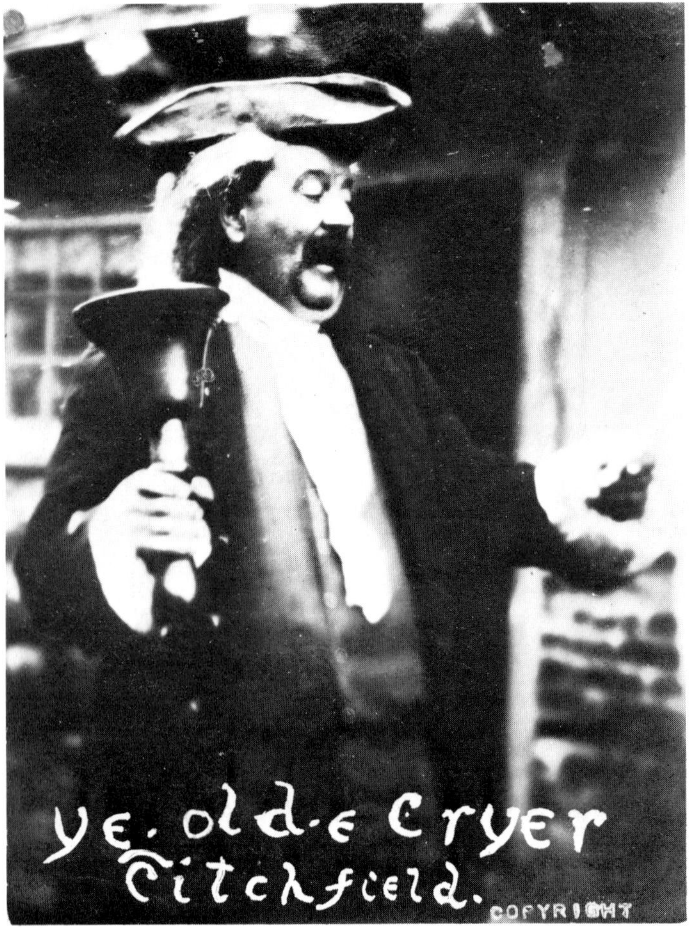

140. What better way to end this book on yesteryear than with a picture of a character right out of the past. The town cryer is believed to have originated as far back as the middle ages. Long before the days of television, radio and even newspapers, news of local or national happenings could only be passed by word of mouth. To keep the man in the street informed of important events, new local byelaws, etc. most of the towns and larger villages appointed their own cryer. These gentlemen were equipped with a bell to summon attention and a voice loud enough to get their message over to the assembled crowd. This postcard showing the Titchfield cryer was posted in 1911. It carries the message 'This is a photo of the Town Cryer. The bell is very ancient and is thought a good deal of'.